BIBLE

FOR NEW

CHRISTIANS

Wilson Harp

Cover Photo
© Jorisvo | Dreamstime.com - *Adam And Eve Photo*

Previously published as *Bible Stories for Grown-Ups*

This book is dedicated to those who have never heard the stories of the Bible

Contents

Early History

Creation and the Fall of Man

Story found in Genesis Chapters 1 to 3

od created everything, and before that, nothing existed. He created all the heavens and the earth with his word. He spoke into the darkness and created light, he separated the sky from the earth, gathered the water into the oceans, made dry land form into earth, and was very pleased at his creation. Then he made plants and set them in the soil. The sun, moon and stars were soon visible from earth, and he created animals to fill its land, sky and oceans. Finally, God made man, male and female, in his own image. When he looked and saw all he had made, he was very glad and took his rest.

This is how the creation of man took place. God reached down into the clay of the earth and formed the shape of man. He then breathed into the form he had made and gave life to his creation. The Lord had planted a garden in the east and placed the man there. In the garden were every tree imaginable, and they bore fruit all the time. In the middle of the garden were two specific trees; the tree of life and the tree of knowledge of good and evil. He gave the man instructions to take care of the garden, but warned him not to eat the fruit of the tree of knowledge because it would cause him death.

After a time, God decided Adam, the name he gave the man, should not be alone. So, he brought to Adam all the birds and animals and had Adam name them. But when no animal was found to be a suitable helper, God caused Adam to fall into a deep sleep, took a rib from Adam's body and formed it into a woman. When Adam woke, he saw the woman, declared his devotion to her, and she became his helper as he tended the garden. They worked in the garden naked and were not ashamed of their nakedness.

There was a serpent in the garden who was cleverer than all other animals. He asked the woman why she did not eat of the tree of knowledge. She replied God had commanded they not eat because it would bring them death. But the serpent told her she and Adam had been deceived. He said if she ate of the tree, then she would have knowledge of good and evil like God, and that would make her God's equal.

So, the woman went to the tree and looked at its fruit. She saw it was pleasing to the eye and looked delicious. She also desired the wisdom she believed it would grant her, so she took the fruit, ate it, and then gave some to Adam who also ate it. They suddenly saw each other's nakedness, grew ashamed, and made clothes out of leaves to cover themselves.

When they heard the Lord moving in the garden, they hid from him and waited for him to pass. But he stopped and called out to Adam because he wanted to speak with the man. Adam answered God and said he had hid himself because he was naked and afraid. The Lord asked Adam if he had eaten from the tree of knowledge and Adam admitted he did, but he blamed the woman for giving him the fruit. When the Lord questioned her, she blamed the serpent for tricking her into eating it.

The Lord was greatly displeased and handed down his punishments. For the serpent, he removed its legs and placed scorn upon it for all time. He made it a detestable creature which had to crawl in the dirt. To the woman, he announced that childbirth would cause great pain and her husband would rule over her. To the man, God informed him working the soil would be hard labor and it would produce barely enough to live on and that Adam's days would be full of sweat and toil. The Lord also pronounced death would be part of their punishment and at the end of their lives they would return to the soil from which they had been made from. Finally, Adam and his wife were banished from the garden, and the Lord set an angel with a sword of fire at the gate to prevent them from returning.

Cain and Abel

Story found in Genesis Chapter 4

fter Adam and his wife, Eve, had been removed from the Garden, Eve gave birth to two sons; the eldest named Cain and the younger named Abel. Cain grew crops and worked the land while Abel tended the flocks. When time came to make sacrifices to the Lord, Cain gathered some of his crops while Abel took some of the fat meats of the firstborn of the flocks. When the Lord saw the sacrifices brought to him, he blessed Abel's sacrifice but not Cain's. Cain was so angry about what happened, the Lord came and spoke to him. He asked Cain why he was angry and warned Cain that sin was sitting at his doorstep waiting for him to act.

But Cain could not get past his anger and asked Abel to go into a field with him. When they arrived, Cain attacked his brother and killed him. The Lord came to Cain again and asked where Abel was. Cain said it wasn't his responsibility to keep track of his brother.

The Lord responded he could hear his Abel's blood call out from the ground. He told Cain the soil which had tasted the blood of Abel would no longer grow crops for Cain, and Cain would become a wanderer and never again succeed in growing crops anywhere.

When Cain heard what the Lord had said, he became afraid and wept because he was an outcast and would be killed by the first person to find him. The Lord had pity on Cain at that moment and placed on him a mark. He told Cain that any who killed the one he had marked would suffer seven times as greatly for his actions.

Cain then left the land of his parents, Adam and Eve, and went into the land of Nod further to the east. He met a woman there and married her and set about building a great city which he called Enoch, after his oldest son.

After Cain had left his parents, Eve had another son named Seth, who the Lord gave her to replace Abel. Through Seth, those who continued to call upon the name of the Lord were born.

Noah

Story found in Genesis Chapters 6 to 9

Noah was born in the eighth generation of Adam's line. In his time, men had become violent and evil. When the Lord observed what humanity had become, he was distraught and sad. He felt it would be best to destroy all he had made rather than have such wickedness in the world. But Noah was righteous and just. The Lord was pleased at what he saw in Noah and decided Noah would be spared the judgment soon to be unleashed upon the world.

The Lord spoke to Noah to let him know the world would be destroyed because of the unrighteousness of the people. He told Noah to build a vessel out of cypress wood with very specific measurements. This ark would house Noah, his wife, his three sons and their wives. It would also house animals of the field and air so they would be spared the wrath of the Lord. Noah went and gathered food and supplies for all the people and animals which would be on the ark and began the construction.

Finally, the ark was complete and the Lord told Noah to enter. He was told to take seven of each kind of bird, seven of each animal they would eat, and two of each animal they would not eat, so when the flood was over, the animals would spread throughout the earth again. Noah did as he was told and gathered his family and all the animals which came to him into the ark.

After seven days, Noah, his family and all the animals had gathered on the ark and the rains came. The Lord closed the door to the ark and the people and animals on board were safe. For forty days and forty nights the rain came down. The sky opened and the vaults of the earth bubbled up and all the land was scrubbed clean of people and animals. But the ark floated on the flood waters and Noah and his family were saved.

Once the rains stopped, the Lord sent a wind to blow across the earth and the waters started receding. The waters of the flood were so deep they covered the mountain tops, but after 150 days, the ark rested on Mount Ararat as the waters slowly lowered. For about seventy-five days, Noah could not even see the peaks of the mountains around him, but eventually there were some points of land sticking up above the water. He took a raven and released it, but the raven did not return. So, he took a dove and sent it from the ark. The dove could find no land to rest on, so it returned to the ark. After seven more days, Noah sent the dove out again, and it returned with a fresh olive leaf and Noah knew the land was returning and the plants were being restored. Seven more days passed, and again the dove was sent out, but this time it did not return and Noah knew the land was now dry.

After about a month, the Lord told Noah to come out of the ark. So, Noah, his wife, his sons, and their wives came out of the ark and set their feet on dry ground. They turned loose the animals and the birds so they could go and replenish the earth. Noah then built an altar and made burnt sacrifices with some of the clean animals and birds to the Lord.

The Lord was pleased with Noah and made a vow that never again would he cleanse the earth of all living things with a flood. He set the rainbow in the clouds as a reminder of his promise to Noah.

The Tower of Babel

Story found in Genesis Chapter 11

oah's descendants spread out and started filling the earth with their children. During this time, there was only one language for all men. On the plains of Shinar, the men of that age came together and decided to build a great city with a tower which would reach the heavens. They learned to make bricks out of mud and they used those bricks, mortared with tar, instead of stones to build their city. They reasoned the city would be a monument to those men who built it and would keep mankind from scattering across the face of the Earth. When the Lord saw what they intended, he confused their language and sent them in all directions. He knew if they were left as one people, they would be able to do anything they could conceive. This is why the Lord gave men many different languages and sent them to all parts of the earth.

Job

Story found in the Book of Job

In the land of Uz there was a man named Job who was upright, just and shunned evil. He was a man of considerable wealth because the Lord had blessed him. He had seven sons, three daughters, many thousand head of livestock and a large number of servants. Each of his sons would take turns throwing extravagant parties each night, and each morning Job would make a sacrifice for each of his children in case one of them had sinned against the Lord.

When the angels came to present themselves before the Lord one day, Satan came with them. The Lord asked Satan where he had been and Satan replied he had been all over the Earth examining things. The Lord asked Satan what he thought of his servant Job, who was upright and blameless. Satan countered the only reason Job blessed the Lord and lived an upright life was because the Lord had always blessed Job and had made him prosperous. So the Lord allowed Satan to do anything he wanted to Job except injure the man himself.

The next day a messenger came to Job and told him an enemy had come upon the men plowing in the fields and they had slaughtered all his servants and taken all his oxen. As Job was hearing this, another of his servants came and said he alone had survived the fire of the Lord coming from heaven and burning up all of the sheep and shepherds of Job in his pasture. As this servant stopped speaking, a third servant came in saying another enemy had raided the herds of camels and he alone was left to tell his master. Finally a fourth messenger appeared and told Job a sudden windstorm had come up and destroyed the house his sons and daughters were in and none in the house had survived.

When Job heard all of these things, he stood up, ripped his robe, shaved his head and fell to the ground worshipping God saying (Job 1:21) "Naked I came from my mother's womb, and naked I will depart. The Lord gave and the Lord has taken away; may the name of the Lord be praised." (NIV)

The next day the angels came to present themselves to the Lord and Satan once again appeared with them. The Lord spoke to Satan and told him even though he had destroyed all of Job's wealth and prosperity for no reason, still Job praised the Lord and did not sin. Satan replied Job was still healthy and whole, and while all of his possessions were taken away, the Lord still protected the man himself. So the Lord told Satan he could afflict Job but he could not take his life.

Satan went and caused great boils and sores to break out on Job from the bottom of his feet to the top of his head. Job was in intense agony and sat and scraped his sores alone. His wife told him to curse God so he might die, and then she left him.

Three of Job's friends decided to go visit him in order to comfort him, but when they arrived at his house, they almost didn't recognize him as he was so afflicted with sores. They tore their robes when they saw him and sat down in the dust with him. For seven days and nights they could not bring themselves to speak due to the amount of agony he was in.

Finally, Job spoke his mind to his friends. Job insisted he had done nothing wrong to be punished so, but his friends insisted he must have sinned because the Lord did not punish the innocent. Job asked several times for proof of his sin, and though his friends could not come up with any example, they did not believe his protests of innocence.

A young friend of Job spoke up after they finished arguing. He criticized Job's friends for their lack of compassion and accusations. He then admonished Job to not question the goodness of the Lord for what has happened. Job acknowledged the Lord was just and merciful, but insisted he had done nothing wrong. He declared if he could, he would question the Lord.

The Lord answered his request and let Job question him. After Job put his case before the Lord, the Lord answered Job by saying a man cannot know the reasons of God nor can he understand fully the answers the Lord would give him. The Lord acknowledged Job never denied the justice and mercy of the

Lord, nor did he curse God or allow his anger to go into sin. For this, the Lord rewarded Job. He blessed Job with twice as much material goods as before and gave him new sons and daughters. Job lived a long and happy life after all of this, living long enough to see his great-grandchildren born.

The Patriarchs

Abraham

Story found in Genesis Chapters 11 to 20

A man named Terah set out from the land of Ur on his way to Canaan with his son named Abram, Abram's wife Sarai, and Abram's nephew Lot. On the way to Canaan, Terah settled in the land of Haran.

After Terah died, the Lord came to Abram and told him to leave Haran and his father's family and go to Canaan. Abram and Sarai packed up their belongings and went to Canaan bringing Lot with them. When they arrived, they wandered Canaan looking at all it had to offer. The Lord came to speak with Abram and told him Canaan would be given to him and his future generations. Abram built an altar to the Lord where he had spoken to him and then went to the hills near Bethel to live.

When a severe famine came, Abram went to Egypt to live for a while. Abram was worried for his own safety because of how beautiful Sarai was. He was afraid the Egyptians would see her and kill him to take her for their own. He told her to tell anyone who asked that she was his sister and then people would treat Abram well to gain favor with Sarai. When they arrived in Egypt it was as Abram believed and the Egyptians were very taken with the beauty of Sarai. News eventually reached the ear of the king of Egypt who sent for Sarai. When he saw her, he decided to take her for himself and gave Abram many sheep, cattle, donkeys and male and female servants in exchange for her. After the king had taken her in, the Lord sent an affliction upon the king's household because he had taken another man's wife. The king summoned Abram and, when he learned the truth of Abram and Sarai's relationship, ordered him to take Sarai and all he was given and to leave Egypt.

When Abram left Egypt, he returned to the place near Bethel where he had settled before. Abram had acquired a great number of flocks and riches, as had his nephew Lot who had traveled with him. Eventually, disagreements came up between

Abram's herdsmen and those men who tended Lot's flocks. Abram came to Lot and suggested they move apart so disputes between them would not keep arising. He told Lot to choose which direction he would go, and Abram would go the other way. Lot looked over the land and saw the plains east of the Jordan were watered like a garden and would make a good place to settle. So, he chose to go to the east and settled near the town of Sodom. Abram went west and settled into the hills of Canaan.

When this had been decided, the Lord came to Abram and told him to look out in all directions. He said Abram's children would be like the dust of the earth and would inherit all the land Abram could see. So Abram gathered his tents, flocks and people and moved to Hebron, to the grove of giant trees of Mamre. There he built an altar to the Lord and settled again.

At this time, the kings of Sodom, Gomorrah, Admah, Zeboiim, and Bela had just gained their freedom from the king of Elam, who had ruled over them for twelve years. About a year after their rebellion, Elam joined with the kings of Shinar, Ellasar, and Goiim and waged war against those who had broken free. Elam led his allies to take the lands of the Rephaites, the Zuzites, the Emites, and the Horites. Once they had been conquered them, Elam and his allies turned and conquered the Amalekites and Amorites. When Sodom, Gomorrah, Admah, Zeboiim, and Bela saw what was happening, they formed up battle lines in the Valley of Siddim.

Elam turned his troops and allies towards the five kings who had broken free from his rule. There in the Valley of Siddim he defeated them, causing Sodom and Gomorrah to flee and leave behind all of their men and plunder. The victorious kings took all of the goods and food of Sodom and Gomorrah, including Lot and his possessions, since he was now living next to Sodom. When Abram heard his nephew had been taken captive, he took the three hundred and eighteen trained fighting men in his house and called upon the rulers who had allied with him named Mamre, Eschol and Aner. Together they went in pursuit of Elam and his allies. They found them encamped at night, and Abram divided the forces to attack. His plan worked and Abram and his men routed Elam and his allies. They took back Lot and his possessions as well as all of the other people, goods and food that were captured.

The king of Sodom heard what had happened and met Abram and his allies in the Valley of Shaveh. The king of Salem, a man named Melchizedek, came and brought bread and wine. He was a priest of the Lord and gave the Lord's blessing to Abram. Abram gave Melchizedek a tenth of all he had taken. When this was done, the king of Sodom told Abram he could keep all of the goods and food he had recovered for the defeated kings as long as he returned the rescued people. But Abram replied he had taken an oath before the Lord not to take so much as a strap from a sandal from him so that Sodom could not claim he helped Abram become wealthy. He told the king of Sodom his men would only take what they ate along the way, but he asked for the share of the spoils to go to his allies Mamre, Eschol and Aner.

Now Abram had grown very wealthy, but he despaired because he did not have any children. He asked the Lord what the promise he had given was worth if his wealth was just going to go to his servants. But the Lord spoke to Abram and promised him an uncountable number of descendants who would possess all the land the Lord had promised him.

When Sarai saw the depths of sadness Abram felt at not having any children, she went to him and offered to let him sleep with her Egyptian maidservant named Hagar. So he slept with Hagar and she soon became pregnant. When Hagar found out she was pregnant, she began to hold it over Sarai. Sarai went to Abram and complained of how Hagar was behaving. Abram told Sarai that Hagar was her servant and she could do whatever she wanted to her.

Sarai began mistreating Hagar, so Hagar ran away from her mistress. When she had traveled some distance, she came to rest near a spring. While she was there, an angel of the Lord appeared to her and asked her why she had run away. When Hagar told what had happened, the angel told her to return home and submit to Sarai. He also told her she would have a son who would be named Ishmael, and he would be like a wild donkey, untamable. Everywhere he turned, he would stir up conflict and his hand would be against everyone. But the angel assured Hagar the descendants of Ishmael would be uncountable, like the sands of the desert. Hagar obeyed the angel and returned to Sarai and Abram where she bore a son who Abram named Ishmael.

Abram was eighty-five years old when Ishmael was born. When he was ninety-nine, the Lord came to him and told him that he was establishing a covenant with him and his descendants. The first thing the Lord did was to change Abram's name to Abraham, telling him he would be the Father of many nations. The Lord promised Abraham the whole land of Canaan would belong to his descendants for all time. The promise of the Lord was to be confirmed by Abraham and his descendants through the ritual of circumcision. Abraham, Ishmael and all men in his household would be circumcised. Each male born into his household, through all generations, would be circumcised when they were eight days old. This would be the sign of the covenant between Abraham and the Lord.

After the Lord spelled out what Abraham would do, he turned the discussion to Sarai. The Lord told Abraham her name was now Sarah. The Lord said she would give Abraham a son and through that son she would become the Mother of many nations. Abraham collapsed in laughter at that and thought it was impossible he should have a son at one hundred years old when his wife was ninety years old. Abraham asked the Lord to put the blessing on Ishmael instead.

The Lord answered Abraham and told him he would bless Ishmael and he would be the father of twelve nations of people, but he repeated that Sarah would give Abraham a son, and his name would be Isaac. It was through Isaac the Lord would keep his covenant with Abraham and his descendants. After the Lord had finished speaking with Abraham, he left him for a while.

Abraham returned to his tents and gathered Ishmael and all of the men in his household. He told them of the Lord's covenant and both Abraham and Ishmael were circumcised that day along with all of the men in the household, whether born there or bought from a foreigner.

A few days later, Abraham was resting at the entrance to his tent in the heat of the day when he saw three men appear before him. Abraham recognized the Lord among the visitors and ran to meet him. He bowed low and asked them to stay for a meal. They agreed and Abraham ran back into the tent and told Sarah to quickly prepare some bread for their guests. Abraham then ran out to the flocks and selected a tender calf and told one of his herdsmen to butcher and prepare it. He returned to his guests with the prepared calf, cheese, milk and bread. When they had eaten, the Lord asked Abraham where his wife was. Abraham replied she was in the tent. The Lord said when he returned the next year, she would have given him a son. Sarah was standing near the entrance to the tent hidden from the men's view. When she heard what the Lord said, she laughed because she did not think it was possible to have a child as old as she was. The Lord asked Abraham why Sarah had laughed. He asked if she thought there was anything too difficult for him. Sarah was afraid of the Lord at that moment and lied to him and said she did not laugh. The Lord replied she did laugh and he would see her with a son the next year.

When the three men were ready to leave, Abraham accompanied them until they came to a place which looked down on Sodom in the distance. It was there the Lord revealed to Abraham that the outcry of wickedness from Sodom and Gomorrah was so great, he was going to go see for himself how bad it was. If it was as he heard, then he would destroy the cities. The two men with the Lord started toward the city of Sodom, but Abraham stayed with the Lord. He asked the Lord if he would destroy the righteous men of the city along with the wicked. He pleaded with the Lord that if he found even fifty righteous men in the city, he would spare the city. The Lord agreed if there were fifty righteous men found in Sodom the city would be spared. Then Abraham said he believed the Lord should spare the city if there were only forty-five righteous men. The Lord agreed with that. Eventually Abraham had the Lord agree if there were only ten righteous men in the whole city, Sodom would not be destroyed. When the Lord had made this agreement, he left Abraham and Abraham returned to his home.

The two men who had been with the Lord were angels sent to see if the city was as bad as the Lord had heard. They arrived around evening at the gates of Sodom where Lot, Abraham's nephew, was sitting in the gate. When Lot saw the strangers, he greeted them and bowed to them. He asked them to come to his house and spend the night. They told him they wanted to stay in the city square, but Lot was insistent and they agreed to stay with Lot that evening.

Lot took them home and fed them, but before they had gone to sleep the men of the town came to Lot's house and demanded he send the two strangers out so they could rape them. Lot came out of his house and begged the men of the city not to do such an evil act, but the men of the city insisted he send his guests out. Lot offered his two virgin daughters to the crowd instead of them taking the strangers, but the men of the city became angry and threatened Lot with worse treatment than the visitors. The two angels pulled Lot back in his house and blinded the men in the crowd so they could not find the doorway. They then informed Lot the Lord was going to destroy the city, and the other cities on the plain, and Lot was to take his wife, daughters, the men engaged to his daughters, and anyone else he could find, and flee the city.

Lot went and spoke to the men engaged to his daughters, but the men thought he was joking and would not come with him. When dawn started to appear in the sky, the two men took Lot and his wife and their two daughters and led them out of the town. They said to run to the mountains to escape the wrath of the Lord. Lot told the men he could never make it to the mountains, but there was a village nearby called Zoar. He asked if they would allow him to go there and be safe. They agreed the Lord would spare the village, but told him to move quickly and not to look back because the destruction was coming soon. When Lot reached the village of Zoar, the sun had risen fully over the land and the destruction of the cities began. Burning sulfur fell from the sky and destroyed Sodom, Gomorrah, and all that lived on the plains, even the plants. Lot's wife had turned back to the city and she was turned into a pillar of salt during the destruction.

After the destruction of Sodom and Gomorrah, Lot and his daughters fled to the mountains from the village of Zoar. They found a cave and lived there apart from all other people because Lot was afraid of what had happened. One day, his oldest daughter convinced the younger daughter since there were no men there and they wanted to continue their father's line, they would get him drunk and sleep with him. The first night they got him drunk on wine and the oldest daughter went in to have sex with him. She left before he awoke and he did not know what had happened. The second night the younger daughter did the same. Eventually both of Lot's daughters became pregnant. The oldest gave birth to a son named Moab, who became the father of the Moabites, and the younger gave birth to a son named Ben-Ammi, the father of the Ammonites.

At this time, Abraham moved into the city of Gerar in the lands of Negav. He again was afraid the men of the city would find Sarah of such beauty he would be in danger if they knew she was his wife. So he convinced her again to refer to him as his sister. The king of Gerar, a man called Abimelech, saw Sarah and took her into his house to marry. When he did so, the Lord shut up the wombs of all of the women of his household and went to Abimelech in a dream and told him he was doomed because he had taken another man's wife for his own. Abimelech pleaded with the Lord pointing out he had not had sex with Sarah yet and he was told she was Abraham's sister. The Lord told Abimelech because of his innocence he would be spared.

The next day Abimelech went to Abraham and confronted him. He said the Lord had come in a dream and told him of the sin he almost committed with Abraham's wife. Abraham confessed he was afraid he would be killed and Sarah taken away, so he had told her to say Abraham was her brother. (This wasn't a complete untruth since Terah was the father of Sarah, but Abraham had a different mother.) Ambimelech was so afraid of what happened, he gave Abraham livestock and servants and told him he could live anywhere around Gerar he chose. He gave Sarah one thousand pieces of silver to make up for the offense against her and vindicate her reputation. Abraham then prayed to the Lord on behalf of Ambimelech. The Lord heard his prayer and the wives and servants of the king's household could once again have children.

In the next few months, Sarah became pregnant as the Lord had said. She bore a son before the year was over and Abraham named his son Isaac. On the eighth day after he was born, Abraham had Isaac circumcised as required by the covenant with the Lord. Sarah was overjoyed she had given Abraham a son and she remained happy as he grew.

Eventually Isaac was old enough to be weaned and Abraham threw a great feast for the occasion, but Sarah saw Hagar mocking Isaac. Sarah told Abraham what had happened and demanded Hagar and Ishmael be sent away. Sarah did not intend for Isaac to share his inheritance with Ishmael. Abraham was troubled by what Sarah wanted because Ishmael was his son. But the Lord came to Abraham and told him to do as Sarah demanded for Isaac's sake. The Lord promised Abraham even though Ishmael would be sent away, he would still be shown favor by the Lord and many nations would come from him because he was Abraham's son.

The next morning, Abraham brought some food and a skin of water to Hagar. He gave them to her and told her she and Ishmael must leave his lands. She started wandering into the wilderness and before long the water ran out while they were in a desert. Hagar left Ishmael crying under a bush and went off a distance to cry by herself so she would not have to see him die. The Lord heard them crying and sent an angel to Hagar. The angel told her the Lord heard Ishmael crying and she was to go and get him. The angel reminded her of the promise of the Lord that Ishmael would be the father of many nations. After the angel spoke to her, she saw a well nearby and she went and got Ishmael and took him to the water. The Lord was with Ishmael as he grew. He lived in the desert and became a great archer. When he was old enough to marry, Hagar went into Egypt and found him a wife.

During this time, Abimelech came to Abraham and asked him to make a treaty between their people for all time. He knew Abraham had been blessed by the Lord in all of his actions, and asked that the same kindness he had shown to Abraham when he was living in Gerar would be shown to his people whenever they lived in the lands of Abraham. Abraham agreed to this. As they spoke, Abraham brought up the issue of a well he had dug, but some men of Abimelech had seized for their own. The two men discussed it and made a treaty over the place of the well which was then after known as Beersheba. Abraham planted a tamarisk tree at the location to mark the treaty.

Some years later, the Lord decided to test the faithfulness of his servant Abraham. The Lord came to Abraham and told him he was to take Isaac into the mountains to a place which would be revealed and sacrifice his son as a burnt offering to the Lord. Early the next morning Abraham woke and took his son Isaac and two servants with him. He saddled his donkey, gathered wood for the burnt offering, and took the oil and coal to start the fire with him. On the third day of the trip, the Lord revealed to Abraham the place in the mountains where he was to make the sacrifice. Abraham told his servants to stay where they were and set off with Isaac to the place the Lord had revealed. Abraham had Isaac carry the wood while he carried the oil and coal. While they were heading up to the place in the mountains, Isaac was curious at the lack of an animal to sacrifice. Abraham assured him the Lord would provide for them. When they got to the location which the Lord had specified, Abraham built an altar and laid the wood upon it. He then bound his son and laid him over the wood. He took his knife in his hand and moved to kill Isaac. The voice of an angel shouted from heaven for Abraham to wait and not harm the boy. The voice told Abraham he had proved the Lord was his only God and he would obey whatever he was told. He told Abraham to look in a nearby tangle of bushes. Abraham searched the bushes and found a ram with its horns caught in the thorns. Abraham took the ram and sacrificed it as a burnt offering instead of his son Isaac. When he was done, the voice of the angel again came from heaven and restated the covenant between Abraham and the Lord because of Abraham's faithfulness.

Eventually Sarah died at the age of 127. When she died, Abraham sought a suitable place to bury her. He called together the leaders of the men in that area and told them he wanted to buy some land to not only bury his wife, but it would be a place for tombs for all of his people. After much negotiation, he bought a cave and field from a man named Ephron for 400 pieces of silver. Abraham buried her in that cave which was close to the groves of Mamre, where they had first settled when they came to Canaan.

After Sarah died, Abraham took another wife named Keturah who gave him six sons. He also had sons by his concubines. Before he died, he gave all of his sons from Keturah and his concubines enough money to move away from the inheritance he was leaving for Isaac. Abraham died at the age of 175 and his sons Ishmael and Isaac buried him beside his wife Sarah.

Isaac and His Sons

Story found in Genesis Chapters 24 to 28

When Sarah had died, Abraham decided to search for a suitable wife for Isaac. He did not want a wife for Isaac from the Canaanite women, so he sent his chief servant back to his homeland and search for a woman among his relatives. He told his servant to take gifts to persuade her and to convince her to come to Canaan. He did not want Isaac to return to those lands, but to continue to live in Canaan, as it would be his inheritance.

Abraham's servant traveled back to the homeland of his master until he came to the town of Nahor, named for Abraham's brother. He had brought ten camels laden with goods and had stopped near the well outside of town near dusk, when the women of the town would come out and draw water for their families. He prayed the Lord would find favor with him and he would find a wife for his master's son that very evening. He prayed if he asked one of the young women for a drink she would reply that she would water the camels too.

When the women came out, he saw a beautiful young woman approach the well and asked her to give him a drink from her jar. When he had finished drinking, she told him she would pour water for his camels as well. Hopeful this woman would be the one he would take back to Isaac, the servant took a gold nose ring and two golden bracelets and gave them to her. He asked if there would be room in her father's house for him to stay. She introduced herself as Rebekah and told him she was the daughter of Bethuel, son of Nahor. She informed the servant there was plenty of room for him and his camels in her father's house. The servant then told her he was sent by Abraham, her relative. When she heard this, she rushed off to let her family know.

A short time later, Rebekah's brother Laban came out to greet the servant. He took the servant and all of the men with him and led them to the house of Bethuel. When the servant had refreshed himself, Laban led him into the house to meet with Bethuel and have a feast. But before the servant would eat, he said he had to tell them why he was there. When they had heard the story of how the Lord had led him to find Rebekah, Bethuel happily agreed to the marriage between Rebekah and Isaac. Abraham's servant was glad his mission was a success and gave Rebekah and her family the gifts from Abraham he had brought.

The next morning the servant rose and prepared for the journey back. He called Bethuel and Laban and asked them to prepare Rebekah for the trip. But Bethuel asked him to allow ten days before Rebekah left. The servant responded he wanted to leave as soon as possible. They agreed to call Rebekah and find out what she desired. When she heard what was happening, she agreed to leave immediately. She gathered her serving girls and her belongings, said goodbye to her family, and left with Abraham's servant.

Isaac was out in the fields meditating when he saw the line of camels coming into his father's lands. He went out to greet them and discover who they were. When Rebekah saw Isaac coming, she asked Abraham's servant who he was. He replied he was his master's son whom she was to marry. Rebekah covered her face with a veil and climbed off her camel to meet him. When he discovered who she was and why she had come to their land, he took her to his father's place and led her into his mother's tent where he married her. Rebekah brought great comfort to Isaac who was still grieved by his mother's death.

Rebekah became pregnant and soon felt her babies struggling within her. She sought the Lord for understanding and the Lord told her there were two babies and they would become fathers of two great nations. They would be separated and struggle against each other and the older would serve the younger. When it came time for her to give birth, the first boy was red and covered in hair and they named him Esau. The second boy was grasping Esau's heel with his hand as he was born and they named him Jacob.

As the boys grew into men, they were very different. Esau was a man of the field, hunting game and roaming widely. Jacob stayed with the tents and was a quiet man. Isaac loved the wild game which Esau brought to him and favored his older son, but Rebekah favored Jacob. One day, when Esau came in from the field very hungry, he saw Jacob had fixed a pot of red lentil stew. Esau came to him and asked for a bowl, but Jacob told Esau he would have to sell his birthright to Jacob before he got a bowl. Esau did not care for his birthright and easily said yes. Jacob then gave him a bowl of the stew and some bread.

A famine came to the land and the Lord told Isaac not to go to Egypt during the famine but to go to the land he showed him. So Isaac went to Gerar, which was ruled by the Philistine King Abimelech who had made a treaty with his father Abraham many years before. When the men of Gerar saw Rebekah, they marveled at her beauty. Isaac decided he would say she was his sister rather than his wife for fear the men of Gerar might kill him to take her. Abimelech was looking out of his window one day and saw Isaac and Rebekah caressing. He called Isaac to him and asked him why he was deceitful in saying Rebekah was his sister instead of his wife. Isaac responded he was fearful he might be killed and Rebekah taken if anyone knew. Abimelech was angry and told Isaac if another man had taken his wife believing she was his sister, then guilt would be on all of the men of the city. The king then issued a decree protecting Isaac and Rebekah on pain of death.

Isaac settled in the area of Gerar and the Lord richly blessed him. He was so blessed the men of the area protested and Abimelech asked him to move away from the city to not stir up any problems. The Philistines had filled in all the wells Abraham had dug, so when he moved into the Valley of Gerar, he found one and restored it, but the Philistines came out and claimed it for their own. Isaac moved further down the valley and restored a second well, but the men of Gerar came and claimed that one as well. The third well he restored was further away from the city and the men of Gerar did not bother him there, so that is where he settled. That night Isaac went up to Beersheba and in his dreams the Lord came and confirmed the promises he had made to Abraham. When Isaac woke, he built an altar and had his servants start digging a well, because that was where he would put up his tents and stay.

Abimelech came to see Isaac that day with some of his officials. Isaac went to meet them and asked why they had come to him after driving him away from their city. They told Isaac they could clearly see the Lord was blessing him and they wished to make a treaty with him. Isaac would promise he would treat them well and they would do likewise. Isaac held a feast for the men and the next morning they swore oaths binding them to the treaty and Abimelech and his men returned to Gerar. Later that day Isaac's servants found water in the well they were digging and the Lord blessed Isaac at Beersheba. While they lived in Beersheba, Esau married two Hittite women who were a cause of grief for Isaac and Rebekah.

Isaac was growing old in age and his eyes were starting to fail when he wanted to give his blessing to Esau. He called Esau into his tent and told him to go and hunt some game and prepare it for him and he would give his oldest son his blessing. Esau left the tent to go into the fields, but Rebekah had heard what her husband had said and hurried to Jacob. She told him what Isaac had said and sent Jacob to get two goats and prepare them and she would cook them the way Isaac liked. Jacob was concerned Isaac would realize who he was because Esau was hairy and he was smooth skinned. Rebekah fastened goat skins to Jacob's neck, arms and hands and sent him into Isaac with the food.

When Jacob entered, Isaac asked who was there and Jacob lied and said he was Esau. When Isaac asked how he had caught wild game that quickly, Jacob answered the Lord had blessed him. Isaac asked again if it was Esau he was talking to, and Jacob confirmed his earlier lie. Isaac then touched Jacob's arm and, feeling it was hairy, believed he was Esau, although he thought it was Jacob's voice. Isaac then ate the food Jacob brought. When he was done eating, he called his son over to kiss him, and when he smelled the field on his clothes, he gave Jacob the blessing he had planned to give Esau.

Jacob had barely been gone from the tent of Isaac when Esau entered with his meal of wild game. When Isaac heard

Esau enter his tent, he asked who was there. Esau answered he had returned with the meal for Isaac. Isaac realized what had happened and told Esau he had given his blessing to Jacob. Esau begged his father for some blessing for himself, but Isaac had already given all his blessings to Jacob. He told Esau he had no blessings left and Jacob had gained all the blessings by deceit.

Esau was angry with Jacob and he promised when the time came that Isaac had died, he would wait only until the mourning period was over before he killed his brother. When Rebekah was told of what Esau had said, she sent for Jacob. She told him of his brother's plot and instructed him to go to her homeland. He was to find Laban, her brother, and stay with him until Esau's anger had calmed. Rebekah then went to Isaac and told him she wished for Jacob to find a wife away from the Hittites since she had so much trouble with Esau's wives. She told Isaac that Jacob should return to her homeland and look for a wife there.

Isaac called for Jacob and told him to travel to Paddan Aram, the land where Laban was, and chose a wife from among the women there. Soon after Jacob left, Esau heard of what happened and realized how much it grieved his parents he had married Hittite women. To soothe them he went and married a woman who was the daughter of Ishmael, his uncle.

As Jacob traveled to Paddam Aram he came to rest one night. He set a rock to use as a pillow and went to sleep. He dreamed of a stairway which rose from the earth all the way to the heavens. He saw angels walking up and down the steps and he saw the Lord stand at the top of the stairway. The Lord spoke to Jacob and reconfirmed the covenant he had made with Abraham and Isaac. When Jacob woke, he declared the location a holy place. He set the rock he had used as a pillow on top of a pillar and covered it with oil. He named the place Bethel and swore to serve the Lord and to give the Lord a tenth of everything he would gain. Jacob then left the lands of his father and did not return for many years.

Jacob's Family

Story found in Genesis Chapters 29 to 33 and 35

Jacob left the land of Canaan and went into the lands of the east where his mother had told him to search out her brother Laban. He came upon a well one day where three shepherds were waiting with their flocks. The well was large and had a great stone over its entrance which took several men to roll away, so the men waited to water all of their flocks at once.

When Jacob talked to the shepherds there, he asked them where they were from and they answered Haran. Knowing he was near his destination, he asked them if they knew Laban. They said they did and Laban's daughter was a shepherdess with a flock which was coming to be watered. As he was speaking with them, Laban's daughter Rachel arrived with her flock. When Jacob told her he was a relative of Laban, she ran home and brought back her father. When they had greeted each other, Laban brought Jacob back to his house and listened to news of Jacob and his mother.

Jacob lived with Laban and his family for a full month helping with the flocks and fields. At that point, Laban came to him and said it was not right he should not be paid for his labor. When Laban asked Jacob to name his payment, Jacob responded he wanted to marry Rachel, Laban's younger daughter, and would work for Laban for seven years if he agreed. Laban decided the arrangement was acceptable, and so Jacob worked for seven years to earn Rachel as his wife.

The day approached for his wedding and Jacob was greatly in love with Rachel, but that night Laban sent his oldest daughter, Leah, to be with Jacob. The next morning Jacob was angry and demanded to know why Leah was sent to him instead of Rachel. Laban explained it was not their custom to allow a younger daughter to be married before her older sisters. He agreed to let Jacob marry Rachel as well, but only if he promised to work another seven years. Jacob loved Rachel and desired to marry her so he agreed to Laban's demands.

The Lord saw what had happened and when Leah was not loved by her husband, he allowed her to have a child; but Rachel was barren. When Leah gave birth to her first son, she named him Rueben which means "the Lord has seen my misery". But Jacob did not love her. She then gave Jacob a second son named Simeon which means "the Lord has heard". And yet Jacob still loved Rachel more. She gave Jacob a third son and named him Levi, "he will be attached to me", and still Jacob did not love Leah. Finally, when Leah bore Jacob's fourth son, she named him Judah and said "I will praise the Lord".

Rachel became jealous of Leah for providing Jacob with so many sons. She became angry with Jacob and fought with him. He told her it wasn't his fault she wouldn't have any children, but the Lord had done that to her. Rachel decided to give Jacob her handmaiden Bilhah so through her, Rachel could give Jacob children and have a family of her own. Bilhah gave Jacob a son and Rachel named him Dan, saying the Lord had vindicated her. A second son from Bilhah soon came, and Rachel was joyous she had won a great struggle against her sister and named him Naphtali.

When Leah realized she had stopped having children and Rachel's handmaiden was giving Jacob more sons, she gave Jacob her handmaiden Zilpah. Zilpah bore Jacob two sons who Leah named Gad and Asher.

Once, when Reuben was working in the wheat fields, he found some mandrakes and took them to his mother, Leah. Rachel wanted some, so Leah traded her some of the mandrakes in exchange for being able to take Rachel's place in Jacob's bed for a while. During this time, Leah conceived two more sons who she named Issachar and Zebulon, and a daughter named Dinah. Rachel a little later gave Jacob his eleventh son and named him Joseph.

After Joseph was born, Jacob decided he wanted to travel back to his father's lands and so he asked his father-in-law Laban if he would allow him to move his wives and children back to the land of Isaac. But Laban asked him to stay and tend his flocks, because Jacob was skilled at tending the animals. Jacob agreed only if Laban would give him all the goats and sheep of the flock which were spotted and streaked, and all the dark colored lambs. Laban agreed and went out to the flocks and separated those he would keep for himself from those he gave Jacob. He then moved his flocks away from Jacob's and left Jacob in charge of all the flocks.

After a few years, Jacob's methods of growing his own flock had been very successful and it was causing murmurs from Laban's sons. They accused him of stealing from their father and even Laban was starting to grow agitated towards Jacob. At this time, the Lord told Jacob to take his wives, children and flocks and go back to Canaan and his father's lands. Jacob told his wives of his decision and they agreed they needed to leave without telling their father. Unknown to Jacob, Rachel went to her father's house and stole all his household idols while they prepared to go. Jacob packed up his entire household and gathered all his flocks and left the land of Haran.

Three days after Jacob and his household had left, Laban learned of it. Laban gathered the men of his household and pursued Jacob, overtaking him in the hill country of Gilead. The night before he was to confront Jacob, the Lord came to Laban in a dream and told him not to speak to Jacob either with promises or threats.

The next morning Laban went to where Jacob had camped and berated his son-in-law. He accused him of running off with his daughters like captives of war, of denying him the chance to kiss his grandchildren goodbye, and of not letting him throw a celebration for Jacob as he left.

Laban told Jacob what the Lord had said in his dream. He told son-in-law he understood that Jacob longed to return to the land of Canaan to be with his people, but he demanded to know why Jacob had stolen his household idols.

Jacob told Laban he was afraid his wives would be kept from him if Laban had heard he was leaving. But Jacob swore he did not steal his idols and if anyone with him had stolen Laban's items, he would put them to death. So, Laban and his men searched the camp of Jacob, but did not find the idols. Rachel had hidden them in the saddlebags of the camel that she sat on and when she was asked to step down, she told her father she was in her time of the month, so Laban's men let her be and did not search her saddle.

When Laban's search was fruitless, Jacob scolded him. He accused him of cheating him through the years, of changing his wages, of toiling him in the heat and cold, and finally of pursuing him even though he had no right.

When their arguing was finished, Jacob and Laban came to an agreement and built a pillar of rocks to signify the end of their bickering and their pledge not to seek to do each other harm. Laban made Jacob promise he would care for his daughters. The two men and all their people feasted and sacrificed together that night. The next morning Laban rose, said goodbye to his daughters, kissed his grandchildren, and went back home.

Jacob packed up his camp that day and continued toward the lands of his father. When he came close to the Jordan River, he sent messengers ahead to tell his brother Esau he was returning. When Jacob's messengers returned, they told him they had met with Esau and delivered Jacob's message and Esau had gathered four hundred men and was coming to meet Jacob.

Jacob was terrified. He divided his people and herds into two so if Esau and his men attacked one group, the other could escape. He selected many his livestock to give as a gift to his brother and had them driven before his family. He sent his family across the river towards his brother and stayed behind alone to come up the next day.

That night, a man came to him and wrestled with him. Jacob would not concede even at sunrise, so the man touched his hip and dislocated his leg. Even then he held fast to the man. The man told Jacob to release him, but Jacob would not until he received his blessing. The man asked Jacob's name and then told him he was no longer Jacob, but Israel, for he had struggled with God and with men and had prevailed. When Jacob asked the name of the man, the man would not tell him but blessed him and left. Jacob realized he had seen the Lord face to face and survived.

Jacob, with a pronounced limp due to the Lord dislocating his leg, then crossed the river in the morning and caught up with his family. When he got to them, he saw Esau coming with his four hundred men. Jacob had his family position themselves as he wanted, then he went forward, alone and bowing, to meet his brother.

Esau ran forward and embraced Jacob and they wept together. Then Jacob brought forward his family so Esau could meet his children. Esau asked Jacob about all the livestock he met on the road and after Jacob explained he had sent them as a gift for Esau, Esau refused and said he had been blessed enough. But Jacob was insistent and Esau finally accepted his gifts.

Once the brothers had met and been reconciled, Esau went back to his home and Jacob promised he would come and visit. He took his people to Succoth and set up an altar to the Lord and shelters for his flocks and people. He took his family to a place near the city of Shechem and purchased a piece of land where he set up his tents and built an altar.

The Lord came to him one day and told him to move to Bethel, where he had the dream while fleeing from Esau. When he moved to Bethel, he had all his people purify themselves and rid their camp of all idols to other gods. He built an altar and sacrificed to the Lord at Bethel, but soon Jacob and his family moved on to Bethlehem.

During his move to Bethlehem, his wife Rachel started giving birth. Her labor was hard, and as she gave birth, she died. Jacob named his son Benjamin and buried Rachel on the way to Bethlehem, and he marked her grave with a large pillar. Eventually Jacob moved back to Hebron where his father Isaac was, and while there, Isaac died. He was 180 years old, and Jacob and Esau buried him in the tomb of their grandfather Abraham and grandmother Sarah, where their mother Rebekah was already buried.

Joseph

Story found in Genesis Chapters 37 and 39 to 50

Joseph was the second youngest son of Jacob. Jacob loved Joseph more than any of his brothers and made an ornate robe for him to wear. Joseph's brothers hated him because their father loved him more and they would not speak a kind word about him. When Joseph was seventeen years old, he had a dream and told it to his brothers. He told them he had dreamed he and his eleven brothers were in a field harvesting wheat. The sheaf of wheat which he had set in the field stayed upright while the eleven sheaves of his brothers bowed down before it. His brothers became upset with him for dreaming he would reign over them and they hated him more.

Later he came to them and told them of another dream he had. In this dream, he saw eleven stars, the moon, and even the sun bowing down to him. When he told this dream to his brothers, he was also with his father. Jacob scolded Joseph for the dream because it suggested not only his brothers, but also his mother and father, would bow to him. This dream only increased the hatred and jealousy of his brothers, but Jacob pondered what it would mean.

One day, Joseph was sent by his father to check on his brothers who were out tending the flocks. He sent Joseph to Shechem, but when Joseph arrived he was told his brothers and the flocks had gone out to the desert near Dothan. Joseph was approaching his brothers from a distance when they saw him and plotted against him. They intended to kill their brother and put him in an old cistern in the ground. When they returned to their father, they would say wild animals had killed and eaten him. Reuben, the oldest son of Jacob, intervened in their plotting. He told them they should not harm Joseph but merely put him in the cistern unharmed. Reuben said this because he planned to rescue Joseph later and bring him back to Jacob.

When Joseph arrived to greet his brothers, they stripped him of the robe which Jacob had given him and threw him into the empty cistern. As Joseph's brothers ate a meal, they noticed a caravan of Midianites loaded down with rich trade goods heading into the desert towards Egypt. Joseph's brother Judah spoke to his other brothers and suggested they should sell Joseph to the Midianites who would sell him as a slave in Egypt. He suggested this as a way to keep Joseph's blood off their hands The Midianites paid twenty silver coins for Joseph and took him as property into Egypt. Reuben had not been with his brothers when they had sold Joseph to the Midianites. When he returned and found out what had happened, he grew upset at what they had done.

The brothers took Joseph's robe and tore it and smeared it with goat's blood. They then took it to Jacob as confirmation of their story that Joseph had been killed and eaten by wild animals. Jacob was distraught when he saw his son's robe bloodied and torn. He put on ashes and sackcloth and mourned Joseph for a long time. He could not be comforted and was in great agony.

The Midianites sold Joseph to an Egyptian official named Potiphar. He was the captain of the guard for Pharaoh, which is what the kings of Egypt were called. He was an important official in Pharaoh's court and bought Joseph to be a servant in his own house. Joseph was successful in every task Potiphar gave him, and even the Egyptian official saw the Lord was with Joseph. Joseph was put in charge of Potiphar's household and the whole house prospered under his direction. Potiphar noticed how even the fields he owned prospered with Joseph in charge, so he gave the young slave control over everything he owned. Potiphar did not concern himself with anything except what he should eat.

Joseph, as a well-built and attractive young man, caught the attention of Potiphar's wife. She tried to lure him to her bed, but he refused. He told her Potiphar trusted him and he would not betray that trust or sin against the Lord by sleeping with her. She continued her attempts at seduction, but he rebuffed her and eventually came to the point of refusing to be around her.

One day he was in the house when no other servants were there. Potiphar's wife found him and grabbed him by the cloak to drag him to her bed. He refused and ran out of the house with her still holding his cloak. She then called for the servants of the house to come to her. She said Joseph had tried to force himself on her and when she screamed, he ran from the house leaving his cloak behind. When Potiphar arrived home, his wife showed him Joseph's cloak and repeated the story to her husband. Potiphar was furious and had Joseph put into the royal prison for his offense.

Joseph quickly found favor with the warden in prison. The warden placed Joseph over all of the prisoners and soon Joseph was running the whole prison. The warden had no worries over anything he had assigned to Joseph.

After some time, the baker and the cupbearer of Pharaoh ended up in the prison because they had offended Pharaoh. One night both officials had dreams, but they did not know the meaning of them. When Joseph saw them the next day, they both seemed depressed. When he asked them why, they said they had dreams they did not understand and there was no one available to interpret the dreams for them. Joseph told them that dreams belonged to the Lord and asked to hear their dreams.

The cupbearer told of a dream where he saw a vine grow and produce three clusters of grapes. He took the grapes and squeezed them into a cup and gave the cup to Pharaoh to drink. Joseph told him it meant in three days he would be brought out of prison and restored to his place as the cupbearer for Pharaoh. Joseph asked the cupbearer to remember who had interpreted the dream when he was released from prison. Joseph explained to them what had happened with Potiphar's wife and why he deserved to be freed.

When the baker heard what Joseph had said to his fellow official, he told his dream. He said he saw three baskets of bread sitting on his head and birds were eating the bread from the baskets. Joseph told him his dream meant in three days Pharaoh would execute him and hang him in a tree where birds would eat the flesh of his head.

Three days passed and it was the Pharaoh's birthday. He held a huge feast as a celebration and called his cupbearer and baker from the prison. When they arrived before Pharaoh, he had the baker hanged but returned the cupbearer to his place. After the cupbearer had been restored, he forgot about Joseph and did not bring his name up before Pharaoh.

Two years later Pharaoh had two dreams none of the wise men in his court could interpret. He dreamed he was standing by the Nile River watching seven healthy cows grazing on the banks. Seven ugly and gaunt cows came to the same place and ate the seven healthy cows. Pharaoh woke from this dream only to fall asleep again and have another dream. In the second dream he dreamed a stalk of wheat with seven full heads of grain was eaten up by a stalk of wheat which had seven heads of grain which looked withered and scorched. The wise men of Pharaoh's court could not tell him what the dreams meant and he remained concerned by what he had dreamed.

The cupbearer heard this and went to Pharaoh and confessed he had forgotten Joseph. He told Pharaoh how Joseph had correctly interpreted his dream and the dream of the baker. Pharaoh sent for Joseph and, after Joseph was cleaned up, he was taken before the king. Pharaoh told Joseph of his dreams and Joseph answered him. He told Pharaoh both dreams warned of the same thing. He said for seven years the lands of Egypt would overflow with food and the people would prosper, but then there would be seven years of famine and hardship.

Joseph then advised Pharaoh to set men in authority to gather one fifth of all of the food and grain produced for seven years and store it in the cities of Egypt so the people would be able to survive the seven years of famine that would follow. Pharaoh and his court saw the wisdom in this advice and decided Joseph had the ability and honesty to be put in that position.

Pharaoh took his signet and placed it on Joseph's hand. He dressed Joseph in fine robes and placed a gold chain around his neck. He gave Joseph a new name and a wife who was the daughter of a priest of Egypt. In this way Joseph was raised to the second highest position in the kingdom and ruled all of Egypt except for what Pharaoh commanded.

For seven years the land of Egypt produced abundant food and grain and Joseph worked hard at storing as much grain as possible. He had two sons in this period, Manasseh and Ephraim, and he grew in favor with Pharaoh and all the people of Egypt. When the seven years of abundance were over, famine swept across all of the nations. When the people of Egypt began to go hungry, Pharaoh sent them to Joseph who oversaw the gathering of the grain and food. He opened the storehouses in the cities and the people of Egypt were able to buy the food they needed. When neighboring nations heard Egypt had stored plenty of food, they sent envoys to buy food for their people.

Canaan was not spared the famine, and when Jacob heard grain could be bought in Egypt, he sent his sons to buy plenty for his household. Ten of Jacob's sons went, but Jacob held back Benjamin because he did not want harm to come to his youngest son.

When Jacob's sons arrived in Egypt, they were directed to Joseph to buy the grain. They presented themselves before Joseph, who went by the name Zaphenath-Paneah which Pharaoh had given him, and was dressed as an Egyptian official. When his brothers came before him, he recognized them and realized they had not recognized him. Joseph had an interpreter speak with the men to continue the ruse he did not know them. Joseph accused them of coming to scout out the land of the Egyptians under the guise of coming to buy food. They denied this by saying they were brothers, ten of twelve sons of their father. They explained one of their brothers was dead and the youngest had been left home with their father.

Joseph told them he would make them prove their words were true. He told the men to send word to bring the youngest brother and he put the ten brothers in prison for three days. After the third day, he had them taken out of prison and told them to choose one to stay in prison while the other nine brothers took the grain back to their households. If they failed to bring back their youngest brother, Joseph declared they would die.

The men spoke among themselves saying they were being punished for what they had done to Joseph. Reuben was upset at the others and told them what was happening to them was because of Joseph's blood. They did not know Joseph could understand what they were saying and when Joseph heard this, he turned away and began to weep. Joseph chose Simeon out of the brothers and had him bound before them.

He sent his brothers back to their lands and told his attendants to not only put the grain they had purchased in the bags to be loaded, but to return the silver they had paid as well. Joseph's men did this and gave the grain over to the nine brothers. They loaded the bags onto their donkeys and left for their father's house.

When they stopped the first night, one of the brothers went to get grain to feed the donkeys. When he opened the bag he saw the silver he had paid to the Egyptians. He told his brothers what he had found. The others checked their bags and found their silver returned as well. They became fearful because they did not understand how their money was returned.

They arrived back to Jacob and told him all which had occurred. Jacob was concerned along with his sons about the strange questions and behavior of the Egyptian official. He was also afraid of the silver showing up in the sacks of grain. When Reuben told Jacob they were to bring Benjamin back to save Simeon, Jacob was distraught. He had already lost Joseph, and now he was afraid to lose Rachel's other son Benjamin. He decided rather than risk any more of his sons, he would mourn for Joseph and Simeon and not send Benjamin to Egypt. Reuben pleaded with his father and pledged his own two sons' lives to guarantee the safety of Benjamin, but Jacob refused.

The famine in the land continued and the food the sons of Jacob had bought was gone. Jacob told his sons to go back to Egypt and buy more food, but his sons reminded him they would be killed if they went back to Egypt without Benjamin. Judah pledged to keep Benjamin safe and offered to take full responsibility if any harm came to Jacob's youngest son. Jacob finally agreed. He told his sons to take not only silver, but also the finest goods they could afford as gifts to the Egyptian official. They were to return the silver they found in their bags on the way back to Canaan as well.

When the sons of Jacob came and bowed before Joseph he told his steward to take them to his house and prepare a feast. When the steward told the brothers they were being taken to the house of the official, they became frightened. They feared because of the silver in their bags, they were being led to a place where they could be overwhelmed and robbed. At the gates of the house, they stopped the steward and told him how they found the silver in their bags. The steward assured them the silver was a reward from the Lord and took them into the house. Simeon was brought to meet them and they were given a chance to refresh after their journey and their animals were taken care of.

The brothers waited at the house until the Egyptian official came home. They bowed before him and gave him the gifts their father had sent. He asked how their journey was and then asked about their father. They reported their father was alive and in good health. He saw Benjamin, his brother from his mother Rachel, and asked if this was their youngest brother. They confirmed it was and Joseph excused himself and found a private place to weep. When he had composed himself, he went back out and told his servants to serve the feast. Joseph sat alone at his table while the Hebrews from Canaan sat at a separate table from the Egyptians who found it unacceptable to eat with Hebrews. The brothers were amazed they had been seated in order of their age and when the food was served, it came to them from the Egyptian official's table. Benjamin received five times as much of each dish as any of his brothers.

After the feast Joseph called his steward to him. Joseph instructed him to fill his brothers' packs with as much food as they could carry and get the packs of grain they were purchasing ready for them to take back to Canaan. He also told his steward to take the silver cup he used as his own and place it along with a sack of silver into the bags of Benjamin.

The next morning the eleven brothers left to return to Canaan. The steward of Joseph caught up with them on the road. He accused one of them of stealing the personal cup of Joseph from his table. The brothers denied the accusation and swore if any of them were guilty, they would serve as slaves to Joseph. The steward watched as they all went through their bags before him. When Benjamin opened his bags, the silver cup and a sack of silver spilled out. The brothers tore their clothes in mourning, reloaded their animals, and returned to Joseph's house with the steward.

Joseph came before them and the brothers threw themselves to the ground. He asked them how they thought they would escape what they had done. Judah spoke for the brothers and told Joseph none of them knew how the cup came to be in their bags but the Lord must have done it to them. Judah declared they were all slaves to him now, but Joseph would not accept that. He demanded only Benjamin, in whose pack the cup was found, would be his slave.

Judah explained to Joseph that Benjamin was so loved by his father that his father had not wished him to travel to Egypt. Since Judah had told his father he would assure Benjamin's safety, he begged to be allowed to serve as a slave in place of Benjamin.

When Joseph heard Judah make these pleas he ordered all of his servants from the room. With only his brothers in the room, Joseph revealed who he was. His brothers were terrified of the wrath he might bring on them, but Joseph was happy to see them and encouraged them by saying it was the Lord's plan which brought him to Egypt so he might save many people, including his own family. He told them to go back to Canaan and tell Jacob that Joseph was alive and a great ruler in Egypt. They were then to gather all of their households and the household of Jacob and come to Egypt where they would be able to settle in the land of Goshen to be cared for during the remainder of the famine.

Pharaoh and his court heard Joseph had been reunited with his family and were glad for him. Pharaoh told Joseph his family could settle in the land of Egypt. He sent carts to help move them from Canaan as soon as possible.

The sons of Jacob left Egypt loaded down with provisions and gifts from Joseph as well as the Pharaoh. Joseph gave each of his brothers a new set of fine clothes. To Benjamin he gave five sets of clothes and two hundred silver coins. He also sent ten donkeys loaded with provisions and food and ten donkeys loaded with the riches of Egypt as a gift for his father Jacob.

The eleven brothers reached Canaan with all of the great gifts and explained to Jacob what had happened and how Joseph was second in power only to Pharaoh in Egypt. Jacob was astounded and disbelieving, but when he saw all of the riches sent to him by Joseph, he believed and prepared himself and his household to go see Joseph while he was still alive.

Jacob, now called Israel, and his entire household gathered to travel to Egypt. The sons of Israel and their households joined together and they made their way from Canaan into Egypt as one group. Israel sent Judah ahead of them to find the directions to the land of Goshen as Joseph had directed. When they arrived in Goshen, Joseph met them there. Israel and Joseph embraced and cried together and Israel declared he was now able to die in peace because he had seen his son again. When their reunion was finished, Joseph explained to his family he had told Pharaoh his father and brothers kept sheep and flocks. He explained the Egyptians had a distasteful view of shepherds and the Hebrews would be allowed to live undisturbed in Goshen.

Joseph took his brothers and father to Pharaoh and informed the king his family had arrived from Canaan. Joseph brought them before Pharaoh who questioned them as to what they did for a living. When he was told they were shepherds and keepers of flocks, he suggested they settle in Goshen were the other shepherds lived. He also told Joseph if any were especially gifted in tending flocks, they should be put over the flocks Pharaoh personally owned. Jacob was taken to Pharaoh and after they spoke for a time, Jacob blessed Pharaoh and left him. Joseph saw his family settled in Goshen and provided them with enough food for each household. He also granted them some lands in the richest parts of Egypt.

The famine continued to get worse in time. Eventually everyone who had come to buy food, both Egyptians and foreigners, had run out of gold and silver. They asked Joseph if he would take livestock in exchange for food and he agreed. Eventually they ran out of livestock and the people of Egypt came to Joseph and begged him to give them food so they wouldn't starve. Since they had already given all of their gold and livestock, they offered to trade their land, and even themselves as slaves, to get the food they needed.

So Joseph ended up buying all of the lands of Egypt and the servitude of the Egyptians for the Pharaoh. The priests in Egypt received an allotment of food from Pharaoh and were not reduced to selling their land or themselves, but all other Egyptians were starving and sold their lands and themselves to Joseph. In exchange for the land and labor of the Egyptians, Joseph established a law that one-fifth of everything produced in Egypt would be paid to the Pharaoh. This law was not just for the generation which sold themselves to the king, but for all of their future generations as well.

Joseph's family settled in Goshen where they prospered and expanded their households. Israel lived there with his sons for seventeen years before the time came for him to die. When Joseph heard his father was ill, he went to him along with his sons Manasseh and Ephraim. Israel declared his love for Joseph and promised Joseph that Manasseh and Ephraim would be treated like the sons of Israel when it came to the blessing he would give. Joseph took his sons over to Israel where Manasseh would be under Israel's right hand and Ephraim would be under his left hand. But when Israel reached forward to bless them, he put his right hand on the head of Ephraim and crossed his left arm over to touch the head of Manasseh.

Joseph moved his father's hands so Manasseh would receive the better blessing, but Israel shifted his hands back and declared even though Ephraim was the youngest, he would receive the larger blessing. Israel finished blessing Manasseh and Ephraim and then gave his blessing to Joseph. Joseph left

Israel's tent and the rest of Israel's sons went in to receive his blessing before he died. He gave blessings to each his sons based upon their deeds and temperaments. Israel asked to be buried in the same tomb which held his grandfather Abraham, his grandmother Sarah, his father Isaac, his mother Rebekah, and where he had buried his wife Leah. Israel then died and his sons mourned him.

Joseph was overwhelmed by grief by the death of his father and threw himself upon his body and wept. He ordered his servants to prepare his father's body and embalm him so he might be buried. For forty days the embalmers prepared and preserved Israel's body. Joseph then mourned another seventy days before he went to Pharaoh. He told Pharaoh his father wished to be buried in the tomb of his fathers. Joseph informed Pharaoh he would be gone long enough to bury Israel and then he would return to Egypt. Pharaoh told Joseph to go and bury his father as he planned.

Joseph and all of his brothers were joined by all of the members of Pharaoh's court and many other dignitaries of Egypt. They traveled in a huge procession of chariots and horses and took Israel's body to the tomb which contained Abraham and Isaac. The sons of Israel did as he wished and buried him in the tomb of his fathers and returned to Egypt.

After Israel had been buried, Joseph's brothers became worried Joseph would seek his revenge against them for their betrayal of him as a young man. They sent word to Joseph that Israel had requested Joseph forgive his brothers for their actions. Joseph wept when he heard the message. His brothers came to him and threw themselves at his feet and put themselves under his judgment. But he reassured them he had forgiven them and would care for them and their children.

Joseph lived a long life in Egypt. When he was nearing the end of his life, he made all of the descendants of Israel swear that one day they would take his body and bury it in the lands promised Abraham, Isaac and Jacob. He died at the age of 110 and was embalmed and buried in Egypt.

Moses

Birth, Exile and Return to Egypt

Story found in Exodus Chapters 1 to 4)

The Lord continued to bless the children of Israel and their following generations. Their numbers grew and expanded to the point that the leaders of Egypt became fearful and placed them into cruel bondage. Even under this bondage, their numbers and strength continued to grow. After several generations, Pharaoh demanded the midwives of the Hebrews kill newborn male children as they were born. The midwives feared Pharaoh, but refused to kill the sons of their people. Instead they lied to Pharaoh and told him the women of Israel were so strong they simply gave birth before the midwives could reach them. When confronted with this excuse, Pharaoh demanded the Hebrews throw all of their newborn males into the Nile River.

During this time of oppression, there was a man from the line of Levi whose wife gave birth to a son. She hid the child and kept him secluded for three months. When she realized her son would eventually become discovered, she took a basket and coated it with pitch and placed the baby inside. She then covered it with reeds and set it in the Nile near an Egyptian woman who was bathing with her servants. The baby's sister was set to watch the basket from the reeds of the river and to see what happened.

When the Egyptian woman, who happened to be a daughter of Pharaoh, saw the basket floating in the river, she sent one of her maids to fetch it. When the maid brought the basket to her, Pharaoh's daughter opened it and found the baby inside. Even though she knew it must be one of the Hebrew babies condemned to be thrown into the river to die, her heart went out to him.

When the baby's sister saw the Egyptian woman take the child, she came out from her hiding place and offered to go get a Hebrew woman to act as a wet nurse for the child. Pharaoh's daughter agreed and soon the child's own mother was being paid to act as nursemaid to the new son of Pharaoh's daughter. When he was weaned, he was brought back to Pharaoh's daughter. She named him Moses, meaning "pulled out", and he was adopted as her own son.

One day after Moses was grown, he went out to where the Israelites were working. He saw an Egyptian beating one of the Hebrews and became angry. He carefully made sure he was not seen and murdered the Egyptian and buried his body in the sand. The next day he went out again and saw two Hebrews arguing. He told them they should not be fighting with each other. One of them asked Moses if he was going to kill them like he did the Egyptian. Moses realized his crime had been observed and his life was in danger, so he fled into the land of Midian.

When he arrived in Midian, he found a well and sat beside it for a while. While he was there, the daughters of a priest living nearby came to draw water from the well for their father's flocks. Some shepherds tried to drive them away, but Moses defended the women and watered the flocks for them. When they returned home, their father was surprised as they had not been gone as long as normal. They told him an Egyptian protected them and watered his flocks. The priest told his daughters to go find the Egyptian and invite him to dine with them. When Reuel, also called Jethro, met Moses, he invited him to stay with his household. Eventually Moses married one of the daughters, named Zipporah, and had a son named Gershom.

After many years, Pharaoh died in Egypt, but the next Pharaoh made life even worse for the enslaved Hebrews. They cried out to the Lord because of their suffering and he remembered the covenant he had made with Abraham, Isaac and Jacob.

One day Moses had led the flocks of Jethro onto the far side of the desert all the way to Horeb, called the mountain of God, when he saw a strange sight. There was a bush on fire, but it was not being consumed. Curious about this, Moses approached the bush. When he approached, he heard the voice of the Lord call out to him. When Moses answered, (Exodus 3:5-6) the Lord said "Do not come any closer. Take off your sandals, for the place where you are standing is holy ground." Then he said, "I am the God of your father, the God of Abraham, the God of Isaac and the God of Jacob." (NIV) When he heard these words he looked away in fear and hid his face from the Lord.

The Lord told Moses he would go back to Egypt and free the Israelites and lead them to a prosperous land of their own. When Moses tried to argue he could not do it, the Lord countered him at every point. Even when Moses asked who should he say sent him if the Hebrews asked for a name, the Lord had the answer. (Exodus 3:14) God said to Moses, "I AM WHO I AM. This is what you are to say to the Israelites: 'I AM has sent me to you.'" (NIV)

The Lord continued with his instructions for Moses. He told him he was to go to the elders of the Israelites and have them approach Pharaoh. They were to ask Pharaoh for permission to go into the desert to worship God and make sacrifices. But the Lord told Moses he knew Pharaoh's heart and knew he would deny the Hebrews their freedom to even go worship God. The Lord said he would then stretch his hand out against the Egyptians and the people of Israel would leave their bondage loaded down with the great wealth of Egypt, plundering the land as they left.

Even after the Lord had given his word as to what would happen, Moses was unsure. He asked what signs he could give if the Hebrew elders did not believe him. The Lord told Moses to throw his staff on the ground. When Moses did what the Lord said and threw his staff down, the Lord caused it to become a large serpent. Moses turned to flee, but the Lord told him to grab the serpent by the tail. When he grabbed the serpent, it returned to a staff. The Lord then told Moses to put his hand into his robe and pull it out again. When Moses did, he saw his hand had become diseased and rotting. He put his hand back into his robe and it came out purified and healed. The Lord said if they did not believe the sign with the staff, they would believe the sign of the leprous hand. If they did not believe either of those, he was to take some water from the Nile and pour it on the rocks and it would become blood.

Moses complained to the Lord that he was not a good speaker and had a speech impediment. The Lord said he would use Aaron, Moses' brother, to speak for Moses when he went to the elders and Pharaoh. In fact, the Lord had arranged Aaron should be seeking out Moses at that time.

Moses went to Jethro and asked for his blessing to go back to Egypt and free his people as the Lord commanded. Moses said goodbye to his wife and went back to the mountain of God where he met his brother Aaron, who had been sent by the Lord to find Moses. Moses explained to Aaron what the Lord had commanded and they travelled back to Egypt. When the elders of the Israelites heard what Moses and Aaron had to say, they believed and worshipped the Lord for his answer to their prayers.

Deliverance

Story found in Exodus Chapters 5 to 15

After Moses and Aaron had shown the wonders to the elders of the Hebrews, they went to Pharaoh and spoke to him. They told him the Lord had commanded his people to travel for three days into the wilderness and sacrifice to him. Pharaoh scoffed at this saying he did not know the Lord and would not let the Hebrews go from their labor. Moses and Aaron warned him the hand of the Lord would move against Pharaoh and Egypt if he did not relent, but Pharaoh sent them away saying the Israelites were a plentiful people and had much work to do.

When they had left, Pharaoh called those in charge of the work and told them to make the Hebrews make their bricks without straw, but not to lower the quota for their work. He believed by working the slaves harder they would stop listening to Moses and Aaron and not ask to go sacrifice to the Lord.

When the workers could not meet the quotas set for them by the Egyptians, their foremen were beaten and threatened. So the Israelite foremen went to Pharaoh to complain about their treatment. Pharaoh called them lazy and said as long as they cried out to go sacrifice they must not be working hard enough. So the Hebrew foremen went to Moses and Aaron and told them the trouble they started by speaking to Pharaoh was causing grief and pain to their people.

Moses went to the Lord and complained since they went to Pharaoh only harm and problems had come to his people, not deliverance like the Lord had promised. The Lord answered Moses and told him to be patient and watch what happened to Pharaoh. He told Moses to go to the Hebrews and tell them the Lord had not forgotten his covenant with Abraham, Isaac, and Jacob, and when they leave Egypt, the Lord will lead them to the land he promised their fathers. But the Israelites did not listen to him because of their slavery and cruel treatment.

The Lord told Moses to go back to Pharaoh and demand he free the people of Israel. But Moses was concerned Pharaoh would not listen to him because he had a speech impediment, so the Lord told him Aaron would do the speaking when Moses told him what to say. He also told Moses that even though they would speak to Pharaoh and demand he free their people, Pharaoh would harden his heart against God and not let them go. Then the Lord would move against Pharaoh and the Egyptians would then know it was the Lord who led the Israelites out of their bondage.

Moses and Aaron went back to Pharaoh and demanded the release of their people to go make their sacrifices to the Lord. Pharaoh demanded a sign from them, so Aaron threw his staff on the ground and it became a serpent. Pharaoh sent for the wise men, sorcerers and magicians of Egypt. They also threw their staves to the ground and turned them into snakes. But the snake that came from Aaron's staff ate the rest of the snakes. But Pharaoh's heart was hardened against Moses and the Lord, and he sent them away.

The Lord told Moses to return to Pharaoh the next morning while he was down by the Nile. He told Moses to strike the Nile with his staff and the river would turn to blood. Then Aaron was to lift his hand over all of the canals and waterways of Egypt and they would turn to blood as well. When Moses and Aaron met Pharaoh the next morning by the Nile, they did as the Lord commanded and all of the Nile and flowing waters became blood. But Pharaoh called his magicians again and they did the same as Moses and Aaron, and Pharaoh's heart was hardened and he departed back to his palace.

Seven days after the Nile turned to blood, the Lord told Moses to go again to see Pharaoh. Moses was to tell Pharaoh the Lord would send a plague of frogs against Egypt if he would not let the Israelites go to sacrifice to the Lord, but Pharaoh would not let them go. So Aaron stretched his hand out and frogs sprang up from the Nile and all the canals and ponds. The frogs swept over the land, into house and kitchens, even into the palace of Pharaoh. The magicians of Egypt could do the same, but there were so many frogs Pharaoh finally asked

Moses to call upon the Lord to send the frogs away in exchange for letting the people of Israel go make their sacrifices. Moses and Aaron left Pharaoh and Moses prayed to God to get rid of the plague of frogs. The Lord caused all of the frogs to die and the people of Egypt were freed from the swarms of frogs. When Pharaoh saw this, he allowed his heart to grow hard again and refused to let the Hebrews go.

The next day the Lord told Moses to have Aaron strike the ground with his staff, and when he did so, gnats sprang up from the dust over the whole land of Egypt. The magicians of Egypt could not replicate this sign and were shaken and afraid. They pleaded with Pharaoh to do what Moses wanted because they saw the hand of the Lord at work. But Pharaoh refused and turned his heart further away from the Lord.

The Lord then told Moses to go meet Pharaoh at the Nile the next morning. Moses told Pharaoh what the Lord was going to do if Pharaoh did not let the Israelites go. He told him the whole land of Egypt would be covered in flies except for the land of Goshen where the Israelites lived. There the Lord would hold back the flies so the Egyptians and Israelites could see that the Lord's hand was at work. Pharaoh refused to let them go and Moses departed.

The next morning, thick swarms of flies invaded all of Egypt except for the land the Hebrews lived on. Pharaoh called Moses to his palace and told him the Hebrews could make their sacrifices where they lived, but they could not travel out into the wilderness. Moses said the Lord told them to head to the wilderness to sacrifice; they could not sacrifice in Egypt. Pharaoh finally relented and Moses left and asked the Lord to lift the plague of flies from the Egyptians. The next day, the flies were dead but Pharaoh changed his mind and would not let the Israelites go into the desert to make their sacrifices.

Moses again went to Pharaoh and told him if he did not let the people of Israel go and sacrifice, the Lord would stretch out his hand and plague all the livestock of the Egyptians, but would spare the animals of the Israelites. Pharaoh refused again and the next day all of the livestock in the fields of the Egyptians were stricken with the plague. Pharaoh sent his men to see about the livestock of the Hebrews and it was reported back to him not a single animal of the Hebrews died. Yet Pharaoh would not relent.

The next day Moses and Aaron returned to Pharaoh and took handfuls of soot and threw them into the air in the presence of the king of Egypt as God had commanded them. Immediately, festering boils sprang up on all of the people of Egypt. The magicians of Pharaohs court could not even come out to confront Moses and Aaron because they were covered in the sores. But as the Lord had informed Moses, Pharaoh still refused to let the people of Israel go sacrifice in the wilderness.

The Lord came to Moses and told him to go to Pharaoh again the next morning and give him the word from the Lord. So Moses and Aaron went again into the presence of Pharaoh and his court and announced the next judgment of God against Egypt. They said even when it happened, Pharaoh would still refuse the Hebrews the freedom to go make sacrifices in the desert. They told all assembled that the next day a terrible hailstorm would cover all of Egypt, except Goshen. They explained to all in the court that if they believed their words, they would bring in all of their servants and what remained of their livestock into place of shelter the next day. Some of Pharaohs officials believed the words of Moses and Aaron and rushed their servants and animals into shelter, but some did not.

The worst storm in the history of Egypt struck the next day. Thunder and lightning flashed all day and hail piled high throughout all the land. Every man and animal caught in the storm was killed and all the crops in the field were crushed under the hail. Even the trees were stripped of their leaves. Finally Pharaoh called Moses and Aaron to him and confessed he had sinned against the Lord and against the people of Israel. He said if Moses would pray to the Lord to stop the storm, he would let the Israelites go make their sacrifices in the desert. So Moses prayed to the Lord to stop the destruction and the Lord answered. But after the storms quieted, Pharaoh hardened his heart against the Lord and refused to let the people of Israel go.

The next morning Moses and Aaron returned to Pharaoh and told him because of his stiff-necked ways, the Lord was going to send a plague of locusts to cover the ground and eat whatever crops survived the hail storm. When Moses and Aaron were finished, the officials of Egypt begged Pharaoh to give into their demands. So Pharaoh called them back and asked them who was to go into the desert when they made their sacrifices. When Moses answered all the Hebrews, from the very young to the very old, and both men and women would go. Pharaoh responded he would not allow it. He would only allow the men to go make the sacrifices. He then drove them from his presence.

The Lord then told Moses to lift up his hands and when Moses did, a strong wind out of the east arose. It blew both day and night and by morning it had brought the locusts. The locusts stripped the land of Egypt bare and there was no green plant to be found. Pharaoh quickly had Moses and Aaron brought to him. He confessed again that he had sinned against the Lord and if Moses would only ask the Lord to take away the locusts, he would grant the permission they needed to go sacrifice in the wilderness. So Moses lifted his hands again and asked God to remove the plague of locusts from the land of Egypt. The Lord caused the wind to shift and a west wind took the locusts away from Egypt. But then Pharaoh's heart grew hard and he refused to let the Hebrews go sacrifice to the Lord.

The Lord then told Moses to raise his hand against Egypt and darkness fell across the land. For three days it was so dark men could not leave their houses, and yet in the land of Goshen there was light for the people of Israel. After this time Pharaoh had Moses brought before him. He told them the people of Israel could go sacrifice in the desert, but they must leave all of their animals and livestock behind. Moses said they needed to take their flocks to sacrifice some of them, but Pharaoh grew angry at Moses and denied him this request. He had Moses thrown out of the palace and told him if he ever came into his presence again he would have him killed. Moses told him he would never again come to him.

The Lord told Moses there was one final plague he was going to strike Egypt with. He told Moses on a night soon to come, the firstborn male of every man and animal, from the Pharaoh in his palace to the lowest slave and even to the cattle, would be killed. He told Moses after that happened, the Israelites should go to the Egyptians they knew and ask them for gold and silver for their journey. The Lord said the Egyptians would gladly give it to the Hebrews and the officials of Pharaoh would come and beg Moses and the people of Israel to leave their country.

The Lord told Moses and Aaron to instruct the people of Israel how they should prepare for this plague. He told them each household should acquire a lamb, one year old and without blemish. If needed, several households should buy a lamb together. In two weeks, at twilight, all of Israel should slaughter these lambs and spread the blood of the lamb over the top and sides of the doorposts on the houses where they were to eat the lamb.

The meal itself would consist of the lamb roasted whole over a fire, eaten with bitter herbs and bread which was not allowed to rise. No leftover lamb was to be consumed; any lamb which was still uneaten by morning should be burned. The Israelites were to eat the meal with their coats tucked into their belts, their sandals on their feet, and their walking staves in their hands. The meal was to be eaten in haste as it was time for them to leave the land.

The Lord then explained to Moses that on the night of the feast, he would move across all of Egypt and strike down the first born in every household, but if he saw the lamb's blood on the doorway, he would pass over that house and spare all who lived inside. This feast was to be called the Passover and should be celebrated every year on the same day as a way of remembering the Lord and how he passed by the houses of those loyal to him when he brought his wrath.

The night came and all of Israel did what Moses had instructed. That night the Lord moved throughout Egypt and struck down the first born in every house, from the palace of Pharaoh to those sleeping in prison. But he spared his people who had done what he had instructed. The land of Egypt was wailing and mourning by the end of the night, because not a house of the Egyptians stood where there was not someone dead inside.

During the night, Pharaoh sent a message to Moses and told him to have the Israelites leave his country the next day. The Egyptians urged the Hebrews to leave before the Lord killed them all. The Israelites asked the Egyptians they knew for gold, silver and clothing before they left, and the Egyptians gave generously to the Israelites. Just as God had told Moses, the Israelites plundered Egypt as they left. By the end of the morning, the Israelites had quickly packed up everything they had and started leaving Egypt. They left the country so quickly they didn't even have time to let the dough rise for the bread that day.

Moses told the people at the end of that day the Lord had commanded they were to commemorate the day of their leaving Egypt each year. For seven days they were not to eat any leavened bread and on the seventh day they were to have the feast of the Passover. They were also to sacrifice the first born male of every animal and they were to redeem each of their firstborn sons with a sacrifice to remember how the Lord moved against Egypt.

When they left Egypt, the Lord did not lead them through the lands of the Philistines because the Lord knew if they faced battle they might decide to go back to Egypt. So he led them down toward the Red Sea as a pillar of cloud by day and a pillar of fire by night. This way the people of Israel could travel both day and night and the Lord guided them.

The Lord told Moses the Israelites should go and encamp near a certain point by the sea. He then told Moses Pharaoh's heart was still hardened and he would pursue the people of Israel. When he did, the Lord himself would deal with Pharaoh so the Israelites would know he was their God.

When Pharaoh had been told the Israelites had left Egypt, he changed his mind about wanting them to go. His officials came to him and complained they had lost their slaves. Pharaoh gathered his chariots and soldiers and went after the Israelites to bring them back to Egypt.

When the people of Israel saw the armies of Pharaoh coming, they were struck with fear and complained to Moses. They asked him why he had brought them to their doom saying it was better to serve in Egypt than to die in the desert. But Moses encouraged them to stand firm and see how the Lord would deliver them.

The Lord told Moses to lift up his staff and hand and stretch them over the sea they were camped beside. When he did, the Lord caused a great wind from the east to rise and the sea was split in two. The people of Israel then fled from the Egyptians on the floor of the sea, crossing on dry ground even though there was a wall of water on each side of them. The pillar of cloud which had been in front of the Israelites went to stand between the Egyptian army and the Hebrews crossing the sea. The Lord created confusion and caused delays with Pharaoh's army and the entire nation of Israel reached the other side of the sea while the Egyptians were still in pursuit.

Once the Israelites were across, and the armies of Pharaoh were still crossing the sea, the Lord told Moses to stretch out his staff and arms again across the water. As Moses did what the Lord commanded, the waters flowed back into its place and destroyed Pharaoh and his army. When the Israelites saw the dead Egyptians start to wash up on shore, they finally understood the power of the Lord. They feared the Lord who had freed them from bondage and trusted him, and his servant Moses.

The Ten Commandments

Story found in Exodus Chapters 15 to 40

fter the Egyptians were destroyed in the Red Sea, Moses led the Israelites out to the Desert of Shur where they wandered for three days without finding water. Finally, they came to a place called Marah (which means bitter) but the water there was undrinkable. The people started grumbling about Moses, saying he could not even give them water. The Lord showed Moses a piece of wood lying by the pool and told him to throw it into the water. When Moses did what the Lord had said, the water became sweet and refreshing. Moses then told the people if they were to just do what the Lord told them to do, then he would not allow diseases, like they faced in Egypt, to harm them.

After they left Marah, they came to the Oasis of Elim which had twelve springs and a grove of palm trees. There the Israelites camped and rested a while before heading out to Sinai through the Desert of Sin. When they were in the middle of the desert, the people began grumbling again saying they wished they had stayed in Egypt where they had plenty of food instead of being led into the desert by Moses to die of starvation.

The Lord told Moses he would provide food for the people. Quail would come to their camp that evening and every morning he would bring food from heaven for the people. He told Moses they were to gather the food on the ground every morning, but only as much as they needed that day. The exception was on the sixth day they should gather enough bread to last for two days since he would not send any on the Sabbath.

The Lord did as he told Moses he would and that evening quail covered the ground around the people of Israel. They took as much as they could and feasted. The next morning a heavy dew was on the ground and after it had evaporated, the whole desert floor was covered in a flaky white substance. The people tasted it and found it tasted like wafers of honey. They called it manna, which means "what is it?", and gathered enough for the day. Some took more than a single day's worth, but by the next morning it was rotten and full of maggots. On the sixth day each person gathered two days' worth and the next morning the manna was still fresh. Every day the Lord gave them manna so they would not starve in the desert. He told Moses the people should remember the Sabbath and not travel or work, but stay with their tents.

As the people came out of the Desert of Sin, they came upon a place called Rephidim. When they arrived, there was no water available. Again, the people complained to Moses he had led them to their deaths. The Lord told Moses to take some of the Hebrew elders and walk to the rock of Horeb. There the Lord told him to strike the rock with his staff. When Moses did as commanded, water rushed from the rock and there was enough for everybody in the Israelite camp.

While the Israelites were at Rephidim, the Amalekites came to fight them. Moses sent his young assistant Joshua to gather a force of men from the camps of the Israelites and fight their enemy. Moses, Aaron and Hur went to a high spot to watch the battle. As long as Moses held his arms up, the Israelites were winning the battle, but if he dropped his arms down, the Amalekites gained the advantage. Moses soon grew tired, so Aaron and Hur gathered some stones for him to sit on. Eventually Moses' arms grew heavy and he was not able to keep them up. So Aaron and Hur held his arms up until the Amalekites were defeated. When the battle was completed, the Lord told Moses to write down the account of what happened and promised the memory of the Amalekites would be wiped from history for what they had done. Moses built an altar to the Lord at the spot from where he watched the battle.

Soon after the battle with the Amalekites, Moses received word his father-in-law, Jethro, was coming with Moses' wife and two sons. Moses was happy to hear this news and went out to meet them on the way. Moses told Jethro all about what had happened in Egypt and how the Lord had delivered his people from Pharaoh. Jethro praised the Lord for all of these things and made burnt offerings and sacrifices to God. Then Aaron and the other elders of Israel came out to where Moses and his family were. They met Jethro and ate with him at the place where he had made his sacrifices.

The next day Moses took up his seat of judgment and listened to all who came to him. Jethro watched Moses work and at the end of the day took his son-in-law aside. He told Moses he would wear himself out acting as the only judge for so many people. He encouraged Moses to look for men of maturity and good character and appoint them over numbers of people based upon their experience; some should be over a thousand, some should be over a hundred and some just over ten other men. When disputes arose, the people could go to one of their appointed judges to get a decision, and only the most difficult cases should be brought to Moses. Moses did what his father-in-law suggested and appointed men to act as judges for all the people. It lightened the load of his responsibility and all of the people were happy with his appointments. Seeing how well Moses was handling things, Jethro then said goodbye to Moses and returned to his own lands.

The Israelites left Rephidim and went into the Desert of Sinai and traveled to the mountain there. Moses went into the mountain to be alone with the Lord and to find out what the Lord would do next. The Lord told Moses the people of Israel were to be his special people. That he had pulled them out of Egypt to be a holy people and a nation of priests. The people of Israel were to obey the commands of the Lord and he would bless them. Moses went to the people to give them the word of the Lord. When they heard this, they responded they would obey the Lord's commands and be his people.

Moses went back to the mountain and told the Lord what the people had said. The Lord lowered a heavy cloud over the mountain and the people of Israel could hear the Lord speaking with Moses. Moses came out of the cloud and off the mountain and told the people what the Lord had said. They were to consecrate themselves to the Lord for two days, wash their clothes and prepare themselves during that time, and on the third day the Lord himself would appear before them and bind them to himself as a nation. But none of the people, not even Aaron and the priests, were to step foot on the Mountain during this time. If any man, or even any beast, of the people were to step foot on the mountain, the people were to kill them with arrows and stones or the wrath of the Lord would come down upon the whole nation.

The people did as they were told and consecrated themselves and prepared to see the Lord. On the third morning Moses went to the mountain followed by the people, but none of them set foot on the mountain. The Lord descended like a thunderstorm in a thick cloud over the mountain and lighting flashed and thunder sounded like great trumpets. And Moses spoke to the Lord and the Lord answered back so all the people could hear. Moses again warned the people not to step foot on the mountain as the Lord would strike them down. Then the Lord told Moses and Aaron to come to the top of the mountain to speak with him and they went as commanded.

The Lord spoke to Moses and Aaron concerning the laws the people were to follow. They were to have no gods other than the Lord. They were not to make idols of gold, stone or wood and bow down to them. The people were not to use the Lord's name in casual speech, but always hold it in reverence. The Sabbath was to be a holy day and they were to remember the Lord set it aside for them to rest. Fathers and mothers were to be honored and respected. Murder, adultery and theft were not to be tolerated. Nor would lying for advantage against each another. To desire with envy anything of a neighbor was evil in the eyes of the Lord, whether it was the neighbor's land, possessions or even his wife.

Moses came back to the people and they were afraid. They had heard the words of the Lord from the mountain and begged Moses to bring them the words of the Lord himself from then on, for they were afraid the voice of the Lord would kill them. So Moses went back to the mountain to speak with the Lord. The Lord detailed for Moses the laws the Israelites would live under as part of their agreement. He spelled out the ten commandments he had given them and expanded the law to take in many examples of what was and was not to be done. He set up punishments and rules and set down the basic system of civil and religious laws which Moses would present to the people. Finally, he sent Moses back to the Israelites.

Moses called to him Aaron, Nadab, Abihu, and seventy of the other elders of Israel to come and worship the Lord at a distance. The people were to come no nearer than they were and only Moses was to go up the mountain into the presence of the Lord. When the people heard the words Moses gave them, they cried out they were God's people and would obey his commands. Moses wrote down all the Lord had told him. He then built an altar to the Lord the next morning and built twelve pillars of stone to represent the twelve tribes of Israel. Moses had some young men from the people bring young bulls to sacrifice and make burnt offerings to the Lord. Moses collected the blood from the sacrifices in bowls. He poured half of the blood on the altar. He then read the words of the Lord from the book he had written and sprinkled the people with the other half of the blood collected. In this way the Lord made a blood pact with the people of Israel.

Then Moses, Aaron and the elders of Israel went up the mountain to see the Lord. Under their feet was something like clear sapphire, as blue as the sky, but it supported them like pavement as they went up to the Lord. The Lord did not strike them down when they saw him and all of the elders ate and drank in the presence of the Lord. When they came back down, the Lord told Moses to come and live for a time on the mountain so they could speak together. Moses took his aide Joshua with him and told the people to wait below the mountain. Aaron and Hur were appointed the head judges to settle disputes while he was gone. Moses went up the mountain to live with the Lord for a while. A cloud descended on the top of the mountain for six days, and on the seventh day the cloud appeared to become a consuming fire and the Lord told Moses to go into the cloud.

For forty days and nights Moses stayed at the top of the mountain with the Lord. The Lord told Moses he was to build a tabernacle which the people of Israel would travel with. There would be specific items to go in the tabernacle, including a great chest which would contain the most holy items of the Hebrews.

The Lord spelled out in detail each item and even the clothes which the priests would wear. He specified the materials used in each item and the dimensions of the tabernacle and all of the altars, clothing and items. He described to Moses how the priests of Israel would be consecrated before him and described the oils and incense the priests would use when entering the tabernacle. When the Lord told Moses all of these things, he gave him two great stone tablets which the finger of the Lord had written the laws upon.

When Moses had been on the mountain for some time, the people lost faith he would return. They went to Aaron and told him they wanted him to make an idol for them to worship since they did not know if Moses would ever return. Aaron instructed the people to bring him any gold they wished and he would make them an idol. So they brought him some of the plunder from Egypt and he crafted a large golden calf for them to worship. He built an altar before it and they began celebrating.

When the Lord heard this, he told Moses he would destroy the people of Israel for their unfaithfulness. But Moses implored the Lord to let him go to the people and see what he could find out. As he and Joshua came down from the mountain, they could hear a large disturbance in the camp. Joshua thought it might be a battle and that enemies may have come to the camp, but Moses knew it was the sounds of celebrations. As he got to the base of the mountain, Moses could see the revelry of the people and the golden calf they were worshipping. He became angry and threw the stone tablets to the ground and smashed them. He went to the idol and had it tossed into the fire. Once it had melted, he had the gold ground into powder and scattered it into water which he made the people of Israel drink.

Moses confronted his brother Aaron and asked why he helped the people commit this sin before the Lord. Aaron made excuses for his own actions and blamed the people for forcing his hand. Moses was furious with his brother for letting the people participate in such debauchery. He went to the front of the camp and called all who were loyal to the Lord to come to him. The men from the tribe of Levi came to Moses and he armed them with swords and told them to go through the camp and kill those who were still in sin with their revelry. The Levites took their swords and went through the camp and killed three thousand Israelites that day. Moses commended the men of Levi for their faithfulness, even though they had to kill their own people.

Moses went back to the mountain to seek atonement for the sin of the people. The Lord was angry with them and told Moses he would punish those who refused to obey his commands. He told Moses to follow where the angel of the Lord would lead. The people of Israel were struck with a plague for their disobedience while Moses was on the mountain. The people were afraid of the anger of the Lord and they took off all ornamentation and traveled in fear.

Moses set up a tent outside of the camp as they traveled, where he would go and speak. Each man would watch from the entrance of his own tent when Moses would go into the tent outside of the camp. Moses would speak to the Lord in person as someone would speak to a friend. When he was done, Moses would leave the tent and go back into the camp to instruct the people.

One day, Moses asked the Lord where they were going and if the presence of the Lord would always be with them. The Lord replied he would lead them to the land he had promised Abraham, Isaac and Jacob and he was pleased with Moses and would be with him. Moses then asked the Lord to let him see his full glory as one man would look upon another. The Lord told Moses he could not allow even Moses to see his face but he would do as much as he could. He found a hollow place in a rock where he stood Moses in and covered it with his hand. He passed by the rock and after he had passed he removed his hand so Moses could see him in his full glory, but the face of the Lord could not be seen.

The Lord brought Moses and the people back to the mountain at Sinai and told him to go up alone with no one else. There the Lord told Moses to carve out two new tablets and carve on them the Ten Commandments he had issued when he first made his covenant with the people. He repeated to Moses the rules the people would obey and the blessings he would give them. After forty days and nights Moses came down from the mountain with the tablets in his hand to present to the people. When Aaron and the gathering of Israelites saw Moses, his face shone with a light and they turned away from him. But Moses called them back and gave them the message from the Lord. The radiance of the Lord stayed with Moses, though, and he started wearing a veil to hide his face. The only time he took the veil off was when he entered the presence of the Lord.

Moses gave the people the detailed instructions concerning the tabernacle the Lord had told him to build. The Israelites gathered all of the materials and certain men were given jobs as specified by the Lord. They built the tabernacle and the Ark of the Covenant and all of the other items which were to go in the tabernacle. They crafted the garments of the priests and their tools. They created the incense and oils which were to be used in the sacrifices and ceremonies. After the Israelites had done all of this, Moses blessed them for following the commands of the Lord.

When the tabernacle was set up, a mighty cloud came down on it and the glory of the Lord filled the tabernacle. Even Moses could not enter when the glory of the Lord settled on the tabernacle. Each morning the people would look to the tabernacle and see if the cloud had lifted. If it had not, they were to stay encamped where they were. If it had lifted, they were to pack up all of their things and travel where the Lord would lead them.

Balaam

Story found in Numbers Chapters 22 to 24

As the Israelites moved through the desert and conquered all who opposed them and the Lord, King Balak of Moab sent a message to the sorcerer Balaam. He told Balaam a people had come out of Egypt who were too powerful for the Kingdom of Moab to defeat. The king of Moab wanted Balaam to place a curse on them. Balaam was well known to the people of Moab and Midian as someone who could bless and curse, so a group of men came to Balaam from the King with money to pay him and told Balaam what Balak wanted.

Balaam told the men to stay the night while he consulted the Lord. The Lord came to Balaam and asked him who these men were who had come to him and what had they asked him to do. Balaam told the Lord, and the Lord responded that Balaam should not go with them, because the people who Balak wished to curse were already blessed by the Lord.

Balaam sent the men away the next morning saying he could not come with them. When they reported to Balak what Balaam said, the king of Moab sent even more distinguished men with even more money. He told them to pay Balaam whatever it would take to get him to come with them. These men went to where Balaam was and asked him to come. Balaam responded even if Balak were to give him all of the money of Moab and even Balak's very own palace, he could not come with them because the Lord told him not to. But that night the Lord came to Balaam and told him to go with the men, but only to do what the Lord told him.

Balaam got up the next morning and informed the men he was going with them. He saddled his donkey and gathered two of his servants and went toward Moab. But along the way the Lord became angry with him and sent an angel to bar his path. Balaam's donkey saw the angel of the Lord with a sword and turned off the path into a field, but he could not see the angel so he beat the donkey to put her back on the path. The angel went further ahead and stood in a portion of the path where there were walls on both sides, and the donkey turned and pressed into one of the walls crushing Balaam's foot. Balaam again beat the donkey until she started down the path. The angel finally came to a narrow pass where the donkey could not go around and stood blocking the path. Balaam's donkey just stopped and lay down under him.

He got up and started to beat her with his staff again, when the Lord opened her mouth and the donkey spoke to Balaam asking him why he had beaten her three times. Balaam responded she had made him look like a fool and if he had a sword in his hand, he would kill her. The donkey responded she had been a good donkey who bore him every day and had never behaved that way before. As Balaam considered this, the Lord opened his eyes and he saw the angel with the sword blocking his path.

The angel was angry at Balaam and asked him why he beat his donkey. He told Balaam if his donkey had not turned, he would have been struck down and the donkey spared.

Balaam confessed his sin to the angel and said he did not know the angel was there opposing him. He said if he had displeased the Lord, then he would turn back for home. The angel told him to continue to Balak, but to only do what the Lord told him.

When Balaam finally got to Balak, the King was anxious and frustrated. He asked why Balaam had not hurried to him. Balaam responded he was there, as Balak requested, but he could only speak the words the Lord gave to him.

Balak made sacrifices that night and had a large feast for Balaam and the men who brought him back. The next morning he took Balaam to a large assembly of the people of Moab where they could see some of the camps of the Israelites. Balaam told Balak to set up seven altars and the two of them sacrificed both a bull and a ram on each altar. Balaam told Balak to wait for him to hear from the Lord, and traveled up the mountain to be by himself.

Balaam heard from the Lord who sent him back to Balak with a message. Balaam returned to Balak and those who had gathered and said (Numbers 23:7-10) "Balak brought me from Aram, the king of Moab from the eastern mountains. 'Come,' he said, 'curse Jacob for me; come, denounce Israel.' How can I curse those whom God has not cursed? How can I denounce those whom the LORD has not denounced? From the rocky peaks I see them, from the heights I view them. I see a people who live apart and do not consider themselves one of the nations. Who can count the dust of Jacob or number the fourth part of Israel? Let me die the death of the righteous, and may my end be like theirs!" (NIV)

Balak was angry and told Balaam he had brought him there to curse the Israelites, but instead Balaam had blessed them. Balaam told him he could only say that which the Lord told him to say. Balak then took Balaam and those assembled to a higher place, where all of the Hebrews could be seen. He built seven altars and then sacrificed a bull and a ram on each. Again, Balaam went off a ways to be by himself and when he returned he again blessed the Israelites with the words the Lord had given him.

Balak was angrier and led Balaam and the people to a point even further up in the mountains where there was a good view of the wasteland. This time Balaam did not wait for altars and sacrifices. He looked out on the desert and saw the tents of all of Israel and the Spirit of the Lord came upon him and he spoke the blessings of the Lord over all of Israel.

Balak was furious and demanded Balaam leave them at once. He refused him payment for coming and sent him on his way. But Balaam was not done speaking the words of the Lord. He pronounced the doom of Moab at the hands of the Israelites. He then turned to some of Moab's allies who had come up in the heights with them. Balaam prophesied that the Amalekites, the Kenites and the people of Kittim would all be destroyed by the Israelites. He then left Balak and went home.

Wandering in the Wilderness

Story found in Numbers Chapters 1 to 36
and Deuteronomy Chapters 31 to 34

Two years after the people of Israel had been delivered from Egypt, after the laws and commandments had been handed down to Moses, the Lord commanded a census be taken of the whole nation of Israel. Moses was to not only take the numbers of the men over the age of twenty, but he was to divide them by their family. The tribe of Levi would not be included in the census because of their special assignment of taking care of the tabernacle of the Lord.

After the census was taken, the Lord detailed to Moses how each tribe was to set themselves up as they camped around the tabernacle of the Lord. The Levites were to camp directly around it and the tribe of Judah was to camp directly to the east, the tribe of Ephraim to the west and so on. Each tribe also had an order in which they were to break camp when the nation of Israel would be moving. Moses told the Hebrews the commands of the Lord and they did as commanded.

The Lord then had Moses assign specific duties for each of the clans within the tribe of Levi in regard to the moving of the Ark of the Covenant and the tabernacle of the Lord. Moses and Aaron set up the tabernacle the way the Lord instructed with all of the utensil and items the Israelites had made. The initial sacrifices and rituals were performed by Aaron and his sons for the blessings of the individual tribes of Israel. The Levites left the area of the camp and were purified and consecrated as the tribe which would be the holy priesthood of the Lord.

Finally, the time came for Israel to leave the Desert of Sinai. The cloud which had settled over the tabernacle since it had been set up was lifted and the tribes of Israel departed in the order which was set down by the Lord. The people of Israel started complaining almost immediately and the Lord grew angry with them. Near a place called Taberah, fire came down and consumed some of those on the outskirts of the camp. The people pleaded with Moses to intercede with the Lord on their behalf. When Moses prayed to the Lord, the fires ceased.

Soon after this, some of the people in the camp became angry and complained to Moses he had brought them into a wilderness where they had no variety of food. They were hungry for meat and other food rather than just the manna the Lord had provided. Moses went to the Lord and told him he was having to bear all of these complaints alone and told the Lord what the troublemakers were demanding. The Lord told Moses to gather seventy elders from Israel and bring them to the Tent of Meeting, a gathering place just outside of the tabernacle, and he would bring his Spirit down on the elders to help Moses manage the troubles of the people.

The Lord then informed Moses he would send more than enough meat for all of Israel to eat for a month. He told Moses he would send so much it would come out of the Israelites noses. The next day a wind picked up from the west and quail came with the wind and covered the ground of the encampment up to three feet deep and a day's walk in every direction. The people went out and gathered piles of quail to keep and eat, but even as they started eating the quail, a great plague came among them and those who complained they had no meat, died. When this was done, the camp of the Israelites moved onward to Hazeroth.

At Hazeroth, Moses was approached by his sister and brother, Miriam and Aaron. They started to bring up issues they had with Moses' leadership. It mostly had to do with the fact that Moses had a Cushite wife instead of a Hebrew wife and they argued his word should not be above theirs. Moses went before the Lord and told him of their concerns and feelings. The Lord summoned all three of them to the tabernacle and the Lord appeared in a pillar of cloud. He told Miriam and Aaron to step towards him and when they did, he reprimanded them for speaking out against the one he had chosen to lead the Israelites. The Lord left and Miriam discovered she was covered in leprous sores and white patches. When Aaron saw her, he asked Moses to intercede on her behalf so she would not be diseased and despised by the Lord and his people. Moses prayed to the Lord, but the Lord answered by saying she was disgraced. Moses was told she would be disgraced for seven days and then she would be restored. For seven days Miriam stayed out of the camp and came back in when her skin was healed. When she came back into the camp, the Lord moved them on to the Desert of Paran.

As the Israelites camped in the Desert of Paran, the Lord told Moses to appoint a leader from each tribe to travel into the land of Canaan and bring back reports of what the land and its people were like. The men were sent into Canaan and spent forty days scouting it out. They examined the defenses of the towns, sampled the fruit which was ripening in the orchards and vineyards, and examined the people living in the land. When they returned, they had thoroughly scouted all of Canaan.

Moses, Aaron, and all the men of Israel waited for them to speak of their scouting in the Desert of Paran. The men told of a land which flowed with milk and honey and was rich in food. They showed the fruits they had gathered there and spoke of how prosperous the land was. They then told of the different people who made their homes there and of the great defensive towns and cities. The men of Israel began to talk among themselves and despair. Then Caleb, the scout from the tribe of Judah, declared they would have no problem taking possession of the land. But all the other scouts, except Joshua from the tribe of Ephraim and the aide of Moses, spoke of the strength of the people including the sons of Anak, who was one of the Nephilim, a giant. They declared the Israelite scouts seemed like grasshoppers next to the men of Canaan.

That night the whole camp of Israelites wept and complained they would not be able to go into the land promised by the Lord. They argued they should never have left Egypt and plans were being made to choose a new leader for them who would take them back to Egypt. When Moses and Aaron heard this, they fell on their faces before the assembled people.

Caleb and Joshua, who had been in the land of Canaan, told the people while their enemies were strong, the people of Israel were stronger and just had to take what the Lord had given them. The people grumbled against the two men and were talking about stoning them when the glory of the Lord descended on the Tent of Meeting. The Lord asked Moses how long he would have to put up with the contempt and unbelief of a people who has seen the miraculous works of his hand. He told Moses he would strike down all of Israel with a plague and from Moses he would build a greater nation.

Moses spoke with the Lord and said his forgiveness was known by all people. He asked the Lord not to go back on his word, but to forgive the Israelites as he had since the beginning. The Lord agreed, but he made this decision; not one of the men who were counted in the census when they were in the Desert of Sinai would cross into the lands promised. Only Caleb and Joshua of all of the men over the age of twenty at the time of the census would go into Canaan, because of their great faith in the Lord. The Lord said the promise the men of Israel had rejected would be given to their children, but the men who treated him with such contempt and unfaithfulness would die in the wilderness.

That night, the ten scouts who came back with fear and unfaithfulness died of a plague, but Caleb and Joshua who told of the promise of the Lord were unharmed. When the people saw this, they mourned and agreed they would go to Canaan and take possession of the land. But Moses told them they would never step foot in Canaan because of their complaints and unfaithfulness to the Lord. Many of the men who heard the words of Moses decided to go up into Canaan anyway, but as they approached the land, the Amalekites and Canaanites came against them and drove them back into the Desert of Paran.

At this time a man named Korah, a Levite, conspired with several other men from the tribe of Reuben named Dathan and Abiram. They gathered two hundred and fifty well respected Israelites and went to confront Moses and Aaron. They were upset Moses had set only the Levites apart as holy as they believed the whole nation of Israel was holy. Moses told Korah he was to bring his supporters with him the next day and meet at the Tent of Meeting with bronze censers filled with incense.

Moses summoned Dathan and Abiram to come to him, but they refused to leave their tents. They said Moses had led them from a land of milk and honey into the wilderness and now had failed to bring them into the land promised to them. Moses became very angry with them and told the Lord he owed them no debt and the Lord should not accept their sacrifice.

The next day the two hundred and fifty Israelite leaders went to the Tent of Meeting with their censers filled with incense. The Lord told Moses and Aaron to move away from them because he was going to destroy them all. Moses prayed the Lord would spare them when it was Korah who had rebelled against the commands of the Lord. Moses and Aaron took the assembled men who were watching into the camp. Moses told everybody to move away from the tents of Dathan, Abiram and Korah. He pronounced the judgment of the Lord and told the people the Lord would destroy them in a way they had never seen before.

After he said those words, the ground under the tents of Dathan, Abiram, and Korah split open and all of the households of the rebel leaders were swallowed up. The earth then closed again and all of the men, women, children and property of the leaders of the rebels were destroyed by the Lord.

After the leaders of the rebellion were destroyed, a great fire came down and consumed the two hundred and fifty Israelite leaders who had presented themselves before the Lord. The Lord told Moses to send Eleazer, Aaron's son and the leader of the Levite tribe, to gather the censers from the ashes and pound them into sheets of bronze to cover the altar. The Lord told Moses the censers were presented before the Lord and became holy as a result, so they would remain with the altar as a sign to Israel no one was to perform the priestly duties at the altar except Aaron and his descendants.

The next day the assembly of Israel came against Moses and Aaron at the Tent of Meeting and charged the two men with killing the Lord's people. As they approached the Tent, the glory of the Lord came down on it as a cloud and the Lord told Moses and Aaron he was finally going to kill the entire assembly. Moses and Aaron fell on their faces. Moses told Aaron to hurry and take incense and make a sacrifice for the sins of the assembly. Aaron went to the altar and made the sacrifices as the plague sent by the Lord swept through the crowd. When Aaron was done, the plague stopped, but not before fourteen thousand and seven hundred men had died.

The Lord had Moses go and gather staves from each of the leaders of the tribes and put their names upon their own staff. Aaron also was to put his name on his staff and give it to Moses. When Moses had them, he took the staves into the Tent of Testimony and presented them before the Lord. The next morning Moses went and gathered them and brought them out to show the people. Aaron's staff had budded, blossomed and produced almonds. Moses gave the other staves back to the leaders of the tribes and placed Aaron's staff before the Tent of Meeting as a reminder to Israel the Lord had chosen Aaron and the Levites to be separated out from the others.

The Israelites traveled from there into the Desert of Zin to the town of Kadesh. After a month Miriam, the sister of Moses, died and was buried. There was no good source of water at Kadesh and the people starting complaining to Moses for leading them there. Moses went to the Lord to ask for his help and the Lord answered Moses. He told Moses and Aaron to go to the rock known to all in the camp and command water to come out of it.

Moses and Aaron brought the people together before the rock and scolded the people for their constant complaining. Moses then struck the rock twice with his staff and water came out and the people and their animals had enough to drink. But the Lord was angry at Moses and Aaron for striking the rock instead of just commanding the water to come out. For that act of unfaithfulness the Lord told them they would not travel into the promised land when the time came.

When the Israelites moved from Kadesh into the area of Mount Hor, the Lord came to Moses and told him he was going to take Aaron from his people. The Lord told Moses to go with Aaron and Aaron's son Eleazar to the top of the mountain. At the top of the mountain Moses took the priestly garments from Aaron and put them upon Eleazar. Aaron then died on top of the mountain. When Moses and Eleazar came down from the mountain, the people of Israel realized what had happened and mourned Aaron for thirty days.

The Israelites were directed by the Lord to wander from place to place in the wilderness. When the people started complaining about traveling through a barren area, the Lord sent poisonous serpents into their camp. Moses prayed to the Lord for mercy upon the people and the Lord instructed him to make a large bronze snake and raise it on a staff. When the people would come and look at it, the serpent's bites would not kill them.

Eventually the people came to camp near the land of Moab, where Balak was the king. Balak brought the seer Balaam to come and curse the Israelites, but Balaam ended up blessing them in the name of the Lord instead. Balaam did advise Balak to send Moabite women into the camp of the Israelites to corrupt the men of Israel. When the Israelite men started engaging in sexual activity with the Moabite women, they also began bowing to the idols of the Moabites and worshipping their god, Baal. The Lord was angry and sent a plague among the Hebrews. He told Moses the men who engaged in sexual activity with the women from Moab were to be killed.

Moses called all the judges who were appointed over the tribes to him and told them they were to kill the men under their authority who had been with the Moabite women. As Moses was giving them these instructions, they saw an Israelite man bring a Moabite woman into the camp and lead her into his tent. When Eleazar saw this, he grabbed a spear and went into the tent after them. He thrust the spear through both the man and the woman killing both. The Lord was pleased at the zealousness of Eleazar and the plague stopped, but not before twenty four thousand Israelites had died by the Lord's wrath.

It came time for the wandering to cease and the Lord told Moses to take another census of all of the people. When the census was taken, it was discovered only Caleb, Joshua and Moses himself were alive from those men whose names were written down in the census in the Desert of Sinai. The Lord had said none but Caleb and Joshua would cross into the promised land and they were now the only ones left alive.

The Lord told Moses that Joshua, who had been his aide since a young man, was to lead the Israelites after he had died. He had Moses bring Joshua before the assembly of Israel and commission him as his successor before the priest Eleazar.

When Joshua had been set in place as the successor to Moses, the Lord informed Moses it was time to take revenge upon the Midianites who lived in the land of Moab. It was from the Midianite towns that the women came to seduce the men of Israel. Moses and Eleazar told the commanders of the army to destroy the Midianites. The army went out and destroyed the five cities of the Midianites and all of their camps. They killed all the men including the five kings and Balaam the seer.

When they returned to the Israelite camp, Moses and Eleazar met them. Moses was angry with the commanders because they had taken captive all of the women and children. Moses told them to execute all of the women and boys and only to leave alive the girls who had not slept with a man. The plunder from the Midianites was great and the tribes divided it among themselves as the Lord gave instruction.

The time had finally come for the Israelites to cross over the Jordan River into Canaan and take possession of the land. The Lord set down the boundaries for each tribe and clan and set other laws for living in Canaan such as the building of cities of refuge, rules for the Levites, and of inheritance for daughters. These were all laws and rules given to Moses as the Israelites camped on the plain of Moab near the Jordan River just across from the fortified city of Jericho.

Moses was 120 years old when the Lord called him to bring Joshua and go to the Tent of Meeting. The Lord appeared in a cloud and told Moses the time of his death was near. He had Moses write a song to teach to the people of Israel. Joshua was assured the Lord would be with him when the Israelites crossed into Canaan. Moses had finished writing all of the laws and gave them to the priests who tended the Ark of the Covenant. He told them to place the law beside the Ark of the Covenant to remind them every time they entered the presence of the Lord. He summoned the people to hear his words and recited the song the Lord had given him.

After Moses had done these things, the Lord told him to go up into Mount Nebo by himself. When Moses reached the top of the mountain, the Lord showed him all of the lands promised to Abraham, Isaac, and Jacob. Moses was still strong with good eyesight in his old age, but there on the top of Mount Nebo he died after seeing all of the promised land. The Lord buried him on the mountain and his tomb was unmarked and unknown. For thirty days the people of Israel mourned Moses and then they turned to Joshua to lead them.

Joshua

Story found in the Book of Joshua

fter Moses had died, Joshua assumed the duties as leader of the Israelites. He prepared the tribes to cross the Jordan River and take possession of Canaan. Joshua sent two spies into Canaan to scout the land and, specifically, the fortified city of Jericho which was across the river from where the Israelites were encamped.

The spies entered Jericho and went into the house of a prostitute named Rahab. When the king of Jericho was informed spies from Israel had been seen in the city, he raised the alarm and searched for them. When the soldiers of the city came to Rahab and told her to bring out the men who had been seen at her house, she lied and said the men they wanted had left the city just as the gates were being closed for the night. The truth was, she had hidden the men on the roof of her house.

The soldiers left the house of Rahab and went out of the city in the direction of the Jordan River to try and capture the Israelite spies. Rahab went up to the roof and told the Hebrew men what she told the soldiers. She had heard of the Israelites and knew the Lord was with them and they would soon conquer all of the land of Canaan. Rahab told the spies she hoped they would remember her and treat her and her family well when the Lord gave them victory over Jericho.

When it was completely dark, Rahab lowered the men out of the window of her house, which was built into the wall of the city. The spies told her their promise of the Lord's protection would be honored if she hung a scarlet cord out of the window which she helped them escape from when the Israelites came to conquer Jericho. They told her all of her family needed to stay in her house and if anyone left, their blood would be on their own hands. Rahab assured the spies she would remember and they left the city. For three days they hid in the hills until they saw the search had been called off. They crossed the Jordan River and reported to Joshua what they had seen.

The morning after Joshua heard the report from the spies, the people of Israel prepared to cross the Jordan. Joshua told them to consecrate themselves and they would cross over in three days. He told the priests who tended the Ark of the Covenant they would lead the people. An elder from each of the tribes would walk behind them and then the people would move in an orderly fashion. He told the people when they saw the Ark they should begin their journey.

On the third morning, the priests carrying the Ark came to the Jordan followed by the elders of Israel. When the feet of the priests touched the river, the Jordan stopped flowing and dried up. The priests stood in the middle of the Jordan River on dry ground and the entire nation of Israel crossed while the water was held back.

Joshua told the twelve elders to each take a large stone from the bed of the river where the priests who held the Ark stood. When all of the people were across the river, Joshua told the priests to come across the river and the waters of the Jordan began flowing normally. The people of Israel then made camp at Gilgal near Jericho and the twelve stones taken from the river were set up as a memorial for the miracle the Lord had performed at the Jordan River.

During the time of the wandering in the wilderness, those who were born after leaving Egypt were not circumcised. The Lord came to Joshua and told him all men who had not kept the covenant of Abraham must be circumcised. After the men of Israel had healed from their circumcision, it was time for the annual Passover celebration. At Gilgal, the Israelites celebrated their first Passover in the land of Canaan.

Jericho had shut and sealed its gates when the Israelites crossed the Jordan. Joshua was looking towards Jericho when he suddenly saw a man with a sword in his hand standing near him. He asked the man if he was for the Israelites or their enemies. The man replied he was for no one, but was the commander of the armies of the Lord and he had come to speak with Joshua. Joshua fell to his face and the man told him to remove his sandals because it was holy ground he was on. Joshua removed his sandals and listened to the word of the Lord.

The Lord told Joshua to have all of the fighting men of Israel march around the city. The Ark of the Covenant was to be carried in front of all of the soldiers and seven priests with trumpets made of ram's horns were to walk in front of it blowing their trumpets. For six days the men were to march around the city once, but on the seventh day they were to march around Jericho seven times with the priests blowing the trumpets. As they finished the seventh march, the priests were to blow a long note from the trumpets and the men marching behind were to give a great shout. The Lord told Joshua if they did as they were told, he would collapse the walls of Jericho and the city would be theirs.

Joshua ordered the men to do as the Lord said. For six days they marched around the city once a day and then went back to their camps. On the morning of the seventh day Joshua told the men to shout when he gave the word, but not before. He told them all of the spoils of Jericho were to be devoted to the Lord except for Rahab the prostitute and those she sheltered in her house. She was to be rewarded for hiding the spies. He told them all of the gold, silver and other riches of the city were not to be taken but were to be devoted to the Lord.

The men then went to Jericho and marched around the city seven times behind the Ark. When the priests gave a long blast of the trumpets as they finished the seventh circuit, Joshua signaled the men to shout and they shouted. The walls of Jericho collapsed and the Israelite army rushed in and killed every man, woman, child and even animal in the city. The two spies were sent to go get Rahab and her household and take them to safety. They took her to a place outside of the Israelite camp and kept her there until the city was destroyed.

After the Israelites had slaughtered those who lived in Jericho, they took all of the riches from the city to their camp. They then burned down the city and Joshua cursed the man who would rebuild it. Rahab and her household were brought into the camp of Israel and lived as part of Israel.

Joshua then turned his eye toward the city of Ai and sent men to scout out the enemy. The men returned and said Ai was poorly defended and only two or three thousand men would be needed to take the city. Joshua sent three thousand men, but the enemy was strong and drove the Israelites back. When news of the defeat reached the Israelites, they became fearful. Joshua tore his clothes and lay before the Ark of the Covenant asking the Lord why this happened. He was afraid the other Canaanites would hear of the defeat and join forces to wipe out the Hebrews.

The Lord told Joshua to get up. He said the reason the Israelites failed against Ai was because there was someone in the camp who had stolen items which were devoted to the Lord. Joshua told the people to consecrate themselves and present themselves before the Lord the next morning. When the people had gathered, each tribe was presented before the Lord and he chose the tribe of Judah. The clans of Judah came forward and the Lord chose the clan of the Zerahites. The families of the Zerahites came forward and the Lord chose the family of Zimri. When the men of Zimri each came forward, the Lord chose Achan. When Achan was confronted by Joshua about stealing items devoted to the Lord, he confessed. He had taken a robe he thought was beautiful, two hundred silver coins, and a wedge of gold of some size. He had buried them under his tent.

Joshua sent some men to find the items and they brought them back to Joshua. Joshua presented the items before the Lord and the people. He then had Achan and his entire family taken along with the stolen goods and everything else Achan owned, even his tent, into a valley near the encampment. There they stoned Achan to death along with his children and animals. They piled up rocks over the bodies and burned them and all of the belongings. The Lord allowed his anger with the Israelites to fade when Achan was punished.

The Lord told Joshua to go and conquer Ai. They were to treat the people the same as Jericho, but the livestock and riches would be plunder for the people of Israel. Joshua took thirty thousand of his best troops and sent them behind the city. He told them he would lead the rest of the troops to the front of the city like the first attack. The soldiers of Ai would come out and he would flee with his men into the hills. When the troops behind the city saw Joshua and the troops flee, they were to go into the city and set it on fire.

Joshua took five thousand men with him and approached the city. The king of Ai saw them coming and sent his troops out. When Joshua and his men turned to flee, the men of Ai and their nearby allies in Bethel came to pursue the army of Israelites leaving no one to protect their cities. The Lord told Joshua to give the signal for the ambush he had set. When his men saw the signal, they moved into the city and set it on fire. At the same time the Israelites who were fleeing turned to face the armies of Ai and Bethel.

The soldiers of Ai saw the smoke from their city and realized they had been trapped. Caught between the two forces of the Israelites, the soldiers of Ai were slaughtered. The king of Ai was captured and after Joshua had killed all of the inhabitants of the city, he had the king hanged. At evening the king's body was cut from the tree and tossed onto the rubble which had been the city gates. There they piled rocks on his body and left the city as ruins. The Israelites plundered the riches of the city and the livestock as the Lord had promised.

After the destruction of Jericho and Ai, Joshua built an altar to the Lord on Mount Ebal. There he read the Law word for word in front of the whole assembly of Israel to remind them of the agreement they had with the Lord.

Word spread quickly throughout Canaan of the Israelites conquests. Most of the kings of Canaan spoke of forming an alliance to stop the Israelites, but the Gibeonites were fearful of the Lord of the Israelites and attempted to trick Joshua and the elders. They put together a delegation of men and sent them to Joshua. They loaded up old, patched up gear, wore clothing which was dirty and needed mending. Even the bread they took was dried out and moldy. They told Joshua they were travelers from a far off land who wanted to make a treaty with the Israelites. They told how the story of the Israelites leaving Egypt had reached their lands. The capture of the lands before they crossed the Jordan had convinced their leaders to reach out to the Israelites.

The Israelites looked at their food and clothing but did not ask the Lord before they decided the Gibeonites were telling the truth. Joshua made a treaty with them and the elders of Israel confirmed it. Three days after they had made the treaty, word came that the Gibeonites lived only a few days away in Canaan. Men were sent to find if the rumors were true. The scouts came upon the cities of the Gibeonites just three days away.

The men of Israel were bound by their oath not to harm the Gibeonites. Joshua went to the delegation and told them they had discovered their deception. He said they were bound by oaths, but wanted to know why they had deceived him. The Gibeonites told Joshua they feared the word of the Lord which said the Israelites were to slay all the inhabitants of Canaan. It was because they feared for their lives they lied. Joshua told them they would not be slain because of the oaths they had received, but from that day the Gibeonites would be a source of labor for the Israelites. The delegation agreed to this because the lives of their people were spared.

Adoni-Zedek, the king of Jerusalem, heard about the treaty the Gibeonites made with the Israelites. The king of Jerusalem went to the Amorites, and spoke to the kings of Hebron, Jarmuth, Lachish and Eglon. He convinced them to attack the Gibeonites because they had allied themselves with the Israelites. When the five kings moved their troops against the city of Gibeon, the Gibeonites sent messengers to Joshua at Gilgal asking him to send men to help them. Joshua gathered the entire army and marched through the night to reach Gibeon. The Israelites surprised the five kings the next morning and the Amorite armies were thrown into panic. The Israelites routed the Amorites at Gibeon and drove them towards the towns of Azekah and Makkedah. The Lord sent a hail storm against those who tried to reach Azekah and more Amorite soldiers were killed by the storm than died at Gibeon against the Israelites.

As the battle raged, Joshua called on the Lord to hold the sun high in the sky until they had finished destroying the Amorites. The sun stood at noon for about a full day as the Israelites crushed the Amorite army.

The five kings of the Amorites took refuge in a cave near the city of Makkedah. When Joshua learned they were hiding in the cave, he ordered his men to block the entrance with large stones and guard it so they could not escape. He ordered the pursuit of the Amorite army instead of trying to force the kings of the Amorites from their cave. After the pursuit was over and the Israelites had slain the bulk of the Amorite army, Joshua ordered the five kings of the Amorites be brought from the cave. Joshua had his army commanders come and place their feet on the necks of the kings of the Amorites so his men would understand that even the mighty kings of Canaan would not be able to stand against the Lord's people. Joshua killed the kings and hanged their bodies in trees until the end of the day. At sunset he had the bodies cut down and thrown back into the cave. He then covered the entrance to the cave with a large pile of rocks and stones and left it buried.

The next day, Joshua captured the city of Makkedah leaving none in the city alive. After Makkedah, Joshua took the army and destroyed all of the cities in Canaan which were south of Jericho. He returned to Gilgal after the successful campaign against the Canaanites.

The kings of Canaan to the north of Jericho had heard what happened and gathered all of their forces to fight against Israel, but the Lord was with Joshua and the Israelites and the armies of Canaan were driven before Israel and all of their cities captured and plundered. Joshua did as Moses told him and utterly destroyed all of the nations of Canaan except the Gibeonites. Once the conquest was complete, the Israelites knew peace.

Joshua was well advanced in years when the Lord came to him and told him the lands of the Philistines, the Sidonians, what was left of the Amorite lands, the Gebalites, and all of Lebanon had yet to be conquered. The Lord promised Joshua these lands would be given to Israel in time, and Joshua was to include them when he portioned out the land to the twelve tribes of Israel.

Joshua called the elders of Israel together and divided up the land promised to Abraham among each of the tribes. Joshua also gave the city of Hebron to Caleb and his family for Caleb's faithfulness to the Lord when he and Joshua and the other ten spies first went into Canaan many years before. Joshua received from the people of Israel the town of Timnath Serah for his own. After the land had been divided, Joshua established the cities of refuge and towns for the Levites.

Joshua was very old once this was all done and called for the elders of Israel to come to him at Shechem. He reminded them of their history, of Abraham being called by the Lord to establish a covenant. He reminded them of the promise the Lord made; Abraham would be the father of a mighty nation and the Lord would give him the land of Canaan as an inheritance. Joshua told the people the Lord had given them everything he had promised and he expected Israel to be faithful to him in return. Joshua gave the elders the written copies of the Law and set up a huge stone next to the oak tree at the holy place at Shechem to remind them of his words.

Joshua then sent the men back to their lands. He died at the age of 110 and was buried in the town of Timnath Serah.

Judges and Kings

Gideon

Story found in Judges Chapters 6 to 8

In just a few generations, the Israelites started worshipping the god Baal and other Canaanite gods. The Lord used the Midianites to punish his people by letting them rule over the Israelites for seven years. Every harvest time, the Midianites would move into the lands of Israel and take everything.

One day the Lord came disguised as a man and sat beneath an oak tree where a young man named Gideon was secretly threshing some wheat in a winepress so the Midianites would not discover him. When Gideon saw the stranger, he went over to him and the man greeted him in the name of the Lord and called Gideon a mighty warrior. Gideon said the Lord had left his people to be oppressed by the Midianites. The stranger told Gideon the Midianites would be overthrown by the strength which Gideon possessed. Gideon argued he was from the weakest clan of Manasseh and he was the weakest of his family. The man told Gideon he would be with him, and Gideon alone would strike down the Midianites.

Gideon doubted what the man said and asked for a sign. He asked the stranger to stay until he had prepared an offering and the man agreed. Gideon slaughtered and cooked a goat, made some bread, and brought it to the man under the tree. The man told him to place the food on a large rock and to pour the broth from the goat over everything. After Gideon did this, the man touched the rock with his staff and the rock sprung unto flames, consuming all of the meat and bread. Gideon was stunned and the man disappeared.

Gideon realized it had been the Lord and cried out for his life. The voice of the Lord told Gideon not to fear, he would not die from seeing him. Gideon built an altar for the Lord where they had talked. When he had built the altar, the Lord told him to go to the altar of Baal which his father had set up and tear it down along with the pole raised to Asherah. The Lord told him to bring the wood and burn it along with the second best bull from his father's herds as a sacrifice to the Lord. Gideon was afraid of what would happen to him, but he obeyed they Lord. After nightfall, he went with ten servants and tore down the altar to Baal his father had built and pulled down the Asherah pole. He sacrificed the second best bull of his father's herd to the Lord on the altar he had built.

The next morning, the men of the city saw the altar of Baal destroyed and the Asherah pole cut down. They saw that an altar to the Lord had been built and sacrificed on and they became angry. The men discovered Gideon was responsible for these acts and they told Gideon's father to hand his son over to the mob to be punished. Gideon's father refused and rebuffed them. He asked which of them would fight for Baal over the Lord and said if Baal was so offended by his altar being torn down then he could come and punish Gideon himself.

Soon after this took place, the Midianites and their allies came and gathered in the Valley of Jezreel. The Spirit of the Lord came to Gideon. He went and blew a trumpet so all the men of his town and surrounding area came to him. He sent messengers out to the tribes of Manasseh, Asher, Zebulon and Naphtali and called them to take up arms and come to him.

When the men gathered, Gideon decided to give the Lord a test. He decided to lay out a wool fleece that night. If the fleece had dew on it, but the ground around it was dry the next morning, he would know the Lord would give the Israelites victory over the Midianites. The next morning, he awoke and found the wool was wet enough to wring out an entire bowl of water, but the ground around it was dry. Gideon then decided he would test the Lord again. The next night he laid out the fleece and waited to see if the fleece would be dry while the ground around it would be wet. The next morning the fleece was dry while dew covered the ground around it. Gideon then believed the promise of the Lord.

Gideon and the men of Israel went to Mount Gilead and camped by the spring of Harod. To the north lay the Valley of Jezreel where the Midianites were camped. The Lord came to

Gideon and told him there were too many Israelites. The Lord explained to Gideon that if the Midianites were destroyed by the full force of the Israelites, then the men of Israel would look at their own strength as the cause of the victory. The Lord told Gideon to send away the men who were afraid of battle. Gideon did as the Lord commanded and told the men if they were afraid, they should leave. Twenty-two thousand men left for their homes and only ten thousand remained.

The Lord told Gideon there were still too many men. He had Gideon take them down to the stream to drink. Most of the men knelt beside the stream and drank straight from the water, but some lifted the water in their hand and licked it to drink. The Lord told Gideon to keep the men who had licked at the water and to send the others away back to the camp. When Gideon had finished telling the men this, only three hundred remained.

Gideon and his men took what provisions and trumpets they could carry and positioned themselves above the Midianite camp that evening. The Lord came to Gideon and told him he would give him the Midianites that night, but if Gideon was afraid, he should slip down to the camp with his servant and listen to what the men in the camp were saying. So, Gideon and his servant made their way down to the camp and heard two Midianite soldiers talking. One was telling the other of a dream he had where a loaf of bread rolled down from the mountain above their camp and hit a tent, and collapsed it. The second soldier responded the dream had to mean that Gideon the Israelite would bring his sword down on their camp and kill them all. When Gideon heard what they said, he was encouraged and went back to his men.

Gideon divided his men into three parts and had them each place a lit torch inside of a clay jar and carry a trumpet. He led them down to the camp and had them wait for his signal. Just as the guards started to change at the middle watch in the night, Gideon blew his trumpet and smashed his jar. That was the signal for the other three hundred men. The Israelites all broke their jars and blew their trumpets.

The Lord caused a panic to run through the Midianites and their allies. Each man ran from his tent in terror and they soon turned on each other. The enemies of Israel abandoned their camp that night and fled from the valley.

Gideon called on the men of Manasseh, Naphtali and Asher to come join him in pursuing the Midianites. The men of the tribe of Ephraim, into whose lands the Midianites were fleeing, also joined with Gideon and held the Jordan River against the Midianites. They captured two of their leaders and beheaded them and gave the heads to Gideon when he had reached the river.

The Ephraimites were angry at Gideon for not calling them to help when the Midianites were camped in the Valley of Jezreel. But Gideon soothed them by showing how much favor they had already won and what great feats they had accomplished by killing two of the leaders of the Midianites. Gideon and his three hundred men were tired of their pursuit, but they crossed the Jordan and continued after the main force of the Midianites.

They soon came to the town of Succoth. Gideon called to the elders of the town to bring bread to his men so they could continue their pursuit of the Midianites and their kings. The elders of the town replied they would not help him. Gideon swore to them he would have them beaten with thorns and briars after he had captured the kings of the Midianites.

When he reached the town of Peniel, he was met with more rejection and was sent away with nothing. He swore he would tear down the tower of Peniel when he returned in triumph.

The Midianites and their kings had fortified themselves in Karkor with only fifteen thousand of their soldiers remaining. They had lost one hundred and twenty thousand men fleeing from Gideon. Gideon and his three hundred men used an old nomad path to surprise and route the army of the Midianites. Their kings fled from the field of battle, but Gideon set off in pursuit of them and captured them. On his way back from the battle, he fulfilled his promise to the towns which refused him aid. He tore down the tower of Peniel and killed the elders, while the elders of Succoth were beaten with briars and thorns.

Once back in his camp, Gideon confronted the kings of the Midianites over a personal matter. They had been the leaders of the Midianites at a place called Tabor where Gideon's brothers were killed. When Gideon confirmed this, he told his oldest son, Jether, to kill the kings to avenge his uncles. But Jether was still a boy and was afraid. The kings told Gideon he should show his strength before his people and kill them himself. Gideon took their counsel and killed the kings with his own hand.

After the defeat of the Midianites, the Israelites asked Gideon to be their King, but he refused. He did request each Israelite present give him one gold earring from their share of the plunder. When they did, it was around forty pounds of gold. Gideon took this gold and created an ephod, a garment the Levites wore, and had it placed in his home town. The Israelites worshipped it as an idol, and it became a cause of weakness for Gideon and his family.

For forty years the people of Israel knew peace and they worshipped the Lord, but they returned to their worship of Baal soon after Gideon died.

Samson

Story found in Judges Chapters 13 to 16

Israel once again turned away from the Lord and he allowed the Philistines to rule over them for forty years. At the end of that time, an angel of the Lord appeared to the wife of a man named Manoah. He approached her disguised as a man and told her she was going to give birth to a son even though she had been barren. The angel told her she had to abstain from all wine and fermented drink, and when her son was born, he was to never cut his hair. He would be a Nazirite, dedicated to God. The angel told her that her son would be the deliverer of Israel from the Philistines.

The woman went to her husband and said a man of God came to her and told her she would give birth to a son who would free the Israelites from the oppression of the Philistines. She told him how the man instructed her not to drink wine or other strong drink and had forbidden her from cutting the boy's hair.

Manoah prayed the Lord would have this man return so he could give more information about how the boy was to be raised. The Lord heard Manoah's prayer and sent the man back. Monoah's wife was working in the field when she saw the man return. She ran to get her husband who spoke with the man and asked him what they should do to raise the boy in the way the Lord commanded. The man told Manoah his wife should drink no wine or other fermented drink nor eat anything unclean while she was pregnant. When the boy was born, he was to be consecrated for the Lord and no razor should touch his head.

Manoah rejoiced when he heard what the man had to say and begged the man to stay until they could prepare a meal for him. He did not realize the man was really the angel of the Lord. The man told him he would not eat any food, but he would stay if Manoah would make a sacrifice to the Lord. Manoah went and prepared a young goat and a grain offering and brought them back to the field where the man was.

When Manoah built the fire and sacrificed his offerings, the man suddenly rose into the sky within the flames. Manoah and his wife then fell to their faces on the ground because they realized they had been speaking with an angel of the Lord. Manoah feared they would die since they had seen the angel face to face, but his wife encouraged him and said if the Lord intended to kill them, he would not have accepted their sacrifice. The woman gave birth to a boy named Samson and the Spirit of the Lord stirred in him as he grew.

Samson was a young man when he went to a nearby Philistine town named Timnah and became attracted to a young Philistine woman there. Samson returned home and told his parents he had seen this girl and wanted them to arrange a marriage to her. His parents told Samson he should look to one of his own relatives, or at least a woman of Israel, but he was insistent this was the woman for him. His parents finally agreed and went to Timnah to make the arrangements with her father. While they were on the way to Timnah, a young lion attacked Samson near a vineyard. His parents were not near him, so they did not know what happened. Samson killed the lion with his bare hands, ripping it in half and leaving the carcass on the ground. He quickly rejoined his parents and made arrangements to marry the Philistine girl.

When the time came for the wedding Samson traveled back to Timnah. Along the way, he went to see where the lion had attacked him. The lion's body was still where Samson had left it, but some bees had built a hive in the rotted animal. Samson pulled out some fresh honey from the lion and continued his journey to Timnah. He shared some of the honey with his parents on the way, but did not tell them where he had gathered it from.

When they arrived at the bride's house, Samson's father made the final arrangements and Samson threw a feast to celebrate his marriage. Thirty Philistine men were attending Samson during the wedding when he challenged them with a riddle. He said if he could give them a riddle which no one could answer by the end of the feast on the seventh day, they would each give him a fine linen cloak and a set of fine clothes. If any of them could answer it, he would give each of them a fine linen cloak and set of fine clothes. They agreed to his wager and asked him to give them the riddle. So Samson said (Judges 14:14) "Out of the eater, something to eat; out of the strong, something sweet." (NIV)

For three days the men of the town could not figure out his riddle. On the fourth day, the men went to Samson's bride and told her she must help them figure out the riddle. They threatened to burn her and her father to death if they were not told the answer. She went to Samson and asked him the answer to the riddle. He laughed and said he had not even told his parents so she should not expect he would tell her.

For the next several days she pressed him for the answer, and finally on the last day of the feast he gave in and told her what the riddle meant. She quickly went and spread the answer to the men of the town. When Samson went to the men to ask if they had figured out his riddle, they gave him the answer. Samson was furious. He accused his wife of infidelity with the men. He went to the nearby town of Ashkelon and beat thirty Philistine men of that town and took their clothes. When he returned to Timnah, he gave the clothes he had taken to the men who had won the wager. He then left his father-in-law's house without taking his wife with him. When Samson left, his wife's father gave her to one of the men of the town.

At the time of the wheat harvest, Samson went to Timnah to see his wife. He tried to gain entrance to the house, but her father blocked him. He explained he thought Samson was so angry at his wife that he would never return. Because of that, he had given Samson's wife to another man. He offered Samson his younger daughter as a new wife, but Samson was offended and angry his wife was given to another man. He plotted his revenge and that night caught three hundred foxes. He tied them together in pairs by their tails and set a torch between each pair. He then let them go into the wheat fields of the Philistines near Timnah. When released, the foxes ran around trying to get away from each other and the torch between them. The fire that night not only burned the wheat fields ready to be harvested, but also the olive groves and vineyards nearby.

When the Philistines saw what happened, they demanded to know who was to blame. When they discovered it was Samson, they went to the house of his wife and burned her and her father to death. When Samson saw what they had done, he went and killed many of the Philistines in Timnah, then he hid in a nearby cave.

The Philistines took their army and went into Judah and camped there. When the men of Judah came to them and asked why, they answered they were looking for Samson to punish him for what he did at Timnah. The men of Judah sent three thousand men to seek out Samson. When they found him in the cave, they told him they were going to hand him over to the Philistines. The men of Judah were afraid of their oppressors and they did not want any trouble. Samson told them if they promised not to kill him themselves, but only turn him over to the Philistines, he would go with them. They promised and he allowed them to bind his hands with rope and be led out to the Philistine army.

When the Philistines saw Samson, they came at him with a yell. But Samson tore apart the ropes binding him and picked up a donkey's jawbone by the side of the road. He attacked the Philistines and killed one thousand before their army scattered. When he tossed aside the jawbone of the donkey, he was thirsty and the Lord caused a spring to open right where he stood. The people of Israel then acknowledged Samson as their Judge and Samson ruled for twenty years.

The Philistines never forgave Samson for the men he killed and the things he did to them. Once, when Samson was in the town of Gaza, the Philistines discovered he was in town with a prostitute. They waited until he was in her house and went to the main gate to ambush him when he left in the morning. But Samson left in the middle of the night and tore the door of the gates off of their posts and carried them out onto a hill overlooking the town.

Later, Samson fell in love with a Philistine woman named Delilah. When the rulers of the Philistines learned this, they went to Delilah and offered her five pounds of silver coins from each of them if she would find out the secret of Samson's amazing strength. She agreed to their proposal and asked Samson the secret of his great strength. He told her if he were bound with thongs of leather which had not been cured, he would be as weak as any man. That night while he slept she let the Philistine rulers into her house and she bound Samson with seven thongs of leather which had not been cured. Once Samson was bound, Delilah shouted the Philistines were coming into the house. Samson jumped up and snapped the thongs which bound him like brittle strings.

A few nights later, she complained he had made her look like a fool and asked him again to tell her the secret of his strength. He told her if he was bound with a new rope which had never been used, he would become as weak as any other man. That night after he had fallen asleep, she tied him with a new rope and again shouted the alarm that the Philistines were coming. He woke and snapped the rope like it was a mere thread,

Delilah again came to Samson and said he had made fun of her and lied to her. She wanted to know what made him so strong. Samson told her if the seven braids of his hair were woven into a fabric and pinned to a loom, he would become just as weak as any other man. When he had fallen asleep that night, Delilah brought a loom into the room where he was sleeping. She took his braids and weaved them together into a fabric and then took a pin and fastened his hair to the loom. She shouted the Philistines were coming and he woke and picked up the loom to which his hair was fastened.

Delilah bitterly complained to Samson that he didn't love her if he kept lying to her about his strength. She nagged and badgered him about the source of his strength day after day until he finally gave in. He told her since he was born, a razor has never touched his head because he was a Nazirite, set aside in dedication to the Lord. He said if his head were shaved, he would become as weak as any man.

Delilah sent word to the rulers of the Philistines that she knew for certain Samson had finally told her the truth. They brought the silver they had promised her and hid in her house.

That night, Samson fell asleep with his head on her lap. She had a man come in with a razor and he cut off the seven braids of Samson's hair. Then Delilah bound Samson and cried out the Philistines were coming. When Samson woke, he tried to break his bond, but the Lord had left him and he was tied securely. When the rulers of the Philistines came into the room, they gouged out his eyes and took him prisoner to the city of Gaza. There they bound him in bronze shackles and made him push the millstone to grind wheat in the prison. But Samson's hair started growing again while he was imprisoned by the Philistines.

The rulers of the Philistines planned a huge sacrifice and festival to their god Dagon because of the capture of Samson. During the middle of the festivities, the Philistine people asked their rulers to bring out Samson so they could see their enemy and mock him. The temple was full of people. Even the roof was covered with Philistines looking down into the temple to see Samson. Samson was made to stand between the pillars in the middle of the temple. As he stood there, his right hand found one pillar and his left hand found another. He then prayed to the Lord. He asked the Lord to return his strength so he could punish the Philistines for his eyes. Samson felt his strength return and pushed on the pillars until they fell and the whole temple collapsed. Everyone in the temple was killed, including all of the rulers of the Philistines. In his death Samson killed more Philistines than he had in his life. His body was taken from the ruins of the temple and buried in the tomb of his father.

Ruth

Story found in the Book of Ruth

In the time of the Judges, Elimelech and Naomi, who were Israelites from Bethlehem, took their sons to live in the land of the Moabites when a famine came upon the land. A short while later Elimelech died and left Naomi a widow with two sons. Her sons took wives from among the Moabites; one son married Ruth and the other married Orpah.

After another ten years, both of Naomi's sons had died and she decided to return to her homeland. She called her daughters-in-law to her and told them of her decision. Orpah went back to her family, but Ruth said she would stay with Naomi and help take care of her. When Naomi protested Ruth's decision, Ruth responded (Ruth 1:16-17) "Don't urge me to leave you or to turn back from you. Where you go I will go, and where you stay I will stay. Your people will be my people and your God my God. Where you die I will die, and there I will be buried. May the Lord deal with me, be it ever so severely, if anything but death separates you and me." (NIV)

With this being decided, Naomi and Ruth headed back to Bethlehem to live out their days among Naomi's people. They arrived just as the barley harvest was beginning and as they approached the town, the women of Bethlehem came out and recognized Naomi from many years before. Naomi rebuffed their greetings and called herself "Mara" because the name meant bitter. She and Ruth settled in a small house on a piece of land her husband had owned.

Ruth took it upon herself to care for Naomi, and when the harvest of barley began, she went into the fields to collect small amounts of grain which had been left from the men and women harvesting for the field owners. Naomi had told Ruth a close relative, named Boaz, owned some of the fields nearby and it would be safer for her to try to gather from those fields.

Ruth went to the fields of Boaz and followed after the harvesters and gathered the small amounts of barley which had been left by the hired workers. As she was gathering in the fields, Boaz came to check the work for the day. When he saw Ruth working alone in the harvested field, he had her brought to him. He greeted her and told her he had heard of her good character and the way she had been taking care of his relative, Naomi. He told Ruth he would allow her to gather in his fields and said he would make sure she was safe. He invited her to eat with his workers and told them they were not to object to her gathering grain from behind them. When Boaz and his workers took their meal, he invited Ruth to join them and after eating her fill, he gave her some leftover food.

Ruth threshed out the grain from all she had been allowed to gather that day and was able to take home a full bushel, or around forty-five pounds, of grain. When she had carried the grain home, she showed it to Naomi and shared the leftover food with her. Naomi asked her daughter-in-law where she had worked and how she found this much favor. When Ruth replied it was Boaz and he had instructed her to work only in his fields and to stay near the maidens working for him, Naomi was very pleased. She encouraged Ruth to work in the fields of Boaz and praised him for remembering her family with his kindness.

At the end of the harvest, Naomi decided it was time to help Ruth find a home and a man who would take care of her, so she told Ruth to wash and perfume herself and put on her finest clothes. She explained to her daughter-in-law that Boaz would be at the threshing floor that night as his men winnowed the barley harvest. As her mother-in-law advised, Ruth waited until the work was over and the men had started to go to sleep. She noted where Boaz had chosen to sleep and went to him and lay at his feet.

In the middle of the night, Boaz woke and found Ruth sleeping at his feet. He asked her what she wanted and she asked him to not send her away. She asked him to take her as his wife and give her dead husband's inheritance to their first son so her dead husband's line would not die out. This was known as redeeming a widow in Israel. He responded he would be willing to do so, but there was a relative closer than he was to her dead husband who would need to agree. He then gave her some more barley so she would not have to return to Naomi empty-handed and led her from the threshing floor before the sun had risen so no one else would know she had been there.

When Ruth returned home to Naomi, she gave her the barley and told what had happened. Naomi was pleased and told Ruth to wait a short time for Boaz to settle the matter.

When he rose in the morning, Boaz went to sit in the gate of Bethlehem and soon spotted the man who was closer in relation to Naomi than himself. He called the man over to speak and gathered ten of the elders of the town to listen to their discussion. He told him the widow of Elimelech had returned from Moab and wanted to sell her land. As the closest relative to her, it was this man's right to buy it. He was interested, but when it was explained that buying the land would mean he would have to redeem Ruth to continue her husband's line, he declined and agreed Boaz could buy the land and redeem Ruth.

It was agreed upon by the two men and witnessed by the elders of Bethlehem that Boaz would redeem Ruth, bring her mother-in-law Naomi into his house, and buy the property of Elimelech so his line would not die out in Israel.

Ruth and Boaz had a son named Obed, who had a son named Jesse, who had a son named David, who became King of Israel.

Samuel

Story found in 1 Samuel Chapters 1 to 7

Elkanah was a man of Israel of the tribe of Ephraim who had two wives. One of his wives had many sons, but his other wife, Hannah, was barren. Hannah desperately wanted to have a child. Year after year she prayed the Lord would bless her with a son. Whenever Elkanah and his family would travel to Shiloh to make sacrifices to the Lord, Hannah would spend the entire time weeping and praying before the Lord. One year, Eli, the priest at Shiloh, saw her praying and weeping before the altar and thought she was drunk.

He reprimanded her and told her not to get drunk before she came to pray to the Lord. When she explained she wasn't drunk, but she was calling out to God in her misery, Eli blessed her and told her the Lord would give her what she desired. After Elkanah and his family left Shiloh and returned home, the Lord remembered Hannah and gave her a son who she called Samuel.

Hannah decided the boy would be dedicated to the Lord when he was old enough to leave her. When she finished weaning him, she took him back to Shiloh and presented him to Eli the priest. She told Eli she was the woman who had prayed for a son so earnestly that she appeared to be drunk. The Lord gave her a son and she in return would give her son back to the Lord.

Every year when Elkanah would return to Shiloh to make sacrifices to the Lord, Hannah would bring her son a new linen robe to wear as he served Eli. The Lord continued to bless Hannah and gave her three more sons and two daughters. Samuel grew up in the presence of the Lord and found favor with both men and the Lord.

Eli had two sons by the names of Hophni and Phinehas who were evil men. They were priests of the Lord, having been born of the line of Levi, but they stole and threatened men who they should have been serving. They slept with the women tending the meeting areas of Shiloh and sinned constantly against the Lord. Their father confronted them about their behavior, but they ignored him and continued their ways.

One day a man came to Eli to give him a message from the Lord. He listed out the things Eli's sons were doing and said the Lord would not tolerate it any longer. He told Eli his family line would be destroyed due to his son's sinful behavior and Hophni and Phinehas would die on the same day. He then told Eli the Lord promised to raise up a faithful priest who would do God's will and would establish his line to serve the house of Israel.

One night, Samuel was lying down in the place where the Ark of the Covenant was being sheltered when he heard a voice call his name. He got up and went in where Eli was sleeping and asked his master what he wanted. Eli told Samuel he did not call him and to go back to bed. Three times Samuel rose after hearing his name called and he went to Eli. Finally, Eli told him to answer the voice if it called him again. After Samuel was lying down again, the voice called his name. Samuel answered and the Lord appeared and told Samuel it was time to do what he had warned Eli about. The next morning Eli asked Samuel what had happened and Samuel told him all the Lord had said. When Eli heard these words, he resigned himself to what the Lord would do to his sons. Samuel continued to hear from the Lord and faithfully followed his commands. All of the people of Israel came to recognize him as a prophet of the Lord.

The Philistines came to battle the people of Israel at Ebenezer and defeated them in a fierce battle. The elders of Israel asked why the Lord would allow them to be defeated by their enemy. They decided to send men to Shiloh to bring back the Ark of the Covenant in order to assure the Lord would be with them in the next battle. The men of Israel returned to their camp bearing the Ark of the Covenant along with the two priests Hophni and Phinehas. When the men of the camp saw the Ark of the Covenant, they erupted in joy and cheering.

The Philistines heard the great commotion and went to discover what had happened in the camp of the Israelites. When they heard the Ark of the Covenant had been brought into the camp of Israel, they were frightened. They knew a god had entered the camp and the Israelites had gods who had brought plagues upon the Egyptians while they were slaves in Egypt, had led them through the desert, and established their rule over many Nations. The Philistines were frightened of the god the Israelites had brought into their camp, but they encouraged themselves and said they would fight rather than be slaves to the Hebrews. The Philistines went to the camp of Israel and fought the Israelites. They slaughtered thirty thousand of the Israelite army, captured the Ark of the Covenant and killed the priests Hophni and Phinehas.

Word quickly spread of the defeat of the Israelites at the hands of the Philistines and it wasn't long before a messenger from the battle arrived at Shiloh. Eli by this time was 98 years old and was confined to a chair when the messenger approached. The messenger told him what had happened, including the death of his two sons. When the messenger told Eli the Ark of the Covenant had been captured, Eli fell backwards and broke his neck.

After the Philistines had routed the army of the Israelites, they took the Ark of the Covenant to their city of Ashdod and placed it in the temple of their main god Dagon. They placed the Ark before the statue of Dagon in his temple and started celebrating their great victory. When the morning came, they found the statue of Dagon lying face down in front of the Ark. The people of Ashdod stood the idol back up, but the next morning the body of Dagon was again lying in front of the Ark. This time the head and hands of the idol had been removed and were sitting on the threshold of the temple. Soon the people of the city were being afflicted with tumors which caused great pain and death. They decided to send the Ark to the city of Gath, but devastation visited the people of that city and many were afflicted with tumors like in Ashdod. The elders of the Philistines moved the Ark to the city of Ekron, but the tumors infected the people there as well. Finally, the people of the Philistines begged their elders to just return the Ark of the Covenant to the people of Israel.

Finally, after having held the Ark of the Covenant for seven months, the elders of the Philistines called their priests and diviners and asked them how they should return the Ark to the Israelites. The priests and diviners gave them these instructions. They told the elders of the Philistines not to harden their hearts against the Lord as the Egyptians did, or the Philistines would suffer in the same way as Egypt. They told them to make a new wagon and hitch two cows to it and place the Ark of the Covenant in the back. Then they were to place a guilt offering in the back of the wagon. The offering should be five golden tumors and five golden rats to symbolize the judgment which had come against the five cities of the Philistines.

Once that was done, the elders were to let the cows go without a driver. If the cows headed toward Beth Shemesh, then the plague of tumors and the disasters in the lands of the Philistines was from the God of Israel. If the cows did not head towards Beth Shemesh, then it was merely chance which caused these things to happen. So, the elders of the Philistines watched the wagon and it headed towards Beth Shemesh.

The men of Beth Shemesh were out in their fields harvesting wheat when they saw the wagon with the Ark of the Covenant coming towards them. They rejoiced the Lord had returned the Ark to them. The wagon stopped beside a large rock in the middle of a field near Beth Shemesh and the men of that town used the wood of the wagon to make an altar and sacrificed the two cows pulling the wagon as a burnt offering to the Lord. The Levites came and moved the Ark of the Covenant onto the large rock in the field and the people worshiped and sacrificed to the Lord all day and night. When the elders of the Philistines saw this, they returned to their own lands.

Some of the men of Beth Shemesh looked upon the Ark of the Covenant. This made the Lord angry and he killed them. The people of the town realized how dangerous it was for them to have the Ark with them and sent messengers to the town of Kiriath Jearim to come and take it from them. The men of Kiriath Jearim came and took the Ark of the Covenant to the house of Abinadab and consecrated his son, Eleazar, as guardian of the Ark.

For twenty years, the people of Israel lived under the oppression of the Philistines because they had turned their back on the Lord. Finally, they started calling out to God again and Samuel saw their sincere prayers and went to them and told them if they were serious about turning back to the Lord, then they should rid themselves of their idols of Baal and Ashteroth and worship the Lord alone. The people of Israel turned from their idolatry and destroyed their idols of Baal and Ashteroth.

When he had seen what they had done, Samuel called all of the people to Mizpah where he would intercede for them with the Lord. When they had gathered, he poured out a water offering for them and led them in a day of fasting and prayer.

When the Philistines heard all of Israel was gathering at Mizpah, their rulers called up their armies and marched against the Hebrews. When the people of Israel saw this, they were frightened and told Samuel to keep interceding for them. Samuel sacrificed a new born lamb to the Lord who heard his prayer. When the Philistines came to the Israelites at Mizpah, the Lord thundered at them and caused them to flee in panic. The Israelites pursued them all the way back to their cities. Samuel set a large stone up outside of Mizpah and named it "Ebenezer", which meant "The Lord has helped us".

The Israelites battled the Philistines and took back all of the Hebrew towns the Philistines had conquered. Never again during the time of Samuel did the Philistines invade the lands of the Israelites. Samuel continued to judge all of Israel for the rest of his days traveling from Bethel to Gilgal to Mizpah. He also judged from his home in Ramah where he had built an altar to the Lord.

Saul

Story found in 1 Samuel Chapters 8 to 31

When Samuel was growing older, he appointed his two sons to be judges of Israel, but his sons did evil in the eyes of the Lord. They accepted bribes and were corrupt in their judgments. The elders of Israel were upset Samuel's sons would be their judges, so they told Samuel to appoint a king to rule over them like other nations.

Samuel was upset by this demand and prayed to the Lord for an answer. The Lord told Samuel to be attentive to what the elders said. The Lord pointed out that the people were not rejecting Samuel as a Judge but rather they were rejecting the Lord as their king. He told Samuel to let them know a king would rule over them and use them for his own ends; their sons and daughters would be used by a king as he wished. The Lord warned Israel if he gave them a king, they would eventually ask the Lord to free them of the tyranny of the crown, but the Lord would ignore their pleas.

When Samuel told the elders the words of the Lord, they rejected them and insisted Samuel give them a king. When Samuel went to the Lord again and told them what the elders demanded, the Lord gave them their wish and told Samuel to anoint a king over Israel. Samuel told the elders he would give them a king and the elders returned home.

There was a young man named Saul of the tribe of Benjamin who was powerfully built and attractive. Saul's father had a herd of donkeys run away and he sent his son and a servant to find them and bring them back home. After a three-day search, Saul and his servant could not find the donkeys, but the servant noted they were near a town where a prophet of the Lord was. He convinced Saul to go see the prophet and see if he could convince him to locate the donkeys. They asked some people in the town where the prophet was and they pointed to a high place where the prophet would go to bless sacrifices. As they headed to the high place, they came across the path of Samuel as he was headed to the high place on the mountain.

The Lord had told Samuel the day before that he would meet a young Benjamite who would be anointed king of Israel. When Samuel saw Saul, the Lord spoke to him and confirmed Saul was to be king. Saul went to Samuel and asked if he knew where the prophet was. Samuel replied he was the prophet and Saul was to join him at the high place and then spend the night in his house. He told Saul not to worry about his father's donkeys; they had been found by someone else and returned. Saul was confused as to why the prophet would treat him with such honor since he was a young man of the smallest clan of the smallest tribe of Israel.

Samuel took Saul to the top of the hill and treated him as an honored guest among the men of the town, who had also been invited to the sacrifice. After they had eaten, Samuel took Saul and his servant to his house and spent the remainder of the day speaking with Saul on the rooftop. Early the next morning Saul prepared to return home when Samuel told him to wait and hear a private message from the Lord. Saul sent his servant ahead and waited for what Samuel had to say.

When Samuel and Saul were alone, Samuel took some oil and poured it over Saul's head. Samuel told him the Lord would establish him as King and told him the route to take home. As a sign, he told him he would meet some of his father's servants who would tell him the donkeys had been found and his father was now worried about his son. Later that day he would meet three men going to sacrifice at Bethel who would offer him some of their bread. And finally, he said Saul would come upon a procession of people prophesying and playing music. When Saul heard the prophecies and music, he would become a new man and would be led by the Lord.

Saul left Samuel and the signs the prophet had given the young Benjamite came true. When Saul came upon the procession of musicians and prophets, the Spirit of the Lord descended on Saul and he began to prophesy. When the people saw this they were amazed because they knew Saul and now he was with the prophets. Saul and his servant went to the high place nearby to sacrifice and worship the Lord. When he was returning home, his uncle came and asked him what had happened. They told him everything which had occurred from the time they left to search for the donkeys except for what Samuel had said about the Lord making Saul king over Israel.

Samuel called all of the elders of Israel to him and told them the Lord had not wanted to place a king over them, but because of their insistence he had granted their desire. He ordered the people to present themselves in order of tribes. He then went through the tribes until he came to Benjamin, the smallest tribe. Then he went through the clans of Benjamin until he came to the clan of Matri, the smallest of the clans. He then came to Kish and told him to bring his son Saul forward. But Saul could not be found among the men. When they went to look for him, they found him hiding with the animals and servants. Samuel had him brought forward and declared the Lord had chosen Saul to be king of Israel. The gathered elders rejoiced at God's decision and Samuel wrote down the rules of the kingship. After this was finished, Samuel sent all the people home. Some of the more valiant men of Israel went with Saul but there were others who were not happy with him being chosen king. Saul did not tell anyone of his anointing by Samuel.

One of the rulers of the Ammonites, a man named Nahash, besieged the town of Jabesh in Israel. The men of the town begged Nahash to cease his siege and they would be his subjects. But Nahash replied he would only accept their surrender if they would agree to let him gouge out the right eye of all of the men in town to bring ridicule upon the Israelites. They told him they would answer his demand in seven days. They sent out messengers to seek aid against Nahash, and some of these messengers came to where Saul was returning from the fields behind his team of oxen. When he saw the messengers talking to his people, he approached them and told them to give him their news.

When they told him what happened, the Spirit of the Lord descended upon him and he flew into a rage. He slaughtered two of the oxen and chopped them to pieces. He had the messengers take the pieces to all parts of Israel with the message that anyone who did not come to aid Samuel and Saul in lifting the siege at Jabesh would suffer the same fate as the oxen. The fear of the Lord compelled the men of Israel to come to Saul's call. Over three hundred thousand men had come to free Jabesh. They sent the messengers back into town with instructions to tell Nahash the city would surrender the next day. That night Saul divided his men into three parts and attacked the Ammonites in the early morning while it was still dark. By the time the sun had started warming the day, the very few survivors of Nahash's men were far away from Jabesh.

The next day the men of Israel called for the deaths of those who had questioned Saul's appointment as king, but Saul forbid any bloodshed on the day of victory. Samuel told those gathered to go to Gilgal and reconfirm Saul as king. They went and made sacrifices and held a great celebration before the Lord declaring Saul was king of Israel.

When Samuel saw Saul was finally accepted as king of Israel, he went to the people and told them they would now have to follow Saul. He warned them to not abandon the laws of the Lord and to follow the Lord with all of their heart. He warned against worshipping false idols and against following the ways of the people which surrounded them. He told them he would continue praying for them as long as he lived.

Saul decided the Philistines, who were always a threat to the people of Israel, needed to be driven back from the borders of Israel. His oldest son Jonathan attacked one of the Philistine outposts at Geba. When the Philistines heard about this, they gathered their armies. Saul called the men of Israel back to him, but when they saw the number of Philistines who were camped and ready for battle, they melted back into the countryside and hid from their enemies. Saul had been told to wait for seven days for Samuel to come and make sacrifices to the Lord on behalf of the soldiers. As the seventh day came and Samuel had not arrived, Saul sacrificed and offered the burnt offerings to the Lord himself. Samuel arrived just as Saul finished. He was very angry with Saul for not waiting. He told Saul his disobedience to the Lord would lead to the downfall of his line and the Lord had already chosen another for the throne.

As Saul and Jonathan waited for the men of Israel to come back to them, the Philistines went through the countryside and captured all of the blacksmiths they could find. Even the Israelite farmers had to go into the land of the Philistines to have their equipment repaired because no one in Israel was left who could work with metal. The armies of Israel were in such disrepair that when it came time to take the field of battle only Saul and Jonathan had serviceable weapons.

Jonathan set out one morning with his armor bearer, the man who helped outfit him for battle, and headed towards a small Philistine outpost. He told his servant they were going to approach the outpost and let themselves be seen by the Philistines. If they told him to stay back, he would head back to his father's camp, but if they told him to come up and face them, then he would take it as a sign from the Lord that he was to go up and kill them. When Jonathan and his armor bearer made it to the hill below the outpost, some of the Philistines laughed at him and said the Israelites were starting to climb out of the holes they had been hiding in. They called to Jonathan to come up so they could teach him a lesson about battle. Jonathan and his servant climbed the hill and started killing the Philistines. They killed about twenty enemy soldiers in a short period of time.

The Lord caused a panic among the Philistines. The ground started shaking and fear gripped them. The Philistine army started to flee from their outposts and camps. When Saul's lookouts saw this, they went and told the king. Saul ordered an accounting for all of the men in his camp. When they checked, only Jonathan and his armor bearer were missing. Saul told the priests who were with him to bring the Ark of the Covenant, but even as he was telling them his instructions, panic overwhelmed the Philistines. Saul ordered his men to assemble for battle and went into the Philistine camp. When they arrived at their enemy's camp, they found the Philistines were fighting each other in confusion and the Hebrews which had sided with the enemy switched sides to support Saul. The Israelites who were hiding from the Philistines in the countryside heard what was happening. They came and helped Saul and Jonathan pursue the Philistines out of the land of Israel.

Saul made an oath while pursuing the enemy that none of those in his army would eat any food until nightfall or be put to death. His son Jonathan did not hear of the oath because he did not meet up with the army until after the pursuit began. When they were going through a forest, Jonathan saw some honeycomb and stopped and ate some honey. The other men of the army warned him of the oath his father swore. Jonathan disagreed with the oath his father had sworn believing that if the men could eat, they could kill more Philistines.

When the sun had set, the men of Israel fell onto the livestock of the Philistines, slaughtering the animals and eating them before they had been properly drained of blood. When Saul heard this, he ordered his men bring the animals to a large rock in their camp to properly prepare the animals for eating. Saul built an altar to the Lord at that location and made sacrifices as his men ate. When he said they should continue the pursuit that night, the priests with him encouraged him to seek guidance from the Lord. Saul sought the Lord's answer to his proposal, but the Lord did not answer him.

Saul called all of the leaders of his army together and said he believed someone had sinned against the Lord that day and he would have that man put to death. The leaders of the army knew Jonathan had eaten honey despite his father's oath, but they said nothing. Then Saul took Jonathan and stood apart from the leaders of his army and cast lots (used the divination of the priest) to find the sinner. The results pointed to Saul and Jonathan. Then Saul cast lots again between himself and his son. The results pointed to Jonathan. Saul was grieved but he had said even if it were Jonathan, he would put him to death. The leaders of the army argued with Saul that it was his oath, not Jonathan's actions, which had brought them to that point and they refused to allow Saul to kill Jonathan. Jonathan's life was spared that night and the Israelites stopped their pursuit of the Philistines and went back to their homes.

Samuel went to Saul with a word from the Lord. When Israel came up out of Egypt, the Amalekites were the first to try to destroy God's chosen people. Because of their actions, the Lord told Saul to gather the men of Israel and to utterly destroy the Amalekites; every man, woman and child was to be put to death. The Lord said even every animal the Amalekites owned was to be wiped out. Saul gathered the armies of Israel to him and marched to the city of Amalek. There he told the Kenites to leave the land, as the Kenites had shown some kindness to the Israelites when they left Egypt. Saul set an ambush in a ravine outside of the city of the Amalekites and utterly destroyed their army. The Israelites then wiped out all of the towns of the Amalekites from the desert to the Red Sea.

But Saul took the Amalekite king, Agag, captive and the men of Israel took the fatted calves and lambs. That night the Lord came to Samuel in a dream and said he was grieved Saul was made king. The Lord told Samuel that Saul refused to obey his commands. The next morning Samuel went to find Saul. He was told Saul had been up on the mountain at Carmel where he had built a monument to himself. He then planned to travel to Gilgal to make sacrifices to the Lord. When Samuel found him, Saul was glad and told him he had followed the commands of the Lord. But Samuel pointed out the men of Israel had broken the command by bringing back livestock, which should have been destroyed, and Agag, the king of Amalekites, who should have been slain.

Saul argued he only brought back the livestock to sacrifice to the Lord and he had killed all but Agag of the Amalekites. But Samuel responded that the Lord was angry with him. He said the Lord preferred obedience over sacrifices and because Saul rejected the Lord, the Lord had rejected Saul as king of Israel. Saul confessed his sin and asked Samuel to go and sacrifice to the Lord with him. Samuel refused and started to leave, but Saul grabbed his robe, tearing it, and begged Samuel to go with him to the elders and sacrifice. Samuel responded in the same way Saul had torn his robe, the Lord would tear away the kingdom from Saul. Saul finally persuaded Samuel to go together and make sacrifices at Gilgal. When the sacrifices were finished, Samuel called for King Agag of the Amalekites to be brought forth. Agag believed he would be ransomed because so much time had passed since his capture, but Samuel killed him with a sword in front of all of the elders of Israel. Samuel and Saul then went their separate ways. Although Samuel prayed for Saul until he died, he never went to see Saul again.

David the Anointed

Story found in 1 Samuel Chapters 16 to 20

Samuel mourned for Saul because the Lord had rejected him as king of Israel. The Lord told Samuel to stop his mourning and take his horn full of oil to Bethlehem and look for a man named Jesse. Samuel was afraid Saul might find out he was looking for a new king, so the Lord told him to take a cow and tell the people of Bethlehem he was going to make a sacrifice to the Lord.

When Samuel went to the town, the elders came out to meet him, afraid of what his presence would mean for them. He reassured them he was there to sacrifice to the Lord and they should consecrate themselves and join him. The elders went to prepare themselves for the sacrifice and Samuel consecrated Jesse and his sons when he found them. When the sacrifice was taking place, Jesse sent his first son to Samuel. He was tall and big and Samuel was sure he was the one he was to anoint. But the Lord told Samuel he was not to look at outward appearances. Samuel sent him back to his Father. Jesse sent each of his seven sons forward, but the Lord rejected them all. Samuel then asked Jesse if he had any more sons, and Jesse replied his youngest was barely a man and was out tending his flocks of sheep. Samuel had Jesse send for him and they waited until he arrived before they finished the sacrifice. When David walked in, the Lord told Samuel to anoint him. Samuel anointed David as king of Israel in the presence of his brothers and the others in attendance. From that day, the power of the Lord was with David.

King Saul was tormented by an evil spirit after the Spirit of the Lord had left him. This spirit would cause him pain and anguish and his attendants determined he needed someone who could play the harp to soothe him when the evil spirit would come. Saul agreed he would try what they suggested and asked them to find a harpist. One of the men said he had heard of a brave young man. The young man was said to be well spoken and had a warrior's spirit. His name was David and he tended the sheep of his father near the town of Bethlehem.

Saul sent word for David to come to him and Jesse sent David with a donkey, bread, wine and a kid goat to Saul. David would play the harp for the king when the evil spirit would come and Saul would feel relief and calm. Saul came to like the young man very much and sent word to Jesse he would keep his son in his service as one of his armor-bearers.

The armies of the Philistines came to battle Israel at the Valley of Elah. The Philistines were camped on the hill on one side of the valley and the Israelites were camped on the hill on the opposite side. The Philistines had a giant of a man with them named Goliath. He was one of the champions of their army. He stood over nine feet tall and was dressed in fierce armor for battle. He wore a huge bronze helmet, his coat of bronze scales weighed one hundred and twenty pounds, and the bronze point of his spear weighed fourteen pounds. Goliath would go down into the valley and taunt the men of Israel, challenging any of them to come out and face him in a one on one fight. He mocked and taunted the men of Israel and told them if any man would come and defeat him, then the Philistines would become servants of Israel, but if the man Israel sent forth was slain, then the Philistines would rule over Israel. Saul and his men were terrified at the giant's challenge.

For forty days Goliath came out and challenged the men of Israel who were in the camp. David, one of the king's armor-bearers, was tending the flocks of sheep for his father during this time. His three oldest brothers were in the army of Israel and his father sent David with some bread and cheese for them and their commanders. David left early in the morning and by the time he reached the valley both armies were taking their positions along the battle lines outside of the camps. David left his packages at the camp and ran out to the warriors to find and greet his brothers. As he was talking to them, Goliath came out from the lines of the Philistines into the valley and issued his daily challenges and taunts. When the men of Israel saw him, they pulled back from their lines and they started talking among themselves about Goliath and how he frightened them. They said King Saul had promised great rewards to go and meet Goliath's challenge and defeat him. The king had promised great wealth and his daughter's hand in marriage to the man brave and skilled enough to kill the giant.

When David saw Goliath make the challenge and heard the men talking, he asked several other men to make sure he knew what the rewards would be for the man who would rid Israel of this threat and mockery. When David's oldest brother heard what he was asking, he became angry with David and accused him of only coming to watch the battle. But David said he had a right to ask and question the men, and he continued to do so.

Word of David being in the camp and asking after the reward reached the ears of the king and Saul sent for David. When David was brought before Saul, he volunteered to go and kill Goliath for Israel. When Saul heard this, he told David he was being ridiculous. He said David was still a boy and Goliath had long years of killing men in battle. But David spoke of how he defended his father's flocks from both lions and bears when he was a youth. He said if the Lord had delivered him in victory over the wild beasts which wanted his sheep, then the Lord would deliver him in victory over a man who came to mock the Lord and the Lord's army. Saul agreed to let David answer the challenge. He had the king's armor and weapons brought for David to wear. After David had put on the helmet and coat of armor, he strapped on the sword of Saul, but he could barely move in it. He took them off and told the king he was not used to wearing the trappings of a warrior, but he would go face the Philistine champion with what he was used to wearing and carrying while tending the flocks.

David took his staff in his hand and gathered five smooth stones from a nearby creek. He then walked out from the lines of battle towards the Philistine champion with his staff in one hand and his sling in the other. When Goliath saw a man coming towards him from the Israelite lines, he started moving forward. When he came closer, he saw it was little more than a boy with a staff. He cursed the Israelites and became angry with them. He said they treated him like a dog by sending a boy with a stick after him. He then spoke to David as he came closer and told him he would leave his body for the vultures and wild animals. (1 Samuel 17:45-47) David said to the Philistine, "You come against me with sword and spear and javelin, but I come against you in the name of the Lord Almighty, the God of the armies of Israel, whom you have defied. This day the Lord will hand you over to me, and I'll strike you down and cut off your head. Today I will give the carcasses of the Philistine army to the birds of the air and the beasts of the earth, and the whole world will know that there is a God in Israel. All those gathered here will know that it is not by sword or spear that the Lord saves; for the battle is the Lord's, and he will give all of you into our hands." (NIV)

When Goliath heard these words, he came toward David. David ran at the giant, dropped a stone from his satchel into his sling, and let it fly. The stone hit the Philistine champion in his forehead, killing him. Goliath toppled face down in the dirt and David ran over to his body. He took the sword from the Philistine's belt and made sure he was dead. David then cut off the giant's head. When the Philistines saw what happened, they fled in terror. The Israelites immediately gave chase and pursued them all the way back to their own lands. Many Philistine bodies lined the roads out of the lands of Israel as the Israelites slaughtered them during the chase. When the army of Israel came back to the valley they looted the camp of the Philistines. David took the head of Goliath to Jerusalem and kept the weapons of the giant for himself.

Saul's commander, Abner, brought David to meet Saul with the giant's head still in his hand. After this, Saul told his advisors to find out more about David and his family. After David had killed Goliath, he stayed with Saul instead of going back to his father's house. Saul's oldest son Jonathan and David became very close friends, and Jonathan dressed David in his robes and placed the symbols of his position on David to show their bond. David accomplished every task Saul set before him, so the king gave David more and more power and prestige in the army of Israel. All of the people of Israel, even the officers in the army of Israel, were greatly pleased with David's success.

When Saul and his army finally returned after their success against the Philistines, the women of Israel came out with tambourines and lutes. They sang and danced in the streets as the army triumphantly came into the city. One of the refrains they sang was "Saul has killed his thousands and David his tens of thousands." When Saul heard this, he became jealous because he feared David only needed to ask for the throne and the people would give it to him. From that time on, Saul kept a watchful eye on David and remained jealous of the people's love for him.

The next day, the evil spirit tormenting King Saul came and David was called in to play the harp to soothe the king. When Saul heard David start to play, he grabbed his spear and attempted to kill David, but David was able to escape from the room. Saul became fearful when he realized the Spirit of the Lord who had left him was now with David.

Saul placed David over one thousand soldiers and sent him out wherever there was battle. But Saul grew more fearful of David as news of success after success continued to come in. All of Judah and Israel loved David for his campaigns against their enemies, so Saul sought to tie himself to David as a snare. When David killed Goliath, one of his prizes was to be the hand of Saul's daughter. Saul thought if he married her to David, the Philistines would seek to kill a member of the king's household in battle. But David declined to marry the king's oldest daughter because he did not feel his family had high enough standing for him to marry the king's oldest daughter.

But David and Michal, who was the king's youngest daughter, had met and fallen in love. Saul knew the snare would not be as strong as if David had married his oldest daughter, but even this marriage might cause the Philistines to look for a chance to kill David. Saul had no wish to raise his own hand against someone who the Lord had blessed, so this situation appealed to him. He offered to give Michal, his youngest daughter, as a wife to David. But again David did not feel he was worthy of becoming a son-in-law to the king. So Saul set a clever trap. He said if David felt he had to pay a price for his bride, then the cost would be nothing less than one hundred foreskins of Philistine warriors. David viewed that as a respectable price to pay and agreed. Saul was hoping David would be killed by the Philistines trying to complete this task. David took his men out and within the time specified by the king, they slew two hundred Philistine warriors and David presented Saul with the full number of foreskins he requested. Saul had no choice but to give Michal to David as his bride and he saw his daughter loved David. From that time on Saul was gravely afraid of David and viewed him as his enemy.

The Philistines and the Israelites continued to wage war against each other, and David continued to be more successful than any other commander of the army of Israel. His fame and exploits grew with each success and his reputation flourished.

Finally, Saul decided he would kill David. He told his close advisors of his plan and Jonathan, his son, heard it as well. Jonathan loved David like a brother and warned him of the plot. He told David to go hide in a field the next day and he would go there with his father and discover how deeply these feelings went. So the next day David hid in the field and Jonathan and Saul came out to talk. Jonathan implored his father not to look upon David as a threat and not to bring death to him because David was innocent of any wrongdoing. Saul agreed David had done nothing wrong and would not be put to death. Jonathan called David to him and told him the whole conversation. He then took David to his father and the relationship between David and Saul seemed to be mended.

War with the Philistines started again, and David went out with his men and won great victories. Soon after this, the evil spirit which tormented Saul came to him again. When David came with the harp, Saul took his spear and again tried to kill David. That night David's wife Michal told David he must flee at once because her father was sending men to kill him in the morning. His house was being watched by Saul's men, so Michal lowered him out of a window and he was able to slip away. Michal took an idol and put some goat hair on it and stuck it in David's bed. The next morning the men Saul had sent ordered her to go get David. She told them he was ill and in his bed. Saul came when he heard this and told his daughter to lead him and his men up to David's room. When she did, they discovered the idol with goat hair on it instead of David. Saul was angry at his daughter and asked her why she would deceive him this way. She said that David threatened her and she was frightened of him.

When David fled his home, he sought out Samuel. He found the prophet in the region of Ramah and told him everything which had occurred. Samuel took David to the village of Naioth in the area and stayed there with him. When Saul heard where David had fled, and he was with Samuel, he sent men to bring David back. But as the men approached the village, a group of prophets led by Samuel came out prophesying. When the men approached, the Spirit of the Lord came upon them and they began prophesying as well. When Saul heard about this he sent a second group of men, and then a third, but each time they came near Samuel, the Spirit of the Lord came over them and they joined the prophets in prophesying. Finally Saul went himself, and when he approached Samuel, the Spirit of the Lord came over the king and he began prophesying as well. Saul stripped off his kingly robes and lay before Samuel prophesying for an entire day and night.

David fled from Saul at Naioth and found Jonathan. He spoke with Jonathan about the king's intentions, but Jonathan had not been included in any discussions concerning David. David came up with a plan to determine what action Saul's mind was bent toward. There was to be a New Moon feast which David was to attend, but David would not be there. If Saul missed him and asked where he was, Jonathan was to tell his father David had to return to Bethlehem to make sacrifices as was the custom. If Saul meant David no harm, then he would say "Very well", but if the king had meant to kill David at the feast, he would become angry because David wasn't there for his plans.

Jonathan agreed to do as David asked. David asked Jonathan how he would let him know whether it was safe to enter Saul's presence or not. Jonathan told him to hide in the field during the feast and wait. Jonathan would go out to practice with his bow and he would send a boy out in the field to gather the arrows. If it was safe for David to come back, he would shoot his arrows short so the boy would have to come in to gather them. But if it was not safe for David to appear in the city, then he would send his arrows past the boy in the field. That was how he would tell David to flee from his father.

When the feast of the New Moon was celebrated, David's seat was empty. The first night of the feast, Saul said nothing because he thought David must be consecrating himself in the city and he would join them for the second day of the feast. But on the second day, David's seat was still empty. Saul asked those at the feast where David was and Jonathan answered David had asked permission to go to Bethlehem and join his family in the sacrifices they were making. Saul became furious at Jonathan and insulted him. He claimed Jonathan betrayed him and was willingly giving up his own place as king because of his love for David. When Saul picked up the spear by his side and tried to kill Jonathan, the king's son understood Saul wished David dead and there would be no persuading him otherwise.

The next day Jonathan took a servant boy to the field where David was hiding. He sent the boy out and then shot arrows at a spot beyond the boy. When the boy had gathered the arrows and brought them back to Jonathan, he was given Jonathan's bow and told to take them back into the town. Jonathan then went out to where David was hiding and they cried together because they knew David had to flee. They reaffirmed their friendship and they spoke words binding their families to each other. Then David left to flee from Saul and Jonathan went back to his home.

David's War with Saul

Story found in 1 Samuel Chapters 21 to 31
and 2 Samuel Chapters 1 to 5

David traveled to the town of Nob and went to Ahimelech the priest. Ahimelech was nervous to see David traveling alone and asked him where his men were. David said the king had sent him on a secret mission with just a few of his men and they were hidden nearby. He asked the priest if he had any food for him and his men. Ahimelech told David he only had a few loaves of consecrated bread, but they could only be eaten by those who had purified themselves. David said he and his men had kept themselves from women, so the priest gave him the bread. David then asked if there were any weapons available. Ahimelech told him the sword of Goliath was kept there and it was David's if he wanted it. David gladly took the sword of Goliath and the consecrated bread and left Nob. Doeg, the head shepherd of King Saul, was in the town and heard what David said to Ahimelech.

After David left Nob, he headed for the town of Gath, but the guards of the town recognized David and sent for the king. When David realized he was in danger, he feigned madness and started clawing at the gates, slobbering all over his face and beard. When the king saw this, he told his men to leave David alone and not take him into the city because Gath had enough madmen as it were.

David found shelter in the cave of Adullam. When his father and brothers learned where he was hiding, they went to see him. Many men in the area who were deep in debt, rebellious, or downtrodden went to David as well. David had about four hundred men with him when he went to Moab and asked the king to allow his father and mother to stay protected in Moab until David could figure out what to do. While David was staying in Moab, a prophet named Gad came to him with a word from the Lord. David was not to stay in Moab, but he was to go back to the land of Judah. David obeyed the word of the Lord and found shelter in the forest of Hereth in Judah.

When Saul discovered David had fled, he met with the elders of the tribe of Benjamin. Saul accused them of conspiring with Jesse and his son David. Doeg was at the meeting and told Saul about David meeting with the priest Ahimelech in the town of Nob. Saul sent men to bring Ahimelech and the rest of the priests of the town to him. Nob was a city of priests and there were eighty-five priests brought back to Saul. Saul accused Ahimelech of providing food and weapons to a fugitive and rebel. Ahimelech argued David was a loyal servant of the king. He said he believed David was on a mission for the king and he did not know he was a fugitive. But Saul did not care about his reasons. He sentenced Ahimelech and all of the priests to death for aiding David.

The king's officials would not raise their hands against the priests, so Saul ordered Doeg to kill them. Saul then took his troops to the town of Nob and destroyed every living thing in the town; men, women, children, sheep and cattle. But one of the sons of Ahimelech, a young man named Abiathar, escaped and made his way to David and told him what happened.

David told Abiathar to stay with him since they were both being hunted by Saul. He also confessed his guilt in the death of the people of Nob. He had seen Doeg there that day and knew he would report back to Saul.

Word came to David the Philistines were attacking the town of Keilah near where he was. He had Abiathar ask the Lord whether he should go and try to rescue the town from the Philistines. The Lord told him to go. David and the men who had joined him defeated the Philistines and saved the people of Keilah. When Saul heard about this, he believed David was trapped in the town. The king sent his army to besiege Keilah and capture David. But David listened to the Lord and did not stay in the town. He moved constantly from place to place so Saul could not corner him.

Once when David was in Horesh, Jonathan came to him and assured him the Lord would keep him safe. He confirmed David would be king one day and Saul would never catch him. Then

Jonathan went back to his father and David stayed at Horesh. Some men from Horesh came to Saul and told him they could deliver David. Saul had the men go and find where David was hiding and then brought his army to hunt for David and his men. But David had left Horesh by the time Saul brought his army and David kept his men moving away from Saul and his troops. Saul was getting close to cornering David when he received an urgent message the Philistines were moving against Israel. Saul broke off his pursuit of David and marched his men to go meet the Philistine threat.

After Saul had dealt with the Philistine threat, he took his best three thousand troops and went to search for David. He discovered David and his men had moved into some rough mountains and started looking for them. One day Saul came to a sheep pen which had a cave. He went into the cave to relieve himself not knowing David and his men were hidden in the same cave but much further back.

David's men told him this was the day the Lord had told David about, when he would deliver his enemy into his hands to do with as he wished. David crept up on Saul and cut off a corner of his robe and returned to his men. He then felt guilty for doing even that to the king who was anointed by God. When Saul had left the cave, David came to the entrance and called to him. He bowed down to Saul and told him he meant Saul no harm. He showed him the corner of the robe he had cut off and said he could have killed Saul then if he wanted, but he loved Saul and did not wish him dead.

Saul realized David could have killed him but didn't. He repented of his anger against David and asked David to swear before the Lord he would not attempt to cut off Saul's line from the earth. David swore an oath he would never do such a thing and Saul left for his home while David and his men stayed in the wilderness.

While David was in the wilderness, Samuel the prophet died and was buried in Ramah. After this happened, David brought his men to the Desert of Maon. There was a man who lived in Maon at Carmel by the name of Nabal. He was surly and hard to deal with, but very wealthy. During the time of shearing, David sent ten of his men to Nabal to see if the wealthy man would agree to give some provisions to David and his followers. David sent the message he and his men were kind to the shepherds and workers of Nabal while they were hiding from Saul in the area of Carmel. He suggested since the time that the sheep were sheared was considered a time of celebration, Nabal could easily help David and his men.

When David's men found Nabal and delivered the message, Nabal was scornful and dismissive. He suggested David was simply a runaway servant of the King and held him in no regard. When the men returned to David and told him Nabal's response, David became angry and told his men to strap on their swords. About four hundred men went with David while two hundred stayed behind to guard their camp. When some of Nabal's men heard what was happening, they went to Nabal's wife, a woman named Abigail. They told her David and his men had been kind to them and protected them when they were at Carmel hiding from the king. They explained Nabal had greatly insulted David and his men and they were afraid David would seek justice for the insults. They begged Abigail to speak to her husband since he was a stubborn and unbendable man.

Instead of speaking with Nabal, Abigail told the servants to gather bread, flour, and even slaughter some livestock and pack it all on some donkeys as quickly as they could. When it was prepared, she mounted a donkey herself and went out to meet David.

David was furious as he headed to the house of Nabal. He swore not a man of Nabal's household would be alive by the next morning as punishment for the insults thrown back at him after his good treatment of Nabal.

When Abigail saw David, she jumped off her donkey and ran to fall at his feet. She took the blame upon herself for not seeing the men David sent and begged him to spare the house of Nabal even though Nabal was a wicked and foolish man. She told David if he kept his hands from bloodshed over this insult and did not take vengeance, then when he became king, he would not have guilt over this day. She begged him to accept the gifts she had brought him and assured him the Lord would make all who stand against him the same as Nabal, foolish and weak.

David thanked Abigail for preventing him from making the rash decision to take vengeance upon Nabal. He gladly accepted her gifts and sent her home in peace. When Abigail returned to her home, Nabal was holding a great feast and was very drunk, so she left him alone that night. In the morning, she told her husband what had almost happened to him and the actions she had taken to prevent David from wiping out Nabal's household. When Nabal heard this, he fell as if struck and was still. Ten days later he died.

When David heard Nabal had died, he praised the Lord for taking vengeance upon Nabal and not letting his own hands become bloody. David sent men to Abigail telling her he wished to take her for his wife. When Abigail heard the news, she went immediately and presented herself to David. Abigail became his wife during this time along with another woman named Ahinoam. While David was fleeing from Saul, the king gave his daughter, Michal, to another man even though she was married to David.

Saul again decided to go find David and kill him. When some men came and told Saul where they had seen David, he gathered his three thousand finest warriors and went down to the Desert of Ziph and made camp along the road. When David saw this from where he was hiding, he sent out scouts who reported back to him the king was indeed camped by the road near the desert. David then went to see for himself and he saw Saul and Abner, the commander of the armies of Israel, resting in the middle of the camp. David asked the men if any would go with him into the camp of the king and a warrior named Abishai agreed to the dangerous assignment.

When Saul and his men had fallen asleep, David and Abishai snuck into the camp and made it to where the king, Abner and their guards were all asleep. Abishai told David he could kill Saul in one thrust of his spear, but David forbade it. He told Abishai Saul had been anointed by the Lord as the king of Israel and he would not lift his hand against one the Lord had raised up. He said the Lord would strike Saul down or he would die in battle, but he would never die at the hands of David. David took the spear of Saul, which was thrust into the ground where the king slept, and a water jug near his head. The Lord had put everyone in the camp into a deep sleep and David and Abishai were able to enter and leave the camp without awaking any of the soldiers.

When David left, he went to the top of a hill nearby and called out to the camp. When the camp was roused, Abner came out to see what was happening. David called to him and scolded him for not protecting the king. He asked Abner where Saul's spear and water jug were and told him there were men near the king that night who could have done him harm. When Saul heard the voice calling out, he came out of the camp and yelled back asking if it was David. David answered Saul that it was David and he asked the king why he was being hunted again. He told Saul his life had been spared because David valued the life of the king. He said if the king valued the life of his servant, he would stop his pursuit of David.

Saul repented and called himself foolish to David. He said since David had once again spared his life, he would never again threaten David's life. He called on David to come back with him. But David told Saul to send a young man to retrieve the king's spear. When they had said their farewells, David went his own way and Saul and his soldiers returned home.

David realized the only way to keep Saul from coming after him again was to leave the lands of Israel. David and the six hundred men with him went to the Philistine city of Gath and made arrangements with Achish, whose father was Maoch the king of Gath. The men of David brought their families just as David had brought his two wives. They lived for a while in the city before David went to the Achish and asked for a small town where he could take his men and their families. The son of the king was pleased by David's request and gave him the small town of Ziklag. When Saul had heard David had taken his men and settled in the lands of the Philistines, he no longer sought to kill David.

David and his men lived in Ziklag for a year and four months. They raided into the deserts south of Gath. David and his men attacked villages and settlements of the enemies of Israel and never left man or woman alive. When they would return from their raids with all of the plunder and livestock, Achish would ask him where he had attacked. David would lie and tell him he was raiding into Israel or one of Israel's allies. Achish was very happy David was making himself so hated among the Israelites because he wanted to bind David to him and make him a malleable servant.

Achish was so pleased by the abilities of David, he decided to take David and his men with him and make war against Israel. When Saul saw the forces the Philistines had brought against him, he panicked and sought guidance from the Lord. But the Lord would not answer his prayers nor could he receive a word from the Lord from the Levite ceremonies or from the prophets of the Lord. Saul had followed the Lord's command to drive all witches and mediums from Israel, but he asked his servants to find one for him.

His servants returned and told him they had located a woman who was a medium in Endor. Saul and two of his servants disguised themselves and went to the woman. Saul approached her at night and told her he wished for her to summon a spirit he would name.

But the woman refused and said the king had sentenced all witches and mediums to death for their practice. Saul swore by the name of the Lord she would not be punished for this. She agreed and asked him to name the spirit he wished to speak with. He named Samuel and as she saw the spirit of Samuel start to rise, the medium was terrified and realized she was in the presence of the king in disguise. Saul reassured her he would not punish her and asked her what she saw. When she said she saw an old man in robes rising from the ground, Saul knew she had summoned Samuel and he fell facedown to the ground.

When the spirit of Samuel had risen, he called out to Saul asking why he had done such a foul thing and disturbed his rest. Saul told Samuel he was afraid of the Philistines and he could not get an answer from the Lord. Samuel rebuked Saul for disturbing him and told him the Lord had turned away from

Saul. He told Saul the Lord was angry for Saul's disobedience concerning the Amalekites and the kingdom of Israel would be stripped out of his hands and given to David. He said the Lord would give the armies of Israel to the Philistines and the land would be conquered by his foes. Samuel told Saul that he and his sons would die the very next day.

When Saul heard this, he threw himself back onto the ground and shook with fear. Saul had fasted for an entire day before he came to Endor and his body was weak. The medium came to him after he spoke with Samuel and urged him to eat something and then leave. He refused at first, but was eventually persuaded by the woman and his own servants. She made him a meal and Saul and his men left her the next evening.

The Philistines were organizing their troops when the commanders of the army noticed David and his men marching with Achish's forces. They questioned Achish about it but he vouched for David and his loyalty. But the other commanders of the Philistine army did not trust David and Achish ordered him and his men back to Ziklag in the lands of the Philistines.

It took three days for David and his men to return home, but when they approached they discovered Ziklag had been attacked. The buildings of the town were burned and the women and children had been taken away. The men with David were angry and bitter and in their weeping David heard grumblings that the men would stone him. But he found strength in the Lord. He called the priest Ahimelech to him and inquired if he should try to overtake the attackers. The word of the Lord came back to David confirming he and his men would be able to successfully catch the raiders and rescue their families. David and his six hundred men started after the raiders, but as they came to a ravine, about two hundred men grew tired and could not continue. The rest of the men and David went ahead and as they were going through a desert area, they came upon a sick Egyptian. David told his men to give the man some food and water and went to talk to him. The Egyptian said he was a slave to an Amalekite master who had left him to die in the desert when he became sick, just three days before. He told David how the Amalekites raided into the lands of the Philistines and Judah and they had burned Ziklag before heading back to their lands. David promised the man he would not harm him or turn him back to his master in exchange for being led to the camps of the Amalekites.

Around dusk, David and his men were shown where the raiding party was camped. The Amalekites were celebrating wildly because of the great wealth they obtained during their raids. David and his men attacked their camp and the fighting raged all that night and through the next day until nightfall. Four hundred young Amalekite warriors fled during the battle, but the rest were killed by David and his men. They recovered all of the plunder and treasure taken by the raiders, including all of the women and children taken as captives. They drove the flocks and herds of livestock ahead of them as they left the place of battle and they were amazed at the amount of plunder they had recovered. When they reached the ravine where the two hundred men stayed having been too exhausted to go with David, some of the men who recovered the goods and captives mumbled these men should not get a share of the wealth. But David said those who stayed behind to guard the camp and baggage should get the same share as those who went to battle. He established that as a law among his people and later as a law in all of Israel. When they returned to Ziklag, they divided the plunder and David sent a portion which had been recovered to the elders of Judah and to the allies of Israel who had been raided as a sign of good favour.

The day after David left the Philistine army to head back to Ziklag, the Philistines attacked the armies of Israel and drove them back to Mount Gilboa. There the Philistines pressed hard into Saul's personal unit and killed his three sons, including Jonathan. Saul was struck by an arrow and mortally wounded. When he saw how badly injured he was, he told his armor-bearer to kill him so the Philistines would not take him alive. His armor-bearer refused to kill the king, so Saul threw himself upon his own sword and took his own life. When he saw what his master had done, his armor-bearer killed himself in the same way.

When the armies of Israel saw the king was dead, they fled the field. When the local Israelites saw their armies had fled, they abandoned their towns and villages and the Philistines came in to occupy them. When the Philistine soldiers went out the next day to strip the dead, they found Saul and his sons. They cut off Saul's head as a trophy and stripped his armor and placed it in the temple of the Ashtoreths. They took the bodies of Saul and his sons and nailed them to the wall of Beth Shan, one of their cities. The Philistines sent messengers out to all of their towns and cities to announce their triumph.

The people of Jabesh Gilead heard about how the bodies of Saul and his sons were being abused. Their valiant men traveled to Beth Shan during the night and removed the bodies from the wall and took them to Jabesh where they burned them. They buried their bones under a tamarisk tree at Jabesh and mourned for seven days by fasting.

David had been back to Ziklag for a couple of days before he heard of Saul and Jonathan's death. On the third morning of his return, a young man came into the ruined town and said he had news of the battle. When David asked him what had happened, the young man said that he had been near where Saul was fighting when the king was wounded. He said Saul saw him and asked him to put him out of his misery, so he took the spear in his hand and killed the king of Israel. He then presented David with the crown of the king and the armband which Saul wore on his arm.

When David and the men with him heard this, they tore their clothes and wept. David asked the young man who he was and the young man answered he was the son of an Amalekite. David then pronounced the young man guilty from his own words of killing the Lord's anointed king and had his men kill the young man. David then composed a lament for Saul and Jonathan and taught it to all of his men.

In time, David inquired of the Lord whether he should return to Judah. The Lord answered and said he should go to Hebron and call the elders of Judah to him. David took his wives and was accompanied by the men and their families who had went with him to Ziklag. When he arrived in Hebron, the people there anointed him king of Judah. When he discovered the men of Jabesh Gilead had recovered the bodies of Saul and his sons, David sent the blessings of the Lord to them.

Abner, the commander of Saul's army, had taken a son of Saul named Ish-Bosheth and declared him king over all of Israel. David was recognized as king in Judah, but Ish-Bosheth was king in the rest of Israel for two years. At that time, Abner came down to the pool of Gibeon with a group of warriors. Joab, one of David's commanders, came down with David's men to the other side of the pool. As they negotiated, Abner suggested they have some of their men fight to show their prowess. Joab agreed and they each chose twelve men to fight. When the signal was given, each man grabbed his opponent by the head and tried to stab him with a dagger. The fighting was fierce, but the men of David defeated the men of Ish-Bosheth.

Joab was the brother of Abishai and Asahel. Asahel was considered as fast as a gazelle and took off after Abner when the men of Ish-Bosheth fled. Abner was running from him and called out to Asahel to give up the pursuit as he did not want to harm him. But Asahel continued his chase. Finally, Abner thrust back with the butt of his spear with such force, he pierced Asahel completely through and the young man died on the spot. The men of David all stopped when they came to the place where Asahel's body lay, but Joab and Abishai continued to chase Abner until dusk.

By that time, Abner had rallied his men and stood with them on a hill. When they saw Joab and Abishai approaching, Abner called out asking for the bloodshed to end. Joab blew his trumpet and signaled his men to halt their chase. In addition to Asahel, David lost nineteen more men that day. But they had killed over three hundred and sixty of the men who had come with Abner. Joab and Abishai gathered the body of their brother and took him to their father's tomb in Bethlehem and buried him. Joab then led the men in a march all through the night and arrived back in Hebron by morning.

The war between the house of David and the house of Saul went on for some time. The house of David continued to grow stronger while the house of Saul grew weaker. One day, Ish-

Bosheth called Abner to him and accused him of sleeping with one of his father's concubines. This was a serious charge as it would be considered a move by Abner to take the throne for himself. Abner became furious with Ish-Bosheth at the accusation and told him he would see the end to his reign. Abner then sent messages to David telling him Abner would like to negotiate giving David the whole kingdom. David agreed, but only if Abner would bring Michal, the daughter of Saul, with him. Abner went to the man who Saul had given her to as a wife and took Michal from his house. Her husband tried to follow but Abner threatened him and he returned home without Michal.

Abner then met with the elders of Israel and told them their rumblings about making David their king had his support now. He went to the Benjamites, who were the most loyal to the house of Saul, and told them it was time for them to support the house of David. When he had secured all of the agreements he needed, he traveled to Hebron with Michal and twenty men. David received him with a feast and sent him away in peace to finish the arrangements which would be needed to crown David king over all Israel.

Soon after David had sent Abner away, Joab and some of David's men returned from a raid with a large amount of plunder. When Joab heard Abner had been to see David and the king had sent Abner away in peace, he became angry and confronted David. He told David Abner was not to be trusted and was afraid Abner was there to spy and plot against David. Joab sent messengers to find Abner and ask him to return to Hebron, but David did not know about this. When Abner returned, Joab took him aside as if he was going to talk with him, but instead Joab stabbed him in the stomach with a sword and killed him. He did this to avenge the death of his brother Asahel.

When David heard what had happened, he was angry at Joab. He declared before all the people the house of David was innocent of Abner's blood and the house of Joab would be forever cursed because of their treachery. He made a public spectacle of Joab by forcing him to tear his clothes and wear sackcloth in mourning for Abner. He also made him walk before

Abner's body in mourning as they buried Abner in Hebron. David refused food for the rest of the day and published a lament for Abner's death. In this way the people were pleased with their king and did not hold him accountable for the death of Abner.

When news reached Ish-Bosheth that Abner was murdered, he became gravely depressed and all of Israel became alarmed at the situation. Two of the men who led raiding parties for the king were brothers named Baanah and Recab. They conspired together and went to the house of Ish-Bosheth. They arrived when the day was at its hottest and went into the house pretending to get some food. Instead they searched the house until they found the king who was taking his afternoon nap. They stabbed him in the stomach while he slept, killing him. They then cut off his head, placed it in a bag, and slipped away from the town. They traveled all night until they reached Hebron the next morning. They came and spoke with David and told them what they had done thinking he would reward them. Instead he explained what had happened to the young man who brought news of Saul's death. He had Baanah and Recab killed and their hands and feet cut off. He hung their bodies by the pool of Hebron so all could see how he repaid murder and treachery. He then had the head of Ish-Bosheth buried with Abner's body.

After the death of Ish-Bosheth, all of the elders of Israel came to David in Hebron. There they made oaths to him and anointed him king of all Israel. David was 30 when he became king of Judah and 36 when he became king of Israel.

King David

Story found in 2 Samuel Chapters 5 to 24
and 1 Kings Chapters 1 to 2

When David became king of Israel, the city of Jerusalem was held by the Jebusites. David took the armies of Israel to conquer this city, but the men of Jerusalem mocked their efforts. They claimed even the blind and lame could defend Jerusalem from attack. But David knew of a water passage which could lead him into the city and he conquered Jerusalem. David called Jerusalem "The City of David", and established it as his capital. King Hiram of Tyre sent messages of congratulations to David along with large amounts of cedar logs. He also sent carpenters and stonemasons who started building a palace in Jerusalem for the new king. David moved his family from Hebron when the palace was finished and took many more wives and concubines. David had eleven children during his years of living in Jerusalem.

When the Philistines heard David had become king of Israel and had taken the city of Jerusalem for his own, they gathered their armies and went to war against him. David asked for advice from the Lord and the Lord instructed him on how to defeat the Philistines. David followed the word of the Lord and drove the Philistines off the field of battle. Later the Philistines gathered their armies and again David asked the Lord for his aid. The next time the Philistines were defeated, they did not try to wage war against David again.

David decided the Ark of the Covenant should be brought to Jerusalem to have a permanent home. He took thirty thousand select men and went to the house of Abinadab where the Ark was resting. They placed it on a new cart and the sons of Abinadab, named Ahio and Uzzah, escorted it along the road to Jerusalem. David and the men of Israel were celebrating with dancing and loud music along the path while Ahio led the cart and Uzzah walked behind it. When they came to the threshing floor of Nacon, the oxen pulling the cart stumbled, and Uzzah reach out to grab the Ark. The Lord became angry at him for this act of irreverence and struck Uzzah dead on the spot.

When David saw this he became afraid and would not take the Ark into Jerusalem because he feared the wrath of the Lord. He had the Ark taken to the nearby house of Obed-Edom. The Ark was at the house of Obed-Edom for three months and the Lord prospered and blessed the man. When David was told the Ark brought blessings to Obed-Edom, he moved it into Jerusalem with a great celebration.

David had dressed himself in a loose linen ephod and was dancing and celebrating wildly with the people of Jerusalem when the Ark was brought into the city and placed in a tent which had been prepared. When it was set into place, the king made burnt sacrifices and offerings for the Lord. When that was finished he blessed all of the people and gave each man and woman a loaf of bread, a cake of dates, and a cake of raisins. When the celebration was over, David sent them home.

When he returned to his palace, his wife Michal confronted him. She had watched from a window as the Ark was being brought into the city and saw David dancing and celebrating wildly in the streets below. She and David fought over his behavior that day and in the end she turned away from David and never had any children.

When the Ark had been in the city for some time, David became concerned. He called the prophet Nathan to him and discussed his feelings. David felt bothered by the fact that he slept in a palace but the Ark stayed in a simple tent. That night Nathan had a vision from the Lord. The Lord told Nathan David should not worry about building a house for the Lord as the Lord would build a house for David which would never fall. The Lord promised David would be the head of a house which would produce a king one day whose kingdom would never end.

When Nathan told David of this word, David went before the Lord in humility and gratitude that the Lord would establish his house in this way.

The Lord blessed David while he was king and David's victories over the enemies of Israel were numerous and impressive. He took cities from the Philistines. He defeated and took tribute from the Moabites, the Arameans, and the Edomites. He defeated Hadadezer who was the son of King Rehob of Zobah. He utterly defeated his army, sent his army home hamstrung, and plundered many articles of silver and gold. He even took several towns from Hadadezer and acquired large quantities of bronze as a result. When King Tou heard of David's victories over his enemy Hadadezer, he sent his son Joram to David with gifts of gold and silver. All of the items which David received as gifts or plunder he consecrated for the Lord.

David told his servants to seek out any relative of Saul who was left alive because he wanted to show kindness to them for the sake of Jonathan. An old servant of Saul named Ziba was found and brought before King David. David asked him about any of Saul's family left alive and finally Ziba told David there was a son of Jonathan, who had two crippled legs, who still lived. David sent for the man, whose name was Mephibosheth, and had him brought to Jerusalem. When he was brought before the king, David reassured him he was not in danger but the king wanted to bless him for the sake of his father, Jonathan. He restored all of the lands of Saul to him and welcomed him to the king's table to eat like one of David's sons. He placed Ziba and all of his family as servants to Mephibosheth and told them the lands of Saul were restored to their master. Mephibosheth lived in Jerusalem and ate with David whenever he sat for a meal.

King Nahash of the Ammonites died and David remembered the kindness Nahash had shown him during his years of hiding from Saul. David sent a delegation of men to Nahash's son Hanun to express his condolences and sympathy. Hanun's nobles did not believe that was the reason David sent his men. They convinced King Hanun David had sent the men to scout out his city and lands. Hanun seized the men David had sent and had them humiliated. He had half of their beards shaved off and cut off their clothes to expose them and sent them back to David.

David heard what happened and sent men to meet his servants on the road and take them to Jericho to stay until their beards grew back and they could return home unashamed. His anger was turned toward the Ammonites and when Hanun realized how angry David was against him, he sought out allies to go to war against Israel. David sent Joab out as the commander of his forces and Israel won a great victory against the Ammonites and their allies.

It was during this time, David woke from his bed and went up on the roof of the palace. Looking out over the city he spied a woman bathing. David was attracted to her because of her beauty and sent men to find out who she was. They returned and told him it was Bathsheba, the wife of Uriah, a soldier under Joab who was away warring against the Ammonites. David sent for Bathsheba and she came to the palace where David had sex with her. After some time, word came to David from Bathsheba letting him know she had become pregnant by the king.

David sent word to the army that he wanted to see Uriah. When Uriah came to Jerusalem, David asked him about Joab, the army, and how the war against the Ammonites was going. When Uriah left the king, David sent a gift with him and told him to go home. But Uriah slept that night in the palace of David with the servants. When David heard this, he asked Uriah why he didn't sleep in his own house. Uriah declared while the army was in the field, he didn't feel right sleeping at home with the comfort of his wife. David asked him to stay another day and to eat with him that night. Over dinner that evening, David made sure Uriah got very drunk and sent him home. But again, Uriah slept with David's servants instead of returning to his wife.

David realized Uriah would not go home and sleep with Bathsheba. He had paper and pen brought to him and wrote a note to Joab. David sent it with Uriah when he returned to the army. The note told Joab to put Uriah into the hottest part of the battle and when things were at their most dangerous, to withdraw so Uriah would be killed.

A messenger came to David a few days later. He recounted an attack Joab made against the city of the Ammonites and said when the men approached, archers from the top of the walls fired at the men, killing several including Uriah. David sent the messenger back to Joab telling him in battle men die by the sword and to press the attack on the city. In this way Joab let David know Uriah was killed and David let Joab know he was pleased.

When she heard her husband was killed in battle, Bathsheba went into mourning. When the time for her mourning was over, David took her into his palace, married her and she soon gave birth to his son. The Lord was displeased at David for what he had done.

After Bathsheba had given birth to David's son, the prophet Nathan approached the king in his court. He told the story of two men who lived in a town. One was wealthy and had many flocks and herds, and the other poor and had a single sheep which he loved dearly. One day a traveler came and the rich man decided to entertain him. Instead of going into his own flocks to feed this traveler, he went to the home of the poor man and took his only sheep.

David became enraged and declared this man should be punished severely. Nathan then scolded the king and told him he was the rich man in the story. He said the Lord was angry at David because while the Lord gave David all success and rewards and held nothing back from him, David gave Uriah death by sending him into the swords of the Ammonites to cover up his taking of Uriah's wife. The Lord declared because David took the woman of another, his women would be taken by someone close to him. And the sin David had committed in secret would be done against him where all of Israel could see.

When David heard this he confessed to Nathan what he had done. Nathan told him the Lord would spare his life, but the life of his son would be taken from him. As Nathan left the palace of David, Bathsheba's son became seriously ill. David tore his clothes and put on sackcloth and wept and prayed to the Lord to spare his son. For seven days he did this and would not eat despite the pleadings of his officials and servants. On the seventh day, his son died and the servants were afraid to tell him because of how much grief he was already showing; they were afraid he might do something to injure himself. When

David saw them whispering, he asked if his son were dead. When they confirmed his suspicions, he rose, washed himself, put on fresh clothes and went to the house of the Lord and worshipped. When he returned, he asked his servants to bring him something to eat. His servants were surprised by his behavior but he explained while the child lived, he had hope the Lord would show mercy on him and take away his punishment, but after the child had died, the punishment had been paid and he was no longer to mourn his sin against the Lord. After he had eaten, he went to Bathsheba and they comforted each other and she bore him another son named Solomon.

During this time Joab had entered Rabbah, the capital of the Ammonites, and secured some important positions in the city. He sent word to David he needed the king to rally more men to come and help him finish the siege. David pulled more men together and went to Rabbah where the city fell completely. The Israelites plundered the land of the Ammonites and forced their men to be laborers for Israel.

David's oldest son was named Amnon and he fell in love with Tamar who was one of his half-sisters. Tamar's full brother was David's son Absalom. Tamar was a virgin and Amnon could find no way to seduce her though he desired her greatly. A friend of his helped him come up with a plan and he feigned illness and stayed in his bed. When his father heard he was sick, he came to see him and asked him what he needed. He requested Tamar make him some bread and bring it to him. David sent for Tamar and told her to make food for her brother. Tamar made him some bread and took it to his house. When she arrived, Amnon sent everyone else away and asked her to come to his room and feed him the bread she had made. When she went into his room, he grabbed her and told her to come to bed with him. Tamar struggled against him and begged him not to take her that way. She asked him to go to their father David who would allow them to be married. But Amnon did not want to listen to her and raped her. When he was done, he hated her more than he had desired her before and sent her away from him in shame.

When Tamar left, she put ashes on her head because of her disgrace. Her brother Absalom found her and had her tell him what happened. He took her into his house and she lived with him as a disgraced woman. King David was furious at his son Amnon and Absalom hated his brother for what he had done to Tamar.

For two years Absalom harbored this hatred toward his brother. He had to go to one of his fields to shear his flocks of sheep. He asked his father to join him along with all of his men and his sons. But David told him it would just interfere with his work. So he asked for his brother Amnon to join him. David thought it unusual, but told Amnon to go with Absalom and he sent the rest of his sons as well. Absalom had planned, with his men, to murder Amnon while they were in the fields. Absalom waited until Amnon was drunk and high in spirits and then he gave the orders to his men and they slew Amnon. When the rest of David's sons saw this, they quickly mounted their horses and rode away from the fields of Absalom.

Word of the attack reached Jerusalem and the rumor said Absalom had killed all of the king's sons. When David heard this he tore his clothes and threw himself on the ground. But one of the king's nephews told him it was likely Absalom had planned on killing Amnon because of the rape of Tamar and the rest of his sons were not harmed in the attack. Soon the guards on the city walls announced riders were coming into the city. As they grew near, they could see the sons of David. When they reached the palace, they told their father what happened. David and his sons wept for the treachery of Absalom and the death of Amnon. Absalom fled to Geshur and stayed there three years.

David wanted to see Absalom as he had come to peace concerning the murder of Amnon. Joab knew David desired to see his son, but he also knew David was still grieved over the murder Absalom committed. He decided he might be able to change the king's mind and developed a plan. He sent some men to get an old, wise woman from a nearby town and gave her a story to tell the king.

She went before the king and claimed she was a widow who had two sons. When they went out into a field they had a fight and one of her sons struck and killed his brother. She knew the men of the town were right to seek punishment of her other son, but her love for him, even though he killed his brother, was still strong and she didn't want to lose both of her sons. David was moved by her plight and told her he would issue a command so her son would not be punished. The old woman then told David he convicted himself with his command because he had not lifted the orders against Absalom and brought him back to Jerusalem.

David saw Joab's hand in this deception and asked her if his commander had sent her to tell this story. She confirmed Joab had told her what to say. David then told Joab to go get his son Absalom from Geshur and bring him back to Jerusalem, but he did not want to see him. Joab brought Absalom back to live in Jerusalem.

For two years Absalom lived in Jerusalem but did not see his father's face. Absalom finally sent for Joab to come and talk to him, but the commander refused. Absalom asked Joab a second time to come, but he refused again. So Absalom told some of his servants to set fire to the barley field of Joab which was next to one of Absalom's fields. When this was done, Joab came to Absalom demanding to know why he had set fire to his field. Absalom told Joab he had repeatedly sent for him and was refused. He told Joab in the two years since he left Geshur to come to Jerusalem he had not seen his father. Absalom said he would accept whatever fate came to him, but he wanted to see the king. Joab arranged for Absalom to see the king. When Absalom came into David's presence, he fell on his face and David came and kissed his son.

During his time living in Jerusalem, however, Absalom had been plotting against his father. Whenever men of Israel would approach the city, Absalom would approach them and ask if they had business with the king. If they sought the king for his judgment and advice, Absalom would tell them the king had no time for their problems and he would sit in judgment for them. He would suggest to them if he were king, he would provide judgment and counsel for all who approached him. In this way Absalom created support for himself and undermined the support of David throughout Israel.

After four years of this behavior, Absalom went to his father and told him he was heading for Hebron to worship the Lord. David sent his son to Hebron with his blessing. Two hundred men from Jerusalem were invited to go to Hebron as well, but they knew nothing of what Absalom had planned. Absalom sent messengers to all of the tribes of Israel telling them when they heard his trumpets, they would announce Absalom was king in Israel. While Absalom was at Hebron making his sacrifices, he sent for one of David's counselors and increased his support.

Word of the conspiracy finally reached Jerusalem. David and his closest advisors and allies fled the city so Absalom would not come and besiege Jerusalem. David left ten of his concubines to take care of the palace, but all of those loyal to him, whether Israelite or foreigner, followed him out into the countryside. When the priests of the Lord brought the Ark of the Covenant out of the city, David waited for them to make sacrifices, but then told them to take the Ark back into the city. He told the priests if the Lord was still with him, he would return one day and see the Ark again, but if the Lord had turned against him he would accept his fate in the wilderness. The priests took the Ark back into Jerusalem and David walked up the Mount of Olives outside the city while dressed in mourning. On the way out of the city, David was informed his counselor Ahithophel was among the conspirators working for Absalom. David prayed to the Lord that the counsel Ahithophel provided Absalom would lead to foolish decisions.

When the people reached the top of the mountain, they were greeted by Hushai the Arkite who had torn his cloths and put dust on his head. David asked him to return to Jerusalem and tell Absalom he would serve the new king. David hoped Hushai would be able to twist any advice Ahithophel gave to Absalom into foolishness. Hushai agreed and went down to Jerusalem just as Absalom arrived at the city.

After David and his followers went over the mountain, they were greeted by Ziba, the steward of Mephibosheth, who had donkeys loaded with food and wine. Ziba told David he had brought donkeys for the king's household to ride on, food for those who did not bring any, and wine to quench the thirst of those who went into the desert. David asked where Mephibosheth was. Ziba told David his master had decided to stay in Jerusalem thinking the people of Israel would restore the house of Saul to the throne. When David heard this, he gave Ziba and his sons all of the lands and properties owned by Mephibosheth.

A man came out to confront the king and his men traveling through the countryside. His name was Shimei and he was of the same clan as Saul. He started throwing rocks and dirt at David and cursing him. He said what had happened to David was payment from the Lord for all of the violence he had done against Saul. Abishai asked if the king should put up with such insults as he wanted to kill the man for his behavior. But David told Abishai to not bother the man. He said if his own son was threatening his life, a man cursing him and throwing rocks was not that big of a concern. So they traveled on, with Shimei following with curses for a while, until they reached their destination.

When Absalom came into Jerusalem, he had his father's counselor Ahithophel with him. Hushai the Arkite approached Absalom and offered his services. Absalom was suspicious of Hushai, but eventually took him as an advisor. Absalom asked Ahithophel what he should do to strengthen his claim to the throne. Ahithophel told Absalom his father had left ten concubines of his to care for the palace, and if Absalom wanted to show his supporters he and his father could not reconcile, he should have sex with them in front of the people. Absalom ordered a tent set up on top of the palace and had sex with his father's concubines in full view of all Israel.

Absalom then asked Ahithophel what he should do about his father. Ahithophel told Absalom he should gather twelve thousand men and strike while David and his men were still fleeing. All of those with Absalom agreed, but Absalom asked Hushai to offer his advice. Hushai told Absalom to wait and gather a much larger force and fall on David like a flood. He said David and his men were true warriors and if Absalom were to send out men and the attack were to fail, then all of the support for Absalom would fade away. After hearing the advice of

Hushai, the men with Absalom agreed his advice was better than the advice of Ahithophel.

Hushai went to the priests who were watching over the Ark and told them what advice both he and Ahithophel had given Absalom. The priests each had a son, one named Jonathan and the other Ahimaaz, who they sent to David with this information. The men tried to slip out of the city but were seen by someone who informed Absalom. When they realized they had been discovered, the sons of the priests fled to the town of Bahurim where they knew a man who would hide them. He had a well in his courtyard and Jonathan and Ahimaaz climbed down into it. Then the wife of the man came out and covered it with a cloth and scattered grain over it so no one could see the well.

When Absalom's men came and questioned those at the house, the woman answered the men had crossed over the brook nearby. Absalom's men searched but could not find the fugitives and went back to Jerusalem. When it was safe, the men left the well and continued on their way to David. They told David all which Hushai had said and encouraged him to move all of his followers across the river in case Absalom changed his mind and followed the advice of Ahithophel. By the next morning all of David's people had crossed the Jordan and were safe.

When Ahithophel realized his advice was not followed, he saddled a donkey and went back to his hometown. He put his affairs in order and then hanged himself.

Absalom sent his army to find David across the Jordan, but David had moved his people toward Mahanaim during the delay. When he reached the safety of that place, allies of his came with bedding and food for the weary people and they were able to rest.

From Mahanaim, David gathered his forces and set up commands. One third of the army was commanded by Joab, one third by Abashai, and one third by Ittai the Gittite who had shown great loyalty to David by following him from Jerusalem with his people. David wanted to go out himself, but his commanders persuaded him to stay behind in the city so he would not be a target for Absalom's men. David reluctantly agreed and sent them out. As he sat in the gates and watched his men leave, he gave orders not to harm his son Absalom if it could be helped. All of the men in his army heard him give this command.

The men of David and the men of Absalom met in the forest of Ephraim and engaged in battle. David's men were fierce and drove the men of Israel before them, slaying twenty thousand that day. Absalom was in the battle when the mule he was riding ran under an oak tree. Absalom's head was caught in a branch of the tree. The mule kept running, but Absalom was stuck hanging in midair. One of Joab's men saw this and reported it to Joab. When Joab asked if he had killed Absalom, the man replied he had not. Joab told him he would give him a vast reward of silver and a warrior's belt as a trophy if he would, but the man refused because he had heard David's command concerning his son.

Joab didn't want to argue about it, so he took three javelins and thrust them into Absalom's heart. Then the armor-bearers of Joab drew their swords and stabbed Absalom. Joab blew his trumpet calling a halt to the pursuit of the enemy. Joab had Absalom's body taken down from the tree and buried in a pit in the woods.

Joab sent runners back to Mahanaim to report about the battle. David was sitting in the gateway waiting for the news when it came. When the king was informed his son was dead, David went up into a room and began weeping and mourning. When Joab returned to the city and heard this was taking place, he went up to the room where David was and confronted him. He told David his army had won a great victory that day and the way he was acting was making his men feel like they should be ashamed. He said those who loved David and were loyal to him came to this city and then fought and died for him, while those who had betrayed David brought men to kill him; and David was saddened by their deaths and not rejoicing over the lives of those who protected him. Joab told David directly if he did not act as a victorious king, then none of his loyal men would be with him by nightfall. David heard the truth in the scolding of

Joab and left his mourning to go sit in the gateway of the city where all of his men gathered to hear his words.

Throughout all of Israel news of the death of Absalom and the victory of David spread quickly. David sent word to the priests in Jerusalem to question the elders of Judah why they have not called for their rightful king to return. He also told the priest to approach the commander of Absalom's forces, a man named Amasa, and inform him David would set him as commander of his army in the place of Joab. The elders of Judah agreed David should be brought back as king and sent for him and all of his men to return. They went out to meet him at Gilgal along the Jordan and Shimei, the man who had come out and cursed David as he fled Jerusalem, came with them. When he saw David coming, he ran forward and threw himself to the ground. He begged forgiveness for what he had done and asked David for mercy. David granted him mercy and swore an oath he would not be punished.

Mephibosheth, the grandson of Saul and son of Jonathan, also came down to greet David as he crossed the Jordan. He had let his beard grow and had not groomed himself since the day David fled Jerusalem. When David saw Mephibosheth, he asked him why he had not joined David in leaving the city. Mephibosheth responded since he was lame, he had ordered a donkey be saddled for him so he could follow the king, but his servant Ziba betrayed him and left him in Jerusalem and then slandered his name by saying he had turned away from David. David ordered half the lands he gave to Ziba be given back to Mephibosheth, but the grandson of Saul told David the return of the king was more than enough reward considering all the kindness David had shown him. He told David Ziba could keep all of the lands, he wanted no reward.

Also at the crossing was a wealthy man named Barzillai who had given great amounts of support to David and his men while they were at Mahanaim. David invited him to Jerusalem to stay in the palace, but Barzillai declined as he was quite old. He did request David take his son Kimham if he wished to show gratitude. David took Kimham with him and had him live as a guest in his palace in Jerusalem.

The men of Judah escorted David across the river which caused the men of Israel to feel offended. They accused the men of Judah of stealing their honor, but the men of Judah said they deserved the honor since the men of Israel had turned away from David. The argument continued until a Benjamite named Sheba blew a horn and told the men of Israel to turn away from the house of David and go back to their homes. All of the men of Israel turned away from the king except for the men of Judah, who stayed with him until he arrived back in Jerusalem.

Upon his arrival at his palace, David had the ten concubines he had left to care for the palace taken to a place where they could recover from what Absalom had done. He set them in guarded apartments in the palace to live as widows and never went to their beds again. He called Amasa to him and said as the commander of the king's army, he wanted Amasa to gather the forces of Judah together within three days.

Three days passed and Amasa had not returned nor had any of the men he was to have gathered come to Jerusalem. David sent Abishai to find Amasa realizing his throne was being threatened once again. Abishai led the most loyal of David's men to go find Amasa. When they came across him in Gibeon, Amasa approached and Joab went out to greet him. As they came forward to embrace, Amasa did not see Joab had slipped the dagger from his belt into his hand. He stabbed Amasa in the stomach and left him in the road to die. Joab and Abishai then left and went after Sheba who had led the men of Israel to turn away from David when he crossed the Jordan.

They followed him to the city of Abel Beth Macaah and started a siege of the city. When the people of the city saw they were in danger, they sent a wise woman up onto the walls to speak to the commander of the army. When she recognized the army and its commander, she called down to Joab and asked why they were threatening a city which had never caused any problems. Joab told her a man named Sheba had taken refuge in the city and they would not leave the city until he had been dealt with. When she heard Joab's demands, she talked with the leaders of the city who found Sheba, beheaded him, and threw his head over the wall for Joab to see. Joab ordered the army to leave and he returned to Jerusalem. When Joab arrived in Jerusalem, the king placed him in command of the army again.

Later in the reign of David there was a three year drought. David sought the Lord to find if this drought was being sent as a punishment. The Lord responded it was for the sake of the Gibeonites the drought came to Israel. The Israelites had sworn to spare the Gibeonites when they came into Canaan, but while he was king, Saul attempted to wipe them out. David called the Gibeonites to him and conferred with them about their grievances. They demanded they be given seven men of the house of Saul they may put to death to show the justice of the Lord before all of Israel.

After this had been done, David gathered the bones of Saul and his son's from Jabesh Gilead and buried them with the seven slain by the Gibeonites in the tomb of Saul's father. Then the drought in the land ended.

Further into David's reign the Philistines came again to make war against Israel. During one of the first battles, David became weary and had to be saved in battle by Abishai. After the battle, David's commanders went to him and told him to not put himself in harm's way. After that day, David did not go into battle again.

Late in David's years, the Lord grew angry with Israel and inspired David to take a census, which would only lead to the Lord's vengeance. Joab tried to stop David from doing such an evil act in the eyes of the Lord, but David's word overruled him and a census of all of the fighting men of Israel took place. When Joab reported back to the king there were eight hundred thousand fighting men in Israel and five hundred thousand fighting men in Judah, David realized the pride which had led him to ask for a census. He confessed his sin to the Lord and begged the Lord to forgive him of his foolishness. The next morning David was met by the prophet Gad who had a word from the Lord.

The Lord sent word to David that Israel would be punished by either three years of famine, three months of conquest by an enemy, or three days of plague. It was David's choice on which punishment to take. David told the Lord to make the punishment swift and chose the plague. For three days the angel of the Lord swept through the lands of Israel killing seventy thousand people. When it arrived at the gates of Jerusalem, the Lord told the angel to stop because the devastation was already immense. David cried out to the Lord to spare his people since it was he and his house who had sinned.

The Lord told David the angel of wrath had stopped at the threshing floor of Araunah the Jebusite near the gates of Jerusalem. He told David to build an altar there and make sacrifices. David went to the threshing floor and met with Araunah. Araunah wanted to give the property to the king when he heard why David was there, but David insisted on paying for the land as he felt he had to incur some cost to himself for what had happened. He bought the property, the equipment and even the oxen from Araunah and built the altar he was commanded. He made the burnt sacrifices at the place the angel of wrath had stopped. The Lord heard his prayer and lifted the curse of the plague from Israel.

After many long years, David was elderly and in such poor health as he could not keep himself warm in his own bed. His servants went searching for a beautiful young virgin to keep the king warm. They found a young woman named Abishag who would lie in the king's bed with David to keep him warm and to serve him in his room, but he never had sex with her.

It was at this point David's son Adonijah put himself forward to succeed his father as king. He sought support for his claim and found the backing of Joab, commander of the armies of Israel, and Abiathar the priest. But others, such as Nathan the prophet, Zadok the priest, Benaiah son of Jehoaida, and David's special guard, did not join with Adonijah.

Adonijah went to make sacrifices before the Lord at the Stone of Zoheleth. He invited many men who he would seek support from including all of the king's sons except Solomon. He also did not invite specific men such as Nathan the prophet. When Adonijah had left to make his sacrifices, Nathan went to Bathsheba, the wife of the king and the mother of Solomon. He told her of Adonijah's plans and told her she needed to go speak with the king.

Bathsheba went in to see David and asked him if he intended for Adonijah to be king instead of Solomon. She reminded David he had promised Solomon would take the throne after him and if he had changed his mind then she and her son would be in great peril as Adonijah would view them as threats to his power. As she was speaking to the king, Nathan the prophet came in and confirmed all she had said. He told David Adonijah had invited all of the powerful men of Israel, except for Solomon, Zadok, Benaiah, and himself. He told how Adonijah was making sacrifices that day and Abiathar the priest would soon anoint him king of Israel.

When David heard this, he went to his throne room and called Bathsheba before him. He spoke before the court telling Bathsheba her son Solomon would follow him as king of Israel and sit upon his throne. He then called Nathan the prophet, Zadok the priest and Benaiah son of Jehoaida before him, He told them to find Solomon, set him on the king's mule, take him to Gihon, and anoint him king.

All of the loyal men of David went with Solomon to Gihon. After Nathan and Zadok anointed him king of Israel, they blew their trumpets and played music loud enough to shake the ground and all of the people declared him king.

Adonijah and all of the people with him were just finishing his feast when they heard the sounds from a distance. Joab heard the trumpets blowing and asked what the sounds coming from Jerusalem meant. As he was asking, Jonathan, son of Abiathar the priest, came to Adonijah and told him Solomon had been made king by their father. When Adonijah heard what had happened, he became greatly afraid and the men at his feast fled.

Adonijah went to the altar and held onto its horns in hopes his life might be spared by Solomon who was now king of Israel. He sent a message to his brother asking to be spared. Solomon sent a message back that if Adonijah acted honorably, no harm would come to him. But if he acted with deception, he would die. Solomon sent men to Adonijah and had him brought to the new king. Adonijah bowed before Solomon and was then sent back to his home.

As David was on his death bed, he called his son Solomon, king of Israel, to him. He gave him advice on how to rule and gave him specific advice to secure his throne. He told him to show kindness to the sons of Barzillai who supported him when Absalom tried to take the throne. He also told Solomon not to let Joab live because he was not to be trusted and to make sure Shimei, who had cursed David, died for his treachery. When David had given his advice to Solomon, he died and was buried in Jerusalem.

Solomon

Story found in 1 Kings Chapters 2 to 11

Soon after the death of David, King Solomon's mother Bathsheba was approached by Adonijah who was the brother of the king. Adonijah asked Bathsheba to see if she could secure the hand of Abishag the Shunammite to be his wife. Bathsheba took the message to Solomon and told him what his brother asked. Solomon became very angry at Adonijah. The king had spared the life of his brother before David had died because Adonijah had sworn he would be loyal to Solomon. Now he was asking to marry the young woman who slept with David to keep him warm in his old age. This would give him another claim to the throne and threaten Solomon's position as king.

Solomon ordered Benaiah to kill Adonijah. He then removed the priest Abiathar from his duties and exiled him to his lands because of his support of Adonijah before David's death. When Joab heard what had happened to Adonijah, he hurried to the tent of the Lord and held onto the altar. When Benaiah came to kill him, he found Joab at the altar refusing to move. When this was reported to Solomon he ordered Joab be killed at the altar if he would not come out of the tent. Joab was killed at the altar and buried in his own lands. When Joab had been killed, Solomon made Benaiah commander of all of Israel's armies.

Solomon sent for Shimei, the man from Saul's household who had cursed David when he fled Jerusalem during Absalom's rebellion. The king told Shimei he was to remain in Jerusalem or be put to death. Shimei agreed, but a short while later went to capture some runaway slaves. When he returned, Solomon confronted him for breaking his word. Solomon had him executed and solidified his hold on the throne.

One night, Solomon had a dream where the Lord came to him and told him to ask for anything he wanted. Solomon blessed the name of the Lord for being kind and loving to his father and then to him. He asked the Lord for discernment so he could lead Israel with sound judgment. The Lord was greatly pleased at the request and promised Solomon riches and success in addition to the wisdom he sought.

Solomon was holding court one day when a case was brought before him to judge. Two prostitutes were brought before him and claimed each tried to steal the other's baby. The two women lived in the same house and had babies three days apart from each other. One of the babies died and each woman claimed the other woman had accidently killed her own child and claimed the living child for her own. Solomon listened carefully to each of the women. He then asked for a sword to be brought to him. When his servant handed him the sword, Solomon declared he would slice the child in two and give half to each woman. One of the women agreed with Solomon's verdict as each woman would be without a child, but the other woman cried out to give the child to the other woman rather than kill him. Solomon then judged the woman who loved the child's life enough to send him away from her was the true mother. The people were in awe of Solomon for the discernment and wisdom he had shown.

Solomon's wisdom grew and all the nations began to send their wise men to question him and listen to what he said. He taught wise sayings and songs as well as teaching about plants and animals. Solomon was widely regarded as the wisest man in the entire world.

Hiram, the king of Tyre, sent envoys to Jerusalem when he heard Solomon was anointed King of Israel. King David and King Hiram had always been on friendly terms and Hiram wished to continue that relationship with Israel. When Solomon received the envoys of Hiram, he sent them back with a request for Hiram to send building supplies for a temple of the Lord in Jerusalem. Hiram was pleased to receive such a request from Solomon and promised him all of the timber from the vast cedar and pine forests which were part of the lands of Tyre and Sidon. Solomon conscripted men from Israel to gather the stone and wood needed to build the temple Solomon had envisioned.

In the fourth year of his reign, Solomon began building the temple of the Lord in Jerusalem. It was grand and ornate, very precisely designed and detailed. It took seven years to build and when it was finished, Solomon had the Ark of the Covenant moved into the inner sanctuary of the temple. When the Ark was set in place, a cloud descended over the temple and stayed there. Solomon went before the altar and lifted his hands toward heaven in front of the assembled people of Israel. He prayed the Lord would be pleased with the temple and answer those who came to the temple to pray.

Solomon led the people in making sacrifices and burnt offerings to the Lord in his temple. Twenty two thousand head of cattle and one hundred and twenty thousand sheep and goats were sacrificed in addition to large numbers of burnt offerings during the time of dedication. For seven days and nights the land of Israel celebrated the building of the temple. After Solomon had dedicated the temple, the Lord appeared to him and told him as long as he and his sons were loyal and obedient to the laws given to them by Moses, the Lord would be with Israel. But if Solomon or his sons were to turn from the Lord then people would wonder why Israel had built such a grand temple to the Lord who had punished them so severely.

The Lord blessed Solomon as he promised. His riches and glory were abundant. He married Pharaoh of Egypt's daughter and built a splendid palace which took thirteen years to complete. He had riches and treasures sent to him from every location on the earth. He received emissaries from kings of distant lands and sent rich gifts for those who found favor with Israel.

The queen of Sheba had heard of Solomon's wealth and wisdom. She traveled from her own lands with a caravan of wealth for Solomon to see if the stories were true. When she met the king of Israel, she was amazed the stories were only half as impressive as the truth she saw with her own eyes. Solomon threw grand feasts and celebrations for her and sent her back to her lands with gifts and wealth from Israel.

Solomon loved many women besides Pharaoh's daughter. He had six hundred wives and three hundred concubines. Many of his wives and concubines were foreign women from nations the Lord warned Israel not to intermarry with. They eventually persuaded Solomon to turn away from the Lord and start building sites for the other gods they worshipped. The Lord was angry at Solomon for not following the ways of David his father by dedicating his worship only to the Lord. Because of his wayward attitude, the Lord decided to split the kingdom of Israel and take it out of the hands of the house of David. But for the sake of David, the Lord would not do it in Solomon's lifetime.

Solomon ruled for forty years before he died. He was buried in Jerusalem, the city of his father David, and was succeeded by his son Rehoboam.

Elijah

Story found in 1 Kings Chapters 16 to 22
and 2 Kings Chapters 1 to 2

ing Ahab of Israel sinned more against the Lord than any king of Israel before him. He married a woman named Jezebel who was the daughter of the king of Sidon and together they led Israel into the worship of Baal. During Ahab's rule, he built a temple to Baal and set up altars to that god. He built Asherah poles and allowed the city of Jericho to be rebuilt.

Elijah was a man of God and a prophet. He went to King Ahab and told him a great drought would come to Israel which would last many years. He told Ahab it would not rain or even have any dew on the ground unless Elijah allowed it to happen. Elijah then fled and hid where the Lord directed him in order to escape Ahab's anger. The Lord led Elijah to a hidden place on the other side of the Jordan River and told Elijah he could drink from the small brook nearby and ravens would come daily with food for him. Every morning and every evening, ravens would come to Elijah and bring him meat and bread.

The drought was so severe that eventually the small brook dried up. When that happened, the Lord told Elijah to go to a nearby town where a widow would take care of him. At the gates of the town, Elijah saw a woman gathering sticks from the ground. He asked her for some water and as she went to get him water, he called out and told her to bring him some bread as well. She came to him and explained she was a poor widow and the reason she was gathering sticks was to go home and make a fire. She had just enough flour and oil left to make a single meal. She told Elijah after she and her son ate that bread they would soon die of starvation.

Elijah told her to make him a small cake of bread and then make whatever she needed for her and her son to live. He told her the Lord would bless her and the flour and oil would not run out until the Lord allowed the rains to come again. The widow made some bread for Elijah and brought it to him. She then made enough food for her and her son, and there was still flour and oil left over. Elijah stayed with her and there was always enough flour and oil to feed them every day.

One day, her son became very sick and stopped breathing. She went to Elijah and asked if this was the Lord punishing her for some sin. Elijah went to the where the boy was laying and prayed to the Lord for his life. The Lord heard Elijah's prayer and restored the widow's son to life. Elijah brought the boy down and gave him back to his mother.

In the third year of the drought, the Lord told Elijah to go to Ahab and the drought would end. Elijah went toward Samaria where Ahab lived. On the way there, Elijah came across Obadiah, one of the king's counselors. Obadiah was a faithful servant of the Lord, even though he had to serve the wicked King Ahab. When Jezebel ordered the deaths of the prophets of the Lord, Obadiah had hidden one hundred of them in caves and kept them supplied with food and water. When Obadiah saw Elijah, he recognized the prophet and fell to his face. Elijah told Obadiah he needed to tell Ahab that Elijah would be on Mount Carmel.

When Ahab heard Elijah had been found, he came to Mount Carmel to confront him. He accused Elijah of bringing the drought to Israel, but Elijah told Ahab it was the worship of Baal which brought the Lord's wrath upon the people. He told Ahab to assemble the four hundred and fifty prophets of Baal and four hundred prophets of Asherah the king allowed in Israel. Elijah said he would meet them at the top of Mount Carmel.

When the prophets gathered at Mount Carmel, many of the people of Israel came to see what was happening. Elijah spoke to them and told them they must choose between the Lord and Baal. But the people were silent. Elijah told Ahab to bring two bulls to be sacrificed. The prophets of Baal could choose their bull and sacrifice it to Baal on an altar they built. They would pray that their god would burn the sacrifice they presented. After they were done, Elijah would do the same for the Lord's sacrifice. The people said they would accept this as a sign of who they would follow.

The prophets of Baal sacrificed the bull in the morning and placed it on the altar. They prayed and cried out to Baal all morning, but the sacrifice did not catch fire. Elijah began to mock them saying perhaps Baal was asleep and they needed to scream louder. The prophets of Baal started cutting themselves in worship to their god and calling out in loud voices through the day, but their altar was without fire.

As evening approached, Elijah gathered twelve stones to represent the twelve tribes of Israel. He built an altar with it and dug a large trench completely around the altar. He arranged the wood on the altar and laid out the sacrificed and butchered bull upon the wood. He told some of the men present to fill four large jars of water and pour it over the altar. They did and he ordered them to douse the altar twice more. Twelve jars of water soaked the altar and even the trench which was dug around the altar was filled. Then Elijah prayed to the Lord and a mighty fire descended from the sky and consumed the meat, the wood, the stones and all of the soil around the altar. Not even the water in the trench was left.

When the people saw this, they fell on their faces and worshipped the Lord. Elijah commanded the people to grab all of the prophets of Baal and Asherah and led them down into a valley where he killed them. Elijah came back to King Ahab and told him to go eat and prepare himself for the coming rain. Ahab went off by himself to eat while Elijah took a servant and went to the top of Mount Carmel. He bowed before the Lord and told the servant to look out to the sea and tell him what he saw. The servant came back and said he saw nothing. Elijah kept sending the servant to check what he saw in the direction of the sea. The seventh time the servant returned, he told Elijah he saw a small cloud coming from the sea. Elijah told the servant to tell Ahab to prepare his chariot and hurry back to Jezreel before the heavy rains overtook him. While Ahab left the mountain on his chariot, the power of the Lord came on Elijah and he ran back to the city before Ahab could arrive.

When the king returned to his palace, he told his wife what had happened at Mount Carmel. Jezebel was angry at Elijah and sent a messenger to tell Elijah she was coming to kill him. Elijah was afraid of Jezebel so he fled from Judah and went into the desert. A day after he left Judah, he came to a broom tree and sat under it. He prayed he might die there and fell asleep. A short while later, an angel of the Lord woke Elijah and fed him some bread and water. Elijah ate it and fell back asleep. The angel woke him a second time and told him to eat because his journey would be long. So Elijah ate and drank again and then went into the desert wherever the Lord guided him.

After forty days and nights, Elijah ended up on Mount Horeb. Elijah found a cave and crawled into it and slept. When he woke, the Lord asked him what he was doing there. Elijah complained bitterly that the people of Israel had turned their backs on the Lord, had killed the prophets and were now trying to kill him.

The Lord told him to go and stand beside the mountain and wait for the Lord to come to him. Elijah stood by the mountain and a mighty wind came and devastated all around Elijah, but the Lord was not in the wind. An earthquake struck after the wind passed, but the Lord was not in the earthquake. Then a great fire came, but the Lord was not in the fire. Elijah then heard a whisper and knew the Lord had passed by him. Elijah returned to the cave and the Lord spoke to him. He instructed Elijah to go back the way he came and when he got to the Desert of Damascus, he was to seek out Hazael and anoint him king over Aram. He was to anoint Jeru as king of Israel, and then appoint Elisha to be his successor as prophet. The Lord promised all who Hazael did not put to the sword in Israel would be killed by Jeru, and anyone Jeru missed would be slain by Elisha. But the Lord comforted Elijah by telling him there were seven thousand Hebrews who had never bent their knee toward Baal or kissed his idols.

Elijah went and found Elisha plowing in his father's fields. Elijah came to him and placed his cloak around him. Elisha knew he was to follow Elijah, but he begged for the chance to go tell his parents goodbye. Elijah allowed him to go back to his home to see his parents. Afterward, Elisha sacrificed some oxen and gave a feast in celebration. Then Elisha followed Elijah and became his attendant.

Sometime later, King Ahab of Israel went to the owner of a vineyard near his palace and asked to buy it from him. Ahab wanted a vegetable garden and the vineyard was in the perfect spot for it. But Naboth, the owner of the vineyard, refused to sell it to the king, or even trade it for a better vineyard. He told Ahab it was his family's vineyard handed down through generations and he could see no way to sell it. Ahab went back to his palace depressed he could not acquire the plot of land he wanted. When his wife Jezebel saw he was upset, she asked him what the problem was. When he told her, she became angry with him and told him he was the king and could just take the land if he chose to. But Ahab became sullen and depressed over the situation.

Jezebel wrote letters to the leaders of the city and ordered them to throw a large feast with Naboth as the guest of honor. When he was being celebrated, the leaders were to sit two men across from him who would then accuse Naboth of blaspheming against the Lord and against King Ahab. The elders were to stir up the people at the feast against Naboth for his crimes.

The elders did what they were told and Naboth was accused of blasphemy against both the Lord and the king at the feast held in his honor. The people took him outside the gates of Jezreel and stoned him to death. The elders sent word to the queen that Naboth was dead and she went to Ahab and told him Naboth's vineyard could be claimed.

When Ahab went to Naboth's vineyard to take possession of it, Elijah met him there. Elijah accused Ahab of murdering Naboth so he could seize his land. He told the king the dogs at the gates of Jezreel would lick his blood up just like they licked up the blood of Naboth. He informed Ahab the Lord would utterly destroy his family line because Ahab had sold himself completely to sin. When Ahab heard these words, he ripped his clothes, dressed himself in sackcloth and fasted. When the Lord saw how humble the king was acting, he told Elijah he would spare Ahab that day and the destruction of his family would come in the days of his sons.

Three years later, Ahab was joined by King Jehoshaphat of Judah to wage war against King Ben-Hadad of Aram. Before they left for the battle, Jehoshaphat asked Ahab if they could get counsel from the king's prophets. Ahab called all of the prophets of Baal he had in the city and they prophesied Ahab would be victorious against his enemies. When Jehoshaphat saw this, he asked Ahab if he had no prophets of the Lord in the city who could give a blessing. Ahab said there was Micaiah, but the king never consulted him because he always prophesied bad fortune. Ahab decided to send for Micaiah because King Jehoshaphat requested counsel from a prophet of the Lord. While all of the prophets of Baal were continuing to give the kings promises of victory, Micaiah arrived. When Ahab ordered him to say what the Lord saw for their fortunes in battle, Micaiah answered he saw the men of Israel scattered among the hills like sheep, because they had no shepherd.

Ahab told Jehoshaphat this was the type of message Micaiah always brought to him. Micaiah then told Ahab how he had seen the Lord in heaven asking all of his attending angels who could lead the king into his own destruction. One of the angels suggested they put false words into the mouths of the prophets of Baal, and the Lord agreed this is how Ahab should go to his doom. The head prophet of Baal then slapped Micaiah and mocked him and the Lord. Ahab had Micaiah confined with nothing except bread and water until he came back. Micaiah told the king the word of the Lord was true and Ahab would never return.

When Ahab and Jehoshaphat came to the site of the battle, Ahab decided he would fight in disguise. He would not dress in his royal robes and he would have his personal bodyguard fight with King Jehoshaphat of Judah. He felt he would be targeted in the battle if the enemy could easily see the King of Israel. When the battle started, the charioteers of Aram came towards Jehoshaphat thinking he was King Ahab. When they saw the king of Israel was not there, they turned and left. But a random arrow struck Ahab in a weak part of his armor and he bled to death in his chariot. The men of Israel, seeing their king was dead, melted away across the hills as the prophet Micaiah had said. When Ahab's chariot was brought back to Jezreel, his officers washed his blood from it with water from a pool at the front gates. Dogs licked up the blood of the king in the same spot where they licked up the blood of Naboth, just as Elijah had prophesied.

Ahab's son Ahaziah took the throne of Israel after his father died. He was a wicked man who took after the ways of his father and of his mother, Jezebel. About two years into his reign, he fell through the lattice work of his palace and lay seriously injured. He sent some of his servants to seek the advice of Baal-Zebub, the god of the people of Ekron. An angel came to Elijah and told him to go meet the king's messengers and have them return to the king and ask why he would seek the advice of a foreign god. Elijah told them because Ahaziah did not seek the Lord but instead sought Baal-Zebub, he would never leave his bed.

When the messengers returned to the king and told him the message, he asked who had sent the message to him. When they described him, he knew it was Elijah. He sent one of his captains and fifty soldiers to get Elijah and bring him back. When they found the prophet of the Lord, he was sitting on top of a hill. The captain called to him to come down. Elijah responded if he was truly a man of God, then fire would consume the men who had come for him. When he said these words a mighty fire came from heaven and consumed the captain and his fifty men.

Ahaziah sent another captain with another fifty men to apprehend Elijah, but like before, a fire came down from heaven and consumed them. A third captain and another fifty men were sent. When this captain approached where Elijah was, he begged for his and his men's lives. An angel came to Elijah and told him he was to go with this captain to see the king.

When they arrived, Ahaziah demanded to know why Elijah had sent such a message to him. Elijah told him the Lord was angry that he would consult a foreign god. For that slight to the Lord, Ahaziah would never leave his bed alive. That night

Ahaziah died in his bed and his brother Joram took the throne of Israel.

Elijah and his aide Elisha had been at Gilgal when Elijah said he was heading to Bethal and he wanted Elisha to stay behind. Elisha refused to leave Elijah because he knew the Lord was going to take his master that day. When they came to Bethel, a group of prophets came out to greet them and asked Elisha if he knew Elijah would be taken away that day. Elisha said he knew, but none of them should speak of it. When Elijah was ready to leave Bethel, he told Elisha to stay behind as he went to Jericho. Elisha refused to leave Elijah so they traveled to Jericho. When they arrived at Jericho, another group of prophets came out and greeted them and asked Elisha if he knew Elijah would be taken away by the Lord that day. Again, Elisha responded he knew, but no one should speak of it. Elijah again told Elisha to stay behind as he went to the Jordan River. Elisha refused and traveled with his master. Fifty of the prophets who had come out to greet them that day followed at a distance and watched. When Elijah came to the river, he took his cloak and rolled it up. He then struck the river with his cloak and the waters parted and he and Elisha crossed the Jordan on dry land.

The prophet then asked Elisha what he would ask for before the Lord took Elijah. Elisha asked for a double portion of the Spirit of the Lord which dwelt in Elijah. Elijah told him if he would watch until Elijah was taken, the blessing would be his. As they were walking and talking, a chariot of fire pulled by horses of fire came from nowhere and separated them. Then Elisha cried out and watched as Elijah was taken away in a whirlwind.

Elisha tore his own clothes because he knew he would never see Elijah again. He took up the cloak Elijah dropped and carried it with him. When he came to the Jordan, he rolled up Elijah's cloak and struck the water with it and crossed on dry land. When the prophets who had followed them from Jericho saw Elisha, they recognized the spirit of Elijah rested on him. They came to him and bowed before him. They asked him for permission to go look for Elijah thinking maybe the Lord had set him down in a distant place. Elisha told them not to go, but they insisted. For three days they searched for Elijah, but could not find him.

Elisha

Story found in 2 Kings Chapters 2 to 13

Elisha went to Jericho for a time and while there the elders of the town came to him and asked him if he could go out to their spring and do something about the water which had gone bad. He had them bring a bowl of salt to him and he threw the salt into the spring and the Lord refreshed the water. When Elisha left Jericho to go to Bethel, some young men came out threatening him. He called a curse down on them and two bears came from the woods nearby and mauled them, killing forty-two of the young men.

During the time of King Joram of Israel, the Moabites broke the treaty they had with Israel and rebelled. Joram did evil in the eyes of the Lord, but not as much as his father Ahab or his mother Jezebel. He destroyed the altar of Baal his father had set up but still did not follow the commands of the Lord. When Moab rebelled, he asked King Jehoshaphat of Judah to go with him to fight the Moabites and hold them to their treaty. They persuaded the king of Edom to join them in the war and headed to Moab through the kingdom of Edom. But when they got to the desert, they lost their way and their armies were without water.

Jehoshaphat asked if there was a man of God nearby who they could seek aid from. One of the officers of Israel told the kings Elisha was nearby and the kings went to him. When Elisha saw Joram he snubbed him and told him to go see the prophets of his father and mother, but the king of Israel told Elisha the Lord had called the kings together to crush Moab. Because of Elisha's respect for King Jehoshaphat, he did not turn the kings away. He had them bring a harpist to play while he sought the Lord. While the harpist played, the word of the Lord came to Elisha. He told the three kings to dig vast trenches all around their encampment and the Lord would fill the trenches with water even though it would not rain. He told them they would completely destroy the land of Moab; its cities, its orchards and its fields.

The kings returned to their camp and ordered the trenches dug. At sunrise the next day, the trenches were filled with water. The Moabites had heard the kings of Edom, Israel and Judah were marching against them, so they gathered their armies and marched into the desert. The morning they came to the camp of the three kings, the water had filled the trenches and in the early morning light it looked like rivers of blood around the encampment. The Moabites believed the armies of their enemies had turned on each other, so they went charging in to destroy and plunder the camp. But the Israelites and their allies were ready in their camp and slaughtered the Moabite armies. They ravaged the land of Moab; they destroyed every tree, spread rocks through every field and tore down every city.

When the king of Moab saw what had happened, he attempted to break through the enemy lines to kill the king of Edom, but failed. He finally retreated behind some walls of a town and sacrificed his own heir to the gods of the Moabites. The Moabites then retreated back into their own lands.

Elisha was approached during this time by the widow of one of the prophets who had been accompanying him. She told Elisha her husband was dead and now one of their creditors was threatening to take her two sons into slavery for her debts. Elisha asked her if she had anything to sell and she said no. He asked her what she had in her house and she said just a little jar of oil. He told her to go to all of her neighbors and borrow as many jars, big or small, that they could spare. When she had borrowed many jars, he told her to start pouring oil from her little jar into all of the empty jars. She did this until all of the borrowed jars were filled. Elisha then told her to sell the oil to pay her debts and she and her sons could live off of the rest of the money.

At various times, Elisha would go to Shunem. A couple who lived there was glad to host the prophet and his servant, called Gehazi, in their house. Eventually they built a guest room on the roof of their house for Elisha and his servant. When he was there one day, he called the woman to him and asked if there was anything he could do for her and her husband for their generous hospitality. She said she was just pleased to host him when he came to Shunem.

When he could speak to Gehazi privately, Elisha asked what could be done for her. His servant replied the woman had always wanted a son, but was unable to have one. Elisha told her she would hold a son by the next time he visited. She urged him not to make the promise, but the next year she gave birth to a son.

One day, when the boy was in the fields with his father, he complained of a severe headache. His father had a servant carry the boy to his mother. She sat with him for hours, but he died. She carried him up to Elisha's room and laid him on the bed. Then she told her husband to prepare a donkey for her so she and a servant could go and look for Elisha and bring him back. The woman and her servant traveled all the way to Mount Carmel before she found Elisha. When he saw her in the distance, he sent Gehazi to ask her what was wrong, but she came to him herself and fell at his feet weeping. The Lord had not told Elisha why the woman had come to him, so he asked her. She told him about her son and asked him to come with her.

Elisha gave his staff to Gehazi and told him to run as fast as he could to Shunem and place the staff on the boy. He then followed the woman back to her house. When he arrived, his servant said the boy was dead and his staff did nothing. Elisha prayed to the Lord and stretched himself over the boy, laying on top of him. The boy grew warm but did not breathe. Elisha walked around the room praying and then stretched himself over the boy again. The boy sneezed seven times and woke. Elisha had his servant call the boy's mother in. When she came in and saw her son, she fell to the ground and bowed before Elisha. She then took her son from Elisha's room.

When Elisha returned to Gilgal, there was a great famine in that part of Israel. He met the prophets there and told his servant Gehazi to gather some wild plants to make a stew. He found a vine of gourds and brought them back and chopped them up for the stew. When the men started to eat the stew, they realized it was poisoned. Elisha took some flour and threw it into the pot and the stew became good and healthy to eat.

Later during the famine at Gilgal, there was a time where one hundred men were gathered and all they had to eat were twenty small loaves of bread. Elisha told Gehazi to set out the bread for the men because the Lord had told him it would feed them all and there would even be bread to spare. All the men ate until they were full, and like the Lord said, there was bread left over after the meal.

The king of Aram had a commander named Naaman who was well thought of and highly respected. His valiant actions as a soldier had won a great victory for Aram, but he was struck with leprosy. During one of his raids into Israel, a young girl had been captured and was serving as a maid to Naaman's wife. When she learned Naaman had been diseased with leprosy, she told her mistress of a prophet in Samaria who could heal him. Naaman went to the king of Aram and asked permission to seek out the prophet so he might be healed. The king agreed and even wrote a letter to the king of Israel seeking help.

Naaman took a vast fortune with him to Israel to find this prophet and pay for his healing. He took thirteen hundred pounds of silver, one hundred and forty-five pounds of gold, and ten sets of very expensive clothes. When he presented himself before the king of Israel and gave the letter from the king of Aram, the king of Israel became angry. He ripped his clothes and accused the king of Aram of trying to start a war by asking he heal this man of leprosy. When word of Naaman and his request reached Elisha, the prophet sent a message to the king. He told the king to stop worrying about the intent of the king of Aram and to send Naaman to Elisha so his leprosy would be healed.

Naaman and all of his men and chariots went to where Elisha was. When Elisha saw him approach, he sent a message to Naaman that he should travel to the Jordan River and go into the waters seven times. Naaman became angry when he heard this. He called the Jordan a filthy river and said if he needed to wash he could do it in some of the clean rivers in the land of Aram. But the servants of Naaman asked their master to reconsider and convinced him to go wash in the Jordan. When Naaman did this, he was healed of his leprosy.

Naaman went back to the house of Elisha and declared there was no god like the God of Israel. He offered all he had brought to Elisha, but Elisha refused any payment. Naaman insisted many times Elisha take some reward, but the prophet stood firm in his refusal. Naaman agreed to go home without rewarding Elisha, but he asked for two things before he departed. He wanted soil from the land, as much as two mules could carry, so he could build an altar to the Lord where he lived. He said he would never sacrifice to any god but the Lord from that day on. He also let Elisha know the king of Aram leaned on his arm when he went into the temple in their lands, and he wanted Elisha to forgive him in advance for bowing in the temple when he went in with the king. Elisha granted him these things and sent him away in peace.

When Gehazi saw what his master had done, he did not think Naaman should have left without leaving a gift. He followed after Naaman and finally caught up with the commander. When Naaman saw Elisha's servant, he came down from his chariot and asked if there was anything wrong. Gehazi told him that soon after he left, two prophets came down from the hills and Elisha wanted to give them each half a talent of silver (about sixty-five pounds) and a fine set of clothes. Naaman was happy to help Elisha and gave Gehazi two talents of silver and two sets of clothes.

Elisha confronted Gehazi when he returned. He asked his servant where he had been and Gehazi said he had not left. Elisha told Gehazi when Naaman came down from his chariot, the spirit of Elisha was beside Gehazi. He rebuked him for taking wealth he didn't need and cursed Gehazi and his descendents with the leprosy Naaman had been healed of. Gehazi left the house of Elisha and did not return.

Soon the king of Aram waged war on Israel, but every time he set a cunning ambush, the armies of Israel were able to avoid it. He called all of his commanders together and demanded to know who among his men was feeding information to Israel. The commanders all told him it was the prophet of the Lord named Elisha who tells the king of Israel all the secrets of Aram's armies. The king of Aram decided he would capture this prophet to prevent him from helping Israel. Spies reported back Elisha was at Dothan so the king of Aram sent a large army to siege the town and take him prisoner.

When the town woke the next morning, they saw the large number of chariots and men set around their town. Elisha and one of his servants went onto a roof to look at the Arameans. Elisha's servant was afraid, but the prophet prayed the Lord would let his servant's eyes see what Elisha could see around them. His servant then saw horses and chariots of fire all across the hills and valleys of the land. Elisha told his servant since the Lord was on their side, they did not have to worry. Elisha then prayed to the Lord to strike the men of Aram blind.

When the soldiers of Aram were struck blind, Elisha went to them and told them they were at the wrong town. He led their army to the gates of Jezreel and then the Lord restored their vision. The king of Israel was perplexed when the large army of Aram walked into the king's city without a struggle. He asked Elisha if he should put them to death, but Elisha told him not to. He said to treat them as if they had been taken captive by the king himself. So the king of Israel had food and drink brought for the army of the Arameans and then sent them home again. For a while, the forces of Aram stopped attacking Israel.

Eventually King Ben-Hadad of Aram built a force strong enough to besiege the king of Israel in his own city. The siege went on for some time and dire starvation came upon the people. One day a woman stopped the king and asked for his justice. She told him another woman had come to her the day before and said if she were to provide her son for their families to eat that day, the other woman would provide her own son for their families to eat the next day. The woman killed her son and the families ate him yesterday, but the other woman had hidden her son to spare him from being killed and eaten.

The king tore his clothes in sorrow and anger. He dressed himself in sackcloth and walked where his people could see his mourning. Finally he decided to go to the house of Elisha and cut his head off for the suffering the Lord was allowing. Elisha was at his house in the city with the elders. He saw the king coming and told them to bar the door as he knew the king was coming to kill him in his anger. The king and Elisha talked through the blocked door. The king accused the Lord of bringing ruin to the city, but Elisha told him tomorrow morning, barley and flour would be bought for pennies at the gates of the city. The king's aide openly doubted even the Lord could do that. Elisha told the man he would see it, but he would never get a bite of the food.

That evening at dusk, four lepers who were by the gates of the city discussed their situation. They decided since the people of the city were starving, they also would die in a short while if they stayed where they were. The lepers decided to go to the camps of the Arameans to beg. They reasoned if the men of Aram put them to death, they would be no worse off than what they faced at the gates of a starving city. When they came to the encampment, they found it abandoned. As the sun was setting, the Lord caused the men at the camps to hear a thundering like the hooves of many horses and the wheels of many chariots. The men of Aram panicked because they thought the king of Israel had brought the Egyptians and Hittites to fight against them. So they abandoned all of their goods, food, and livestock in the camp and fled for their lives.

The lepers went into several tents and took items and hid them away. They ate and drank and rested in the camp of the Arameans. But soon they realized if the people in the city were starving, they needed to let them know the siege was over. The lepers went to the gate and called to the gatekeepers that the enemy camp was empty. Eventually news reached the palace but the king was concerned it was a trap. He thought if he sent his men out, the Arameans would ambush them from where they were hidden. He decided to send two chariots out to locate the armies of Aram. The chariots went out and found the road the Arameans had fled down. They followed it to the Jordan, and discovered clothing and equipment abandoned all along the way as the men of Aram tossed aside anything which was slowing down their flight. The soldiers returned and reported what they had seen.

The king opened the gates for the people and they ran out in a rush to raid the encampment of the armies of Aram. The people who could not go out bought barley and flour for pennies at the gates of the city from those who raided the camp. The aide of the king who had doubted the word of Elisha was put in charge of the gate and was trampled during the rush of people trying to get food.

King Ben-Hadad of Aram became very ill and was confined to bed when Elisha went to the lands of Aram. The king sent his aide Hazael to ask Elisha if he would recover from his illness. When Hazael found Elisha and asked him, Elisha told Hazael to tell the king he would recover, even though both Elisha and Hazael knew the king would die. Hazael became ashamed because Elsiha knew what was in his mind. Then Elisha began to cry and explained to Hazael that Israel would suffer greatly when Hazael had taken the throne of Aram. When Hazael came back to the king, he told him he would recover. The next day, Hazael took a towel soaked in water and smothered Ben-Hadad. Then Hazael became king of Aram.

During the time that Hazael was king of Aram, Israel and Judah both warred against him. During one of the battles, King Joram of Israel was gravely wounded in a battle. Elisha called one of the prophets of the Lord who attended him and gave him a flask of oil. He told him where he could find the commanders of the armies of Israel and Judah and had him seek out Jehu. When the prophet found where the commanders of the armies had pitched their tents, he called to Jehu and asked to speak privately with him. He anointed Jehu as king of Israel and gave the words of the Lord to him. Jehu was to kill off the line of Ahab so no male descendant lived. He was also to kill Jezebel in vengeance for the prophets of the Lord she had killed. Jehu was told dogs would eat her body and she would not be buried. When the prophet left, Jehu returned to the commanders of the army. When he told them what had happened, they laid their cloaks at his feet and proclaimed him the rightful king of Israel.

Jehu told the commanders they needed to keep the camp secure so no word would reach Joram in Jezreel. He took his troops and headed for the city. When he was some distance out, the scouts on the city wall saw the army coming and sent word to King Joram. Joram ordered a horseman to go and see if the army came in peace. When the messenger got to Jehu, he gave him the king's message, but Jehu told him to fall in with the rest of his troops. When the lookouts saw the messenger did not return, Joram sent another. Jehu told this one to join him as well and he continued to the city.

When Jehu came close enough to be seen, King Joram had his chariot brought to him, though he was wounded. King Ahaziah of Judah was in Jezreel with him and also had his chariot brought. The two kings went to meet Jehu and they stopped in the field which was the vineyard of Naboth. When Jehu came up to them, Joram asked if he had come in peace. Jehu responded there would be no peace in Israel as long as the idolatry and witchcraft brought by the king's mother, Jezebel, was still in the land.

When he heard this, Joram called out to Ahaziah that they had been betrayed and tried to flee in his chariot. Jehu pulled his bow and shot Joram in the back and the arrow pierced his heart. Ahaziah turned his chariot to flee as well but Jehu ordered a pursuit. Ahaziah was wounded and died a short time later. Ahaziah's servants took him to Jerusalem to be buried, but Jehu told his men to dump Joram's body in Naboth's field in repayment for what King Ahab did to Naboth.

Jehu then went into Jezreel to claim the throne. When Jezebel heard what had happened, she dressed in fine clothes and put on all of her regalia. When she saw Jehu coming through the gates of the city, she sat in the window and called down to him accusing him of murdering his own master. Jehu looked up in the window and asked if there were any who would serve him. A few of Jezebel's eunuchs looked down and Jehu told them to throw her out the window. They did, and the horses of Jehu's army trampled her body into the ground at the gates. When Jehu had secured the palace, he sent some of his men to recover her body and bury her, but when they returned to the gates they found the dogs had dragged her body off and eaten her. Only her skull, hands and feet remained.

Jehu purged Ahab's line as the Lord ordered. He had all seventy of Ahab's remaining sons killed, he slaughtered all the palace officials who Ahab had appointed, and he killed all of Ahaziah's family as well, because they had been related to Ahab through his daughters.

After Jehu had wiped all of Ahab's blood from both Israel and Judah, he called together all of the people of Jezreel and told them he was going to have a great feast in honor of Baal. He called for all of the prophets, priests and ministers of Baal to come to this grand celebration. He ordered any who were summoned but did not attend would be put to death. When those who served Baal heard this news, they came gladly thinking Jehu would worship Baal and give them great honor and positions. Jehu had robes made for all of the ministers of Baal. When they were all gathered together in the temple of Baal in Jezreel, he had them look around and make sure no one who worshipped the Lord was present and only those who worshipped Baal were in attendance and once the men assembled looked at each other, they agreed that was the case. Jehu stayed with them in the temple as they made their burnt sacrifices. He had stationed eighty soldiers outside the temple and told them upon pain of death they were not to allow anyone wearing a robe of Baal to escape. When they were deep in their ceremonies, he ordered his men to enter the temple and kill them all. His men went in and slaughtered all of the priests, prophets and ministers of Baal. The inner areas of the temple were ransacked and the sacred stone of Baal was taken out into the streets and burned. The bodies of the ministers of Baal were thrown out into the streets and the temple was torn down. Jehu ordered it used as a latrine in the city.

Jehu ended the worship of Baal in Israel, but he did not end some other forms of idolatry during his reign. Because of this, the Lord allowed King Hazael of Aram to continue to take territory from Israel during Jehu's reign.

The prophet Elisha lived to see the promise the Lord had made to Elijah come true. Hazael became king of Aram and punished Israel when it sinned against the Lord, Jehu was made king of Israel and wiped out the line of Ahab, and Elisha became the successor to Elijah. Elisha continued to speak the words of the Lord to the kings of Israel until the day he died.

Jonah

Story found in the Book of Jonah

ne day the Lord told Jonah to go to the city of Ninevah and tell them the Lord was going to destroy their city because of their wickedness. Jonah did not want to go to Ninevah and decided to flee from God. He went down to the city of Joppa and bought passage on a boat which would take him to Tarshish.

As the boat headed out to sea, Jonah went below deck to sleep. As he slept, the Lord caused a storm to rise up and threaten to break apart the boat. The workers on the boat started throwing cargo overboard to lighten the craft and keep them from sinking. Finally the Captain of the boat went and woke Jonah up, telling him of the danger and asking him to pray to the god he served to save them all.

When Jonah went up on deck, he saw the men of the boat all praying to their various gods. They had decided one of them was to blame for the storm, and they cast lots to determine who the gods had become angry with. The lot fell on Jonah and they asked him what he had done. When he confirmed he was a prophet of the Lord and he was running from his command, they became afraid and asked him what they should do. Jonah told them to save the boat and their own lives, they must throw him overboard.

The men on the boat refused to kill a prophet of the Lord and instead tried to row back to shore, but the seas became rougher and the boat was starting to sink. So they cried out to the Lord for forgiveness and tossed Jonah into the sea. Immediately the sea calmed and the men knew they were safe. They were afraid of the God Jonah served and made sacrifices to the Lord to thank him for sparing their lives.

Jonah, in the meantime, had been swallowed by a very large fish the Lord had sent. For three days and three nights, Jonah lay trapped in the belly of this fish. He prayed to the Lord asking for forgiveness and mercy. Jonah came to realize the Lord, even though he was angry with Jonah, had spared his life. Once Jonah realized this, the Lord commanded the fish to vomit up Jonah on the shore.

Jonah traveled from there to Ninevah as commanded by the Lord. The city of Ninevah was so large it took three days to walk across. Jonah walked one full day into the city and started preaching the Lord's condemnation. He told the people of Ninevah they had forty days before the Lord destroyed their city.

The Ninevites believed the message of the Lord and repented of their ways. They put on sackcloth and began fasting and praying to the Lord throughout the city. When the king of Ninevah heard the words of Jonah and the message from the Lord, he left his throne, put on sackcloth and sat in the dirt. He issued a decree mandating a fast for both people and animals, and told the people of the city to wear sackcloth and pray to the Lord asking him to change his mind and spare them for their sinful and violent ways. When the Lord saw this, he felt compassion for the true repentance of the city and spared them from the destruction he was preparing them.

Jonah became angry at the Lord. He complained since the Lord was merciful and compassionate, he should not have forced Jonah to have traveled to Ninevah. Jonah told the Lord if he was not going to destroy Ninevah, he might as well strike Jonah dead. The Lord asked Jonah if he had any right to be angry. Jonah didn't answer the Lord, but instead went outside the city and built a small shelter to wait and see what the Lord would do to Ninevah.

During the night, the Lord caused a great leafy plant to grow over Jonah's shelter providing him with pleasant shade the next day. Jonah was quite pleased at the shade and protection from the heat the plant provided. The next day, the Lord sent a worm to the plant so it withered and faded. The sun came out and heated up Jonah's shelter and a scorching wind blew on Jonah as well. Jonah was miserable and again said it would be better if the Lord were to just let him die. The Lord asked Jonah if he were upset about the vine, and Jonah said he was bitterly upset, enough to die for his anger.

The Lord scolded Jonah for his attitude. He pointed out that Jonah was upset about a plant dying he had neither planted nor tended, but he was unconcerned for the one hundred and twenty thousand people the Lord had showed mercy to instead of killing.

Captivity

Daniel

Story found in the Book of Daniel

When Jehoiakim was king of Judah, the Babylonian King Nebuchadnezzar conquered Jerusalem. He took the King of Judah captive as well as several items from the temple of the Lord. Many of the people of Judah were also taken as slaves. King Nebuchadnezzar ordered the chief of his court officials, a man named Ashpenaz, to have some of the young men from the noble and royal houses of Israel learn the Babylonian language and customs.

Daniel, Hananiah, Mishael, and Azariah were four young men from the tribe of Judah who were chosen. All of the Hebrews chosen were given a daily ration of food from the palace along with wine. But Daniel and his friends did not want to defile themselves by eating food which was not clean. So they asked Ashpenaz to excuse them from eating the food provided. Ashpenaz was not willing to excuse them because he was afraid he would be held accountable for not keeping the young men healthy. Daniel had found favor with Ashpenaz, so he asked him if he would agree to a test. For ten days Daniel and his friends would only eat vegetables and water, and if they were less healthy than the other Israelite men, they would eat the royal food and wine. Ashpenaz agreed to the test and after ten days Daniel and his friends were found to be healthier and in better condition than any of the other Israelite men. After this, Daniel and his friends were no longer offered the royal food and wine and ate only vegetables and water.

The four friends were exceptionally skilled at learning the literature and writings they were being taught. Daniel could also understand visions and dreams. At the end of their training, King Nebuchadnezzar sent for all of the young men to be presented to him. Daniel, Hananiah, Mishael and Azariah were found to be without equal and they entered into the service of King Nebuchadnezzar. He eventually came to realize the advice and council they gave was greater than any of the Babylonian magicians and enchanters who were in his court.

About a year later, King Nebuchadnezzar was tormented by dreams. He called his court magicians, enchanters, sorcerers and astrologers to him. They asked him to tell them his dreams so they could interpret for him. But the king told them they were to not only interpret his dreams, but they were to tell him what they were. He said if they failed to provide the right answers, he would have them cut into pieces and have their houses torn from their foundations. But if they were to tell him his dreams and then interpret it, they would be greatly rewarded and honored. At this the wise men in the court were deathly afraid. They argued with the king that no man could do what he asked. The king flew into a rage and ordered all of his advisors put to death because he believed they were trying to deceive him.

When the order went out, Daniel, Hananiah, Mishael and Azariah were gathered along with the wise men from Babylon. Daniel asked the chief guard what was happening and when he was told of the situation, he went before the king and asked him for one night to pray to the Lord and return with both the dream and the interpretation. The king agreed to give him one night, and Daniel returned to Hananiah, Mishael and Azariah and asked them to pray with him that night. During the night the Lord revealed to Daniel in a vision what King Nebuchadnezzar had dreamed. Daniel praised the Lord for his mercy and wisdom and went to see the king the next morning.

When he approached the throne, the king asked Daniel if he was wise enough to give the answer. Daniel said there was no man wise enough to reveal to the king what he asked, but the Lord in heaven could reveal what was disturbing the king. Daniel described the dream for the king.

He said as Nebuchadnezzar lay on his bed he saw a great statue before him. The statue had a head of gold, a chest and arms of silver, a belly and upper legs of bronze, the rest of the legs were iron, and the feet were a mix of baked clay and iron. While the king pondered the great statue, a rock came flying at it and struck the feet, smashing them. The statue collapsed and as it did all of the iron, bronze, silver and gold turned to dust and blew away. The stone that had struck the statue grew in size until it was a mighty mountain which filled the earth.

When Daniel finished telling the king his dream, he then explained it. He said the Lord had established Nebuchadnezzar as the mightiest of all Kings and he was the head of gold of the statue. The chest and arms of silver was the next kingdom to rise after Babylon. It would not be as powerful or grand. The bronze belly and thighs was the kingdom after that which would rule the entire world. The legs of iron were the fourth kingdom which would be strong as iron and break those around it. But the feet show the kingdom would be divided in the end, with some parts strong and other parts weak. It would break apart and not hold together. The rock which smashed the feet of the statue was not carved by man, but by the Lord and at the time the kingdom of iron divided, he would destroy all kingdoms on earth and establish a kingdom which will never end.

When Daniel finished telling King Nebuchadnezzar his dream and its interpretation, the king fell face down on the ground before Daniel and ordered an offering and incense be given to Daniel. He then declared the god who Daniel served must be the God of gods and the Lord of all Kings because of the words he had given Daniel. The king established a high place for Daniel and gave him many gifts. He placed him in charge of all of the wise men of Babylon. Nebuchadnezzar gave Hananiah, Mishael and Azariah positions in Babylon as administrators, but he kept Daniel in his court.

Sometime later, King Nebuchadnezzar had another dream which disturbed him. He told all of the wise men of Babylon, but they could not tell him what the dream meant. Finally Daniel came to the court and Nebuchadnezzar told him about the dream. He told Daniel he dreamed there was a large tree in the middle of the land. It was so large its top touched the sky and it was visible from every part of the earth. It was a beautiful tree with plentiful fruit which all animals could eat. The beasts of the field were sheltered under its shade, the birds of the air nested in its branches, and all creatures were fed by it. He saw a messenger descending from heaven calling out to cut down the tree. The messenger ordered the tree stripped and destroyed, and all of the animals fled. The stump was bound with bronze and iron and left in the field. The messenger declared it should be left there and be given the mind of an animal until seven times passed over him.

When Daniel heard this, he was confused and then distraught as the Lord revealed to him what the dream meant. Daniel went to the king in great sadness and told King Nebuchadnezzar the meaning of the dream. King Nebuchadnezzar was the mighty tree which filled all the earth and provided food for all those who were under his reign, but the time would come when he would lose the mind of a man and become like an animal wandering the fields eating grass. This would continue until the king acknowledged the Lord places men in position of power. Daniel then begged the king to do what was right and be kind to the oppressed so his rule would continue in prosperity.

A year later, King Nebuchadnezzar was walking on the balcony of his palace when he looked out over Babylon and congratulated himself on how much he had accomplished. As he said this, a voice from heaven spoke to him and he became like an animal in his mind. He was driven away from the palace and sent into the fields where he lived like an animal. For seven years he lived this way until he lifted his eyes toward heaven to praise God. Then his mind was restored and he took back his place on the throne. From that day forward, King Nebuchadnezzar worshiped the Lord and praised him for his justice.

After King Nebuchadnezzar died, his son Belshazzar took the throne and sent Daniel away from his court. He threw a large celebration inviting one thousand of his nobles and was deep into the wine when he ordered the silver and gold cups his father had captured from the temple of the Lord in Jerusalem brought it. He poured wine in them and he, his nobles, and all of his wives and concubines drank from the holy vessels in their revelry. They worshipped their idols and praised the gods of Babylon while they drank from the cups taken from the temple of the Lord.

Suddenly the fingers of a human hand appeared in their presence and wrote words on the plaster near the lampstand in the palace. The king saw the hand as it moved and collapsed in fear. He called the wise men of Babylon to read the words and tell him what they meant. He promised them robes of purple, chains of gold and places of great prominence in the Kingdom. But none of the wise men could read and decipher the message. Belshazzar began to despair but one of his wives reminded him of the Jew named Daniel who had served his father by interpreting dreams and giving wise advice.

King Belshazzar summoned Daniel to him and showed him the writing on the wall. He told Daniel if he could read and interpret the words scrawled on the wall by the moving hand, then he would receive robes of purple, a golden chain of authority, and be made the third most powerful man in the Kingdom. Daniel told him he could keep his treasures and rewards, but he would tell the king what the words meant anyway. Daniel said Belshazzar's father, King Nebuchadnezzar, had been a mighty king, greater than any other on earth. But when his arrogance had become too much, the Lord made him as an animal in the field. Only after Nebuchadnezzar had acknowledged the Lord and realized the Lord sets kings in their places did he recover his mind and his throne. Although Belshazzar knew all of this and witnessed it firsthand, he still acted with more arrogance than his father, even going so far as taking the gold and silver cups from the temple of the Lord and drinking wine in praise of idols made of gold, silver and wood. Because of this, the Lord sent the hand which wrote on the wall the words "MENE, MENE, TEKEL, UPHARSIN". The word MENE meant the Lord had numbered the days of Belshazzar's rule. TEKEL meant Belshazzar had been weighed and found lacking. And PERES (derived from the word UPHARSIN) meant soon Babylon would be divided and conquered by the Medes and the Persians.

When Belshazzar heard the words of Daniel, he had purple robes and a golden chain placed on the Jew and promoted him to the third highest position in the kingdom. That night

Belshazzar was killed and Darius, King of the Medes, conquered Babylon.

When Darius had secured his kingdom, he established one hundred and twenty administrators known as satraps. Above these he placed three men, including Daniel, to manage the daily workings of the kingdom. Daniel's work was so admired and respected by the satraps that Darius decided he would appoint him as chief administrator. But some of the Mede and Babylonian officials grew jealous of Daniel's position and tried to find some scandal or example of corruption to use against him. But they could find no breach of the law or corruption in any of his actions. They decided the only way to charge him would be to use his deep faith against him.

The men who wished to destroy Daniel went to the king as a group. They praised and flattered him and put into his thoughts that for thirty days no one should pray to any god or man except King Darius. They encouraged him to put the decree in writing. The tradition of the Persians and Medes was if the king writes a decree it cannot be overruled or changed. Darius put a decree in writing for thirty days no man should pray to a god or man except the king. If someone were caught doing so, they would be thrown into a pit containing hungry lions.

Daniel heard the decree but when evening came he went to the upper room of his house where the windows opened towards Jerusalem. He prayed to the Lord, praising him and asking him for help. The men who had persuaded the king to issue the decree were waiting and came to Daniel while he was praying. When they had witnessed his violation of the decree, they went to the king and reported what they had found.

King Darius realized his chief administrator had been the target of the decree and he tried to find a way to allow Daniel to escape the punishment which was spelled out in the law. But as evening came, he watched helplessly as Daniel was tossed into the pit of hungry lions. He called to Daniel and said maybe the Lord whom Daniel served would protect him. The stone which covered the pit was replaced and Darius put his royal seal on it so no man could move it until the morning.

That night Darius could not sleep nor eat. He was worried all night about his good servant Daniel and hurried to the pit of lions at dawn. When the stone was pulled away from the entrance, the king shouted to Daniel asking him if the Lord had spared him. Daniel answered the Lord had sent an angel to close the lions' mouths because Daniel was not guilty in the eyes of the Lord. When Darius heard the answer, he had Daniel pulled out of the pit. He then ordered the men who had accused Daniel to be brought with their wives and children. They were thrown into the pit and the lions immediately killed and ate them.

King Darius wrote a decree to all of his provinces that the Lord who Daniel served should be held in fear and reverence because of the mighty things he had done. Daniel served in a place of honor through the reign of King Darius and into the reign of King Cyrus the Persian.

The Three Hebrew Men in the Furnace

Story found in Daniel Chapter 3

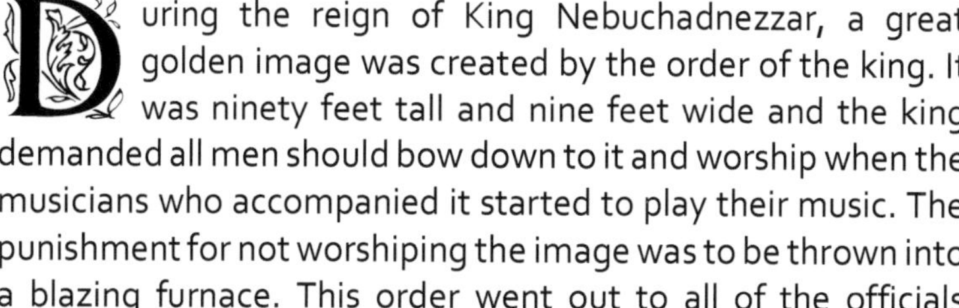

During the reign of King Nebuchadnezzar, a great golden image was created by the order of the king. It was ninety feet tall and nine feet wide and the king demanded all men should bow down to it and worship when the musicians who accompanied it started to play their music. The punishment for not worshiping the image was to be thrown into a blazing furnace. This order went out to all of the officials throughout the kingdom of Babylon.

Some of the king's astrologers came to Nebuchadnezzar and informed him that three of the Jewish men he had placed in positions of authority refused to follow his command. They were Hananiah, Mishael, and Azariah who the king had renamed Shadrach, Meshach, and Abednego. The king sent for them and when they arrived in his presence, he asked if they had refused his command. He warned them if they did not do as he said, he would have them thrown into a blazing furnace where their God would not be able to save them.

They refused to worship his golden image. They further told the king if he did throw them into the blazing furnace their God could rescue them from his hand. They added even if the Lord did not rescue them, they would still never bow and worship any god but the Lord.

Nebuchadnezzar was furious when he heard their response to him. He ordered the temperature in the furnace to be increased seven-fold and the men thrown in. The Hebrew men were thrown in fully clothed and bound with rope. The furnace was so hot, the soldiers who threw the men into the mouth of the furnace were overwhelmed by the heat and died before they could be rescued.

King Nebuchadnezzar sat to watch the three Hebrew men burn to death, but he suddenly leapt to his feet. He knew only three men were thrown in, but he saw four men walking around inside the furnace. All were unbound and the fourth man was shining like a son of the gods.

Nebachadnezzar shouted to the men to come out of the furnace. The three Hebrew men came out of the furnace and all of the king's officials gathered around them to see. Not only were the men unharmed by the fire, but even their clothes and hair were not singed. They didn't even smell like they had been in the furnace.

The king acknowledged the Lord Shadrach, Meshach, and Abednego served had saved them from their fate. He decreed any person in his realm who spoke ill of the God these men served would be cut to pieces and their house torn to rubble. Nebuchadnezzar then promoted the three men to even higher positions of power within his kingdom.

Esther

Story found in the Book of Esther

During the third year of his reign over the Persians, King Xerxes held a grand celebration. All of the leaders of the Persians and Medes came to Susa, where the king had his palace, and observed his wealth and power. After one hundred and eighty days of this display, Xerxes held a banquet for his most important officials which lasted seven days. Xerxes told his stewards to let each man drink as much as he wanted of whatever was available.

On the seventh day of the feast, Xerxes was high in spirits from drinking. He sent for his eunuchs to bring his wife, Queen Vashti, from where she was holding her own feast with some of the powerful women of the kingdom. He ordered them to dress her in her crown and bring her so all the men could see how beautiful she was. Queen Vashti refused the king's demand to be presented in that manner.

King Xerxes was furious at his queen and consulted with his closest advisors on what should be done about her refusing one of his public commands. One of them, a man named Memucan, suggested to the king if she were to get away with such behavior it might encourage other women to disobey their husbands. His recommendation was to forbid Vashti to ever be allowed in the king's presence again and to give her position of queen to someone else. This, he told the king, would let all of the women of the land know what would happen to disobedience. The king and his nobles agreed with his advice. Not only did Xerxes do as Memucan recommended regarding Vashti, he sent a proclamation to his entire kingdom that men should be the rulers over their households.

After the king's anger faded, he realized what he had done to his queen. His servants encouraged him to bring many beautiful young virgins to the palace to be groomed for him and the woman who pleased him best would become his new queen. Xerxes agreed with this advice and had his kingdom searched for suitable women. They would be brought to Susa and placed under the supervision of Hegai, the king's eunuch who was in charge of the king's harem.

Mordecai was a Jew who lived in Susa. His grandfather had been taken into captivity when Nebuchadnezzar conquered Judah and captured King Jehoiachin. Mordecai had a young cousin named Hadassah, also known as Esther. He had her taken in when her mother and father died. She was a child when she came to Mordecai and he raised her as his own daughter. She was very lovely to look at and had fine features. When the decree went out to gather beautiful, young virgins, she was taken to the king's palace and put under the care of Hegai. When she was taken, Mordecai made sure she understood not to tell anyone she was Jewish.

Esther quickly won favor with Hegai who gave her special foods and beauty treatments. He assigned her seven maids and placed her in the best housing of the harem. Hegai would check on her every day to see how she was doing.

For an entire year the selected young women underwent the beauty treatments; six months of oil of myrrh and six months of perfume and cosmetics. The young woman would then be taken to the king with anything in the harem she requested. She would go to the king in the evening and the next morning she would be taken to another section of the harem and placed under the charge of Shaashgaz, the eunuch who was in charge of the king's concubines. Once there, she would only be taken back to the king if he asked for her by name.

When Esther's night came, she took exactly what Hegai told her to take and pleased the king greatly. Soon he had decided she was the young woman who had pleased him above all others and put the crown on her head and she replaced Vashti as queen. Xerxes gave a great banquet to honor Esther and invited all of his officials and nobles. The king declared the day a holiday throughout his kingdom and gave great numbers of gifts.

Mordecai had begun sitting in the king's gate while Esther was in her training. After she had become queen he was in the king's gate when he heard two of the king's guards plotting to assassinate Xerxes. Mordecai went to Esther with what he had heard and she informed the king and told him who had uncovered the plot. Xerxes had the plot investigated and it was discovered the report was true. The king had the two guards hanged.

An official named Haman had gained great favor with King Xerxes at this time and the king elevated him to a position of great power. The king ordered all around Haman to bow to him and show him honor because he had pleased the king so greatly. But Mordecai refused to bow or give honor to Haman because Mordecai was a Jew. When Haman heard about Mordecai's refusal and heard the reason, he became angry and decided for this insult he would destroy all of the Jews in the kingdom. He counseled together with others who hated the Jews and they cast lots, called in Persia the *pur*, to determine when their plot should be carried out. The day landed on the thirteenth day of the twelfth month.

Haman went to King Xerxes and described a people who would not comply with the king's commands nor would they adapt the culture of the Persians. Haman told the king it would be in the kingdom's interest to wipe out these people and he offered ten thousand silver coins to the king for an decree declaring the death of every man, woman and child from these people. The king trusted Haman and determined the decree would be given even without payment from Haman. Xerxes gave his signet ring to Haman and allowed him to write and send the decree as he wished. It was on the thirteenth day of the first month when Haman sent the message out to all the provinces that on the thirteenth day of the twelfth month all the Jews were to be killed by the people in the kingdom.

The city of Susa was confused by the decree and all of the Jews in the city were gravely concerned by what had been proclaimed. Mordecai dressed himself in sackcloth and wept in the king's gate for the fate of his people. When Esther was told by her servants that Mordecai was weeping in the city and had dressed himself in sackcloth, she sent them to find the reason. Esther sent clothes for Mordecai to put on as people dressed in mourning were not allowed past the king's gate, but Mordecai refused to stop his mourning. Esther then sent one of her trusted servants to ask Mordecai why he was in such grief. Mordecai told everything which Haman had done, including the offer to pay the king for his decree. He even showed the servant a copy of the decree to prove what he was saying.

When Esther was informed, she sent a message back to Mordecai that there was nothing she could do. She explained if she were to enter the presence of the king without him having summoned her, the punishment was death unless the king raised his scepter to her. The king had not called for her in thirty days and she had no way of knowing if he would call for her again.

When Mordecai heard these words, he responded back to Esther saying when the decree was enforced, she would not be spared even though she was the queen. Mordecai said if she did not try to help rescue her people, then the Jews would find rescue some other way but she would still be destroyed. He told her perhaps she was put into her position for just this purpose.

Esther replied to Mordecai and told him to gather the Jews in Susa and fast for her. She would prepare herself for three days and then go into the king's presence and make her request. She said she would accept her fate regardless of the consequences.

On the third day, Esther dressed herself in her royal robes and entered the inner courtyard. When King Xerxes saw her, he was pleased and extended his royal scepter towards her. She approached him and touched the end of his scepter. Xerxes asked her what her request was. He promised nothing would be held back from her. She requested the king and Haman attend a banquet she was preparing that day and she would put her request before the king at that time. He agreed, and that night they dined at a banquet with Haman in attendance. While the king and Haman ate with Esther, the king asked her again for her request, but she asked him and Haman to attend another banquet the next day before he heard her request. The king agreed to come the next day and dine with her again.

Haman left the king and queen in a good mood and high spirits. But as he left the king's gate to head home, he spotted Mordecai who did not rise to greet him or act fearful of him. Haman was enraged at Mordecai, but he restrained himself and went home. Once there, Haman called for his friends and wife to come to him and hear about how he was prospering. He told them how he had been honored because King Xerxes and Queen Esther invited him to dine with them. He then told how Mordecai had made him angry by not giving him the honor he deserved. Haman's wife and his friends encouraged him to build a gallows seventy-five feet high and the next day when he was in the presence of the king, he should ask a favor. He should request the king to allow Mordecai to be hanged for his insults. Haman was happy with the suggestion and ordered the gallows built that day.

During the night, King Xerxes had trouble sleeping so he called for some things to read concerning his kingdom. As he was reading, he ran across the account of Mordecai the Jew alerting the king of a plot to assassinate him. He asked his attendants if any reward had been given to Mordecai for his service to the throne. They told the king nothing yet had been done for Mordecai. It was at this time Haman entered the court. When he came in, the king asked what should be done for a man who had greatly pleased the king. Haman believed the king was referring to himself, so he answered the man should be dressed in a royal robe, placed upon a royal horse, and led through the streets of the city with loud proclamations that this is how a man who pleases the king will be treated. The king agreed with Haman's ideas and commanded him to go and find Mordecai the Jew. He was to dress Mordecai in royal robes, put him on a royal horse, and lead him through the streets of Susa proclaiming loudly that this is how a man who pleases the king is treated.

Haman did what the king commanded and afterwards he ran to his house to tell his wife and friends the strange turn of events. They were scared for him and told him he should not appear to stand against Mordecai or any of the Jews because of the favor shown by the king. As Haman was talking with his family and wife, the king's men arrived to take him to Queen Esther's banquet.

While the king and Haman were drinking wine at the banquet Esther had thrown for them, Xerxes asked Esther again what her request was. This time she answered him. She asked the king to spare her life and the life of her people. She told him all her family and people of her ancestry were being threatened by someone within the kingdom. She said if her people were just being sold into slavery, she would not have bothered the king, but they had been targeted for death and destruction. When Xerxes asked who had done this, she accused Haman.

The king left the banquet in a rage and went into the garden to think. Haman realized his fate was sealed, so he threw himself on the queen to beg for his life. Xerxes came back just in time to see Haman laying on Esther's couch with her and he was furious Haman would molest the queen in such a manner. One of the eunuch's present at the banquet informed the king a gallows had been recently built at Haman's house in order to hang Mordecai. Xerxes ordered Haman to be hanged on his own gallows.

Esther then revealed to the king the relationship between her and Mordecai. The king summoned Mordecai into his presence and gave him the signet ring he had taken from Haman when he ordered him to be hanged. Esther begged the king to issue another decree which would nullify his original decree concerning the Jews. Xerxes told her a decree issued by the king and sealed with his ring could not be overturned. He then told Mordecai to issue another decree which would find a solution to the fate facing the Jews.

On the twenty-third day of the third month, Mordecai sent out an decree in the king's name and seal to the entire kingdom. The decree declared the Jews could assemble and arm themselves against any enemy who sought to do them harm. They were to be allowed to do this on the thirteenth day of the twelfth month, the same day the original decree ordered the destruction of the Jews. Throughout the kingdom the Jews celebrated and rejoiced at this decree and those who opposed the Jews were afraid.

When the thirteenth day of the twelfth month finally arrived, the Jews in all of the cities of the kingdom had come together to defend themselves against those who would do them harm. Even though many of the people were afraid of the Jews, some of their enemies attacked them anyway. The Jews were victorious in each city, however, and even the officials of the king sided with the Jews because Mordecai the Jew was growing in power and influence in the king's court.

In the city of Susa, five hundred men were killed when they attacked the Jews living there, including the ten sons of Haman. Mordecai asked the decree be extended for one more day in the city of Susa. Xerxes agreed and the next day another two hundred and fifty men were killed by the Jews of Susa.

Mordecai sent messages to all of the Jews throughout the kingdom that the fourteenth and fifteenth day of the twelfth month should be celebrated from that day onward as a time to remember when their certain destruction was turned into triumph over their enemies. The name "Purim" was given to the time of celebration from Haman's consultation of the "pur" to determine when he would destroy the Jews. After these events, Mordecai continued to serve King Xerxes and Queen Esther as the second most powerful man in the kingdom.

Jesus

The Birth and Childhood of Jesus

Story found in Matthew Chapters 1 to 2
and Luke Chapters 1 to 2

During the time of King Herod, there was a priest by the name of Zechariah living in Judea. He was married to a woman named Elizabeth and they had no children because Elizabeth was barren. One day, he had been chosen to light incense in the Temple while people outside the sanctuary prayed. When he had lit the incense, an angel of the Lord appeared beside the altar and Zechariah was scared. The angel was named Gabriel and he told Zechariah the Lord had heard his prayers and his wife would have a son named John. He told him John would grow to be a powerful man of God, filled with the Spirit of the Lord from birth. Gabriel told Zechariah his son would live a devout and strict life. He informed the priest that John's words and actions would lead many back to the ways of the Lord.

Zechariah doubted, though, because both he and Elizabeth were growing older and had passed the age for children. The angel struck Zechariah mute because of his disbelief and told him he would be able to speak again once his son was born. Elizabeth soon discovered she was pregnant and rejoiced.

Elizabeth had a young cousin named Mary, who was betrothed to a man named Joseph. One night the angel Gabriel came to her. She was afraid and fell before him, but he told her to rise and not be afraid. He said the Lord had found favor with her and she would be considered the most blessed woman in the world. She would give birth to a child, a son who would be called Jesus. He would be called the Son of God and would take David's throne and his kingdom would never end. Mary was confused by this as she was a virgin. The angel told Mary the Spirit of God would come to her and she would become pregnant without having sex with a man. Gabriel then told her that her cousin, Elizabeth, was in her sixth month of pregnancy even though she had been barren. He told Mary this to show nothing was impossible for the Lord.

Mary went to see her cousin and when Elizabeth saw Mary, she was filled with the Holy Spirit and her child leaped in her womb. She greeted her cousin loudly and called herself blessed that Mary should visit her, because she knew Mary was pregnant and her child would be the most blessed among all mankind.

Mary stayed with her for three months until Elizabeth was ready to give birth. During this time, Joseph, the man betrothed to Mary, had heard she was pregnant. Since he knew the child was not his, because had not had been with her, he was torn between marrying her and sending her away in disgrace. While he was considering what to do, an angel came to him in a dream. The angel told Joseph that Mary had conceived the child through the Holy Spirit and Joseph should marry her. Joseph continued with his plans to get married and brought Mary into his house, but he did not have sex with her until she had given birth.

It came time for Elizabeth to give birth to her son and on the eighth day the people came to Zechariah and Elizabeth's house to circumcise and name the boy. When they gathered, the people decided he should be named Zechariah after his father, but Elizabeth insisted he should be called John. When the people asked Zechariah, he asked for a writing tablet and confirmed the boy's name was John. When he had written those words, he could speak again. Zechariah started praising the Lord and prophesied over his son, saying he would prepare the way for the salvation of mankind. All the people were in awe of these signs and wondered what the child would be.

As Mary approached her delivery date, Caesar Augustus called a census for the entire world and each family in Judea traveled to their home to be counted. Since Joseph was of the line of David, he traveled to Bethlehem. When they arrived, the town was crowded and the only place he could find for him and Mary to sleep was with the animals. That night she gave birth to Jesus, wrapped him in clothes, and laid him in a feeding trough to rest.

The same evening shepherds were in the nearby fields watching over their flocks when an angel appeared to them and the light of the Lord shone about him brightly. The shepherds were afraid, but the angel said (Luke 2:10-12) "Do not be afraid. I bring you good news of great joy that will be for all the people. Today in the town of David a Savior has been born to you; he is Christ the Lord." (NIV) and suddenly a large crowd of heavenly inhabitants appeared and praised the Lord and wished peace upon all mankind.

The shepherds left their flocks and went into Bethlehem. When they found Joseph, Mary and the baby wrapped in clothes in the feeding trough, they told the town what the angels had said. The people of the town were amazed and the shepherds returned to their flocks praising the Lord for what he had let them hear and see that day.

On the eighth day, the baby was circumcised and given the name Jesus, as the angel had instructed. Joseph and Mary then took the child to the temple in Jerusalem to be consecrated before the Lord. While they made the sacrifices, there were two people who approached them. One was named Simeon, a very old man, who had heard the voice of the Lord tell him he would not die until he had seen the Christ. He was urged by the Holy Spirit to enter the courts of the Temple that day and saw the family. Taking the child in his arms, he lifted him up and blessed him, calling him the salvation of mankind, the glory of Israel, and the revelation to the Gentiles. He then spoke to Mary, blessing her and speaking words of prophecy about her son. While this was happening, a very old prophetess named Anna approached. She praised the Lord for the child and spoke to everyone in the Temple about the Lord's blessing on him. Mary and Joseph were astonished at what they heard and saw and returned to their town of Nazareth.

On the night Jesus was born, a great star shone in the sky which powerful and wise men from the east discerned to mean the king of the Jews was born. They traveled to Judea and sought King Herod. When he welcomed them, they asked to see the child. They wanted to worship him and give him gifts, as he had been born to be the king of the Jews. When Herod heard this, he became quite upset and consulted with the priests of the temple to determine from prophecy where the king of the Jews might be born. When he heard the child would be born in Bethlehem, he sent the men of the east to find the child and then to send for him so he could go and worship as well. The wise men followed the star in the sky until they came to the house the child was in. They worshipped him and gave him gifts of gold, incense and myrrh. Being warned in a dream not to return to King Herod, they left the house of the child and went back to their lands.

After they had left, an angel appeared to Joseph in a dream and warned him King Herod would be looking for the child. He was to take Mary and Jesus and flee to Egypt. When Herod realized the men from the east would not return to him, he ordered all children under the age of two in Bethlehem and nearby be killed. After Joseph had heard Herod had died, he brought Mary and Jesus back to Nazareth.

When Jesus was twelve, he and his parents traveled to Jerusalem to celebrate the Passover as was their custom. But on the way back, neither of his parents could find him among the various relatives. So they went back to Jerusalem. After having searched for him they found him sitting among the teachers in the temple, asking them questions and listening. The men there were amazed at Jesus' answers and wisdom. When his parents told him they had been looking for him, he responded (Luke 2: 49) "Why were you searching for me? Didn't you know I had to be in my Father's house?" (NIV) He went with his parents back to Nazareth and grew in wisdom and favor with the Lord and with men.

Baptism and the Calling of the Disciples

Story found in Matthew Chapters 3 to 4
and Mark Chapter 1
and Luke Chapters 3 to 4
and John Chapter 1

John, the son of Zechariah and Elizabeth, had taken the Nazarite vows. He never drank wine or other fermented drink, he never cut his hair or trimmed his beard, and he lived in the wilderness and ate locusts and honey and whatever food he could find. He preached repentance to the people of Israel, both high and low, and baptized them in the Jordan River as a symbol of devotion to the Lord. The teachers of the law and the priests of the temple came to him and asked if he was a prophet from old or Elijah returned from heaven. They asked him if he was the Messiah, the Christ, who would deliver Israel from its enemies and establish the kingdom of God. John denied all of these things. He told the people he came to prepare the way for the Messiah and while he baptized them with water, the Messiah would baptize them with fire and the Holy Spirit.

John's cousin Jesus came to be baptized during this time. As he approached, John spoke to those around him declaring Jesus to be the Lamb of God who takes away the sins of the world. When Jesus asked John to baptize him, John said he should be baptized by Jesus. Jesus told John he must be baptized in order to fulfill the calling of righteousness. When John took Jesus into the Jordan and baptized him, the Holy Spirit descended on Jesus in the form of a dove and a voice from heaven called out (Luke 3:22) "You are my Son, whom I love; with you I am well pleased." (NIV)

After he was baptized, Jesus went into the wilderness to pray and fast for forty days. While he was there, the devil came to him. He saw Jesus was hungry from his long fast and said if he was truly the Son of God, he could turn the rocks into bread and be satisfied. Jesus rebuked him and quoted the scriptures that taught man does not live on bread alone. The devil then led him to a high place and showed him all of the kingdoms of Earth. He told Jesus he would give him dominion and authority over all of them if Jesus would only bow and worship the devil. Jesus spoke of the first commandment of God that man should only worship and serve the Lord. The devil then took Jesus to the highest point of the temple of the Lord and told him he should throw himself down if he were the Son of God, because the angels would be there to protect him against any harm. Jesus responded it was a sin to tempt the Lord. The devil took him back to the wilderness and left him alone until he could find a way to tempt him again.

After Jesus left the wilderness, John saw him passing by. John was with a couple of his disciples who were also present at the baptism of Jesus. When John saw him, he again declared Jesus was the Lamb of God. One of these disciples was named Andrew. When John confirmed what he had heard and seen at the baptism of Jesus, Andrew ran home and found his brother Simon and told him he had seen the Messiah and knew who he was.

Soon after this occurred, John the Baptist publicly criticized King Herod. John was arrested and thrown in prison. When Jesus heard this, he moved from Nazareth to Capernaum on the Sea of Galilee. There he started teaching the law and preaching repentance. Those who heard him were first amazed and then upset at his teaching. They drove him out of their gathering places and refused to listen to him.

One day as Jesus was walking along the banks of the Sea of Galilee, he saw John's disciple Andrew and Andrew's brother Simon. He called to them and told them to leave their nets and follow him. When Andrew brought Simon over to meet Jesus, Jesus told him his name was no longer Simon, but was now Peter. Another pair of brothers named James and John, the sons of Zebedee, were nearby fishing from their boats. When Jesus saw them, he called them to follow him. They left their boats and followed Jesus. The next day Jesus decided to leave the area of Galilee. That morning he saw Philip and called him to follow. Philip agreed but ran to get his friend Nathaniel. When Nathaniel came, Jesus called him to follow as well.

Jesus started teaching in many areas afterward and gathered many more disciples to him.

The Miracles of Jesus

Story found in Matthew Chapter 8 to 9 and 14 to 15 and 17
and Mark Chapters 2 and 4 to 7 and 9
and Luke Chapters 5 and 7 to 9 and 17
and John Chapters 2 and 6 and 11

fter Jesus began calling his disciples to follow him, he was invited to a wedding in the town of Cana. Jesus, his disciples, and his mother went to the celebration. During the feast, his mother told him the groom throwing the party had run out of wine. Jesus told her it wasn't yet time for him to perform miracles, but she went to the servants and told them to do whatever her son instructed. When they went to Jesus for instructions, he had them fill six large jars with water. Each jar was between twenty and thirty gallons. After they had done as Jesus said, he told them to take some from the jars and present it to the man in charge of the banquet. Jesus had turned the water into wine and when the man in charge of the banquet drank from the jars, he went and questioned the groom. He wanted to know why the groom had held back the best wine so late in the celebration when most people serve the cheap wine near the end. This was the first miracle of Jesus. He revealed his glory and his disciples began to believe in him.

Jesus went back to the region of Galilee and began preaching repentance and teaching the word of God. While he was near Capernaum one day, news came to Jesus that a centurion had heard of his preaching and sought his help. Jesus was told one of the centurion's servants was sick and at the point of death. The Roman officer had heard Jesus could heal the sick and wanted Jesus to come heal his servant. The men who came to tell Jesus the news were Jewish leaders in Capernaum who were impressed this centurion had supported them in building a synagogue and had treated the Jews in the town fairly. Jesus decided to go to this man's house. While he was still on the way, he met messengers from the centurion who told him he did not need to come to the house. The centurion knew Jesus had the authority, by his word, to heal his servant, so if Jesus would just speak the word, the man would be healed. Jesus marveled at the faith of this centurion and told the messengers to go back and find the man healed.

One day on the shores of the sea of Galilee Jesus had been teaching a great crowd. After he was finished, he and his disciples got into a small boat to cross the sea. Jesus was tired and went to sleep in the back of the boat away from the others. A sudden storm caught the boat while it was crossing and nearly swamped the vessel. The disciples went to Jesus and woke him in a panic. When Jesus got up, he rebuked the wind and sea and the storm came to an immediate end and the sea was calm. Jesus admonished his disciples for their lack of faith. The disciples wondered what kind of man Jesus was that even the wind and waves obeyed his command.

When Jesus and the disciples had finished their trip across the sea, they came to the region of Gerasenes. When they left the boat, they were met by a demon possessed man who had lived among the tombs nearby. This man was wild and dangerous to the people of the region. They had tried to chain him and subdue him many times, but he would break the chains and escape. When he saw Jesus, he ran to him and fell on his knees. He addressed Jesus as the Son of God and the demons in the man begged Jesus not to torture them. Jesus felt pity for the man and asked which demon dwelt within his body. The man answered the demon was Legion, which was saying there were many demons who lived in him. Jesus prepared to free the man from this possession of demons, but the demons begged Jesus not to send them to the abyss which was created for them. They pointed out a herd of pigs on a nearby hill and asked Jesus send them to the pigs instead. Jesus agreed to their request and sent them away from the man and into the pigs. The herd of pigs panicked at the sudden possession of the demons and ran into the Sea of Galilee and drowned themselves. When the men tending the herd saw this, they ran into the nearby town and told what happened to the pigs. The people of the town came to see Jesus and his disciples. When they saw the possessed man dressed normally and in his right mind, they became afraid and asked Jesus to leave their region. The demon possessed man wanted to go with Jesus and his disciples, but Jesus told him to go home to his family and tell everyone what had happened to him.

When Jesus returned to Capernaum, he began to draw larger crowds because news of his teachings and miracles were spreading through the region. Religious teachers of the law came to him on one occasion in a house which was very crowded. There was a man who was completely paralyzed who lived nearby. His friends thought if they could get him close enough to Jesus, he might be healed. Four of his friends carried him on his mat and brought him to the house. But the crowds were too big and they could not get close enough to speak with Jesus about their friend. They went up to the roof of the house and cut a hole in the ceiling over where Jesus was sitting. They then lowered their friend into the room. When Jesus saw the faith of the man's friends, he told the paralyzed man his sins were forgiven. When the teachers of the law heard him say this, they murmured among themselves at the audacity of Jesus saying someone's sins were forgiven. Jesus heard their murmurs and asked if it was harder to forgive sins or to heal someone who was paralyzed. When they didn't answer, Jesus turned to the paralyzed man and told him to stand up, gather his mat, and go home. When he did, the crowd was amazed and praised God. They were in awe of Jesus because he wielded that much power.

While Jesus was teaching one day, a local synagogue ruler named Jarius came to him and begged him to come to his house to see his daughter who was dying. Jesus agreed to go with the man and the crowds followed him into the town. There was a woman who had a condition where she bled for twelve years. The physicians could do nothing for her, but when she saw Jesus moving through the streets, she thought if she could just touch the edge of his clothes she would be healed. As he passed where she stood, she pushed her way through the crowd and touched the bottom of his robe. Jesus felt power leave him. He stopped and looked around and asked who had touched him. The disciples pointed out there were many people touching him as they were in the middle of a large crowd, but Jesus insisted someone had touched him. When the woman realized he meant her, she fell to her knees and confessed what she had done. Jesus told her her faith had healed her and sent her home. As this was happening, servants came to Jarius and told him there was no longer any need to bring Jesus, as his daughter had died. Jesus told Jarius not to worry and he took Peter, James and John with him and continued to the house. When he arrived, there were musicians and mourners gathered. Jesus told them to stop their mourning because the girl was simply asleep. The people there laughed at Jesus but he had them removed from the house. He went to the room where the girl was lying and took her by the hand and told her to get up. She stood up and Jesus walked with her out to her family. He told them not to tell anyone about this and to get her some food. When he left, the crowds outside were astonished at what happened.

Once as Jesus was heading to Jerusalem, he passed a town which had ten lepers begging at the gate. When they saw him, they cried out for him to show mercy to them. Jesus called over to them that they were healed and they needed to go present themselves to the priests so their cleanliness could be confirmed. They went and did as they were told. One of the men, a Samaritan, later came to Jesus and fell to his knees and thanked him. Jesus told him to go in peace because his faith had healed him. After he left, Jesus wondered out loud to his disciples why the only man to return and thank him was a foreigner.

News came to Jesus that his cousin, John the Baptist, had been beheaded by King Herod. When Jesus heard this, he and the twelve disciples he had appointed as his apostles boarded a boat and headed for a remote area near the town of Bethsaida on the Sea of Galilee. Jesus wanted some time to rest and be with his apostles. When the people saw where he was going, they raced around the Sea gathering people as they went. Jesus wanted to head to the mountain in that area to be secluded, but when he saw the groups of people coming, he felt pity for them.

So he and his apostles ministered to the people and their needs. When it came to the end of the day, the apostles told him to send the crowds home because they could not feed them all. Jesus told them to talk to the people and see if they had anything to eat. A small boy was brought to Jesus. He had five small loaves of bread and two small fish for his meal. Jesus had the people sit down in groups and he took the bread and fish and blessed them. Then he broke them into pieces and gave the pieces to his apostles who distributed them to the people sitting down. When everyone was finished eating, he sent his apostles each with a basket and had them gather up any leftover food. When they returned to Jesus, each of their baskets were full of bread and fish. Jesus had fed five thousand men with five small barley loaves and two fish. When the people realized what had happened, they began muttering they wanted to make Jesus king. When he heard this, he told the twelve to go by boat to Bethsaida, and he went up the mountain to be alone and pray.

The apostles set off in the boat, but there were strong winds that night and rowing was difficult. Jesus saw the boat was a good distance from shore, so he walked out across the water to them. When he approached the boat, the men cried out in fear because they thought it was a ghost. When Jesus told them who he was, they recognized him. Peter yelled out and said if it were truly Jesus, then he would walk out to him. Peter climbed out of the boat and started walking to Jesus across the water, but he saw the wind and the waves, he became afraid and started sinking into the water. Jesus reached out and pulled him up. He criticized him for his lack of faith and they climbed into the boat. The wind calmed as Jesus came aboard and the apostles dropped to their knees as they declared him the Son of God.

As crowds would follow him, Jesus and the twelve would sometime go to distant places to find solitude. Once they headed to the area of Tyre and Sidon and quietly stayed in a house, but news spread of Jesus being there. A Greek woman from that area had heard the stories about Jesus and came to beg him to help her daughter who was possessed by a demon. Jesus ignored her loud cries for help until his disciples asked him to send her away. He told the woman he had been sent for the

Jews, not for the other people of the world and it wouldn't be right to take bread from the children and throw it to the dogs. She replied even the dogs can eat the scraps which fall from the children's table. Jesus was amazed at her faith and told her to go because her daughter was delivered from the demon.

Jesus went to a remote area of a mountain with Peter, James and John to pray and to teach them. When they returned to the rest of the disciples, they saw a crowd gathered around. A man had brought his son who was possessed with a demon and as he asked Jesus for help, the demon threw the boy to the ground and he started foaming at the mouth. Jesus asked the father if he had faith and when he answered he did, Jesus drove the demon out of the boy and returned the boy to his father. When the disciples saw this, they asked Jesus why they could not drive the demon out. He replied with faith, even as small as the size of a seed of mustard, they could do anything. He then revealed to them he would be betrayed and killed, but would rise again on the third day. The disciples could not understand what he was saying and did not speak of it to others.

Mary and Martha were sisters who had supported Jesus in his early days of ministry. Jesus was very fond of the women and of their brother Lazarus. When Lazarus become seriously ill, the sisters sent word to Jesus to come and see him because they were afraid he would die. Jesus sent a message back to the sisters that Lazarus would not die. Jesus stayed where he was for two more days, then he told the disciples he was heading back into Bethany just outside of Jerusalem. The disciples with him discouraged this because the last time he had been there some of the teachers of the law had threatened him because of his preaching. Jesus told them their friend Lazarus had fallen asleep so he needed to go wake Lazarus. When they didn't understand clearly what he meant, he spoke plainly and said Lazarus had died and they needed to go to strengthen their faith.

When they finally arrived at Bethany, they discovered Lazarus had been dead and in the tomb for four days. Many people from Jerusalem had gathered at the house of Mary and Martha to mourn with them. When Martha saw Jesus coming, she left the house to meet him while Mary stayed behind with their guests. After they greeted each other, she mourned the fact Jesus had not been there to save Lazarus. Jesus told her Lazarus would rise again. She agreed at the end times Lazarus would reawaken and join all who believed. But Jesus stopped her and told her he was the resurrection. He asked if she believed in him. She said she believed he was the Son of God and whatever he wanted would come true. After they had spoken, Martha left him and ran into the village. She came to her house and told Mary that Jesus was just outside the village and wanted to see her. Mary ran from the house and the people from Jerusalem followed. When Mary saw Jesus, she fell to her knees before him and cried to him if he had come sooner, Lazarus would not have died. Jesus was deeply moved and saddened by Mary's grief and the sadness of those who had followed her from the house. He asked to see Lazarus' tomb and the sisters showed him where it was located.

When Jesus arrived at the tomb, he wept for Lazarus. The men from Jerusalem admired at how much he loved Lazarus but also muttered among themselves that a man would could perform miracles could surely have saved the life of his friend if he had come sooner. Jesus told the men to remove the rock in front of the tomb entrance, but Martha reminded him Lazarus had been buried for four days and his body would stink by then. But Jesus insisted and the men took the stone away. Jesus prayed to God and thanked him for always listening to his prayers. He then spoke in a loud voice commanding Lazarus to come out of the tomb. Lazarus came out, still wrapped in all of his grave clothes. Jesus told the crowd to help Lazarus out of the linen he was wrapped in. When the men of Jerusalem saw what had happened, many of them put their faith in Jesus.

The Crucifixion and Resurrection

Story found in Matthew Chapters 16 to 28
and Mark Chapters 8 to 16
and Luke Chapters 9 to 24
and John Chapters 11 to 21
and Acts Chapter 1

Many men from Jerusalem were present when Lazarus was raised from the dead. While some believed in Jesus after witnessing that event, others went back and reported what they had seen to the Pharisees and other elders of the Jews. They were troubled by the miracles Jesus was performing and they felt something had to be done about it. The High Priest was named Caiaphas and said clearly the death of Jesus might be needed to save the nation from ruin. From that day onward, there were those in the high levels of the Jewish leadership who plotted to kill Jesus.

As the time for Passover came near, the leaders of the Jews set men to watch for Jesus and his apostles in Jerusalem. They knew he would come to the city to celebrate Passover and were looking for a chance to arrest him.

Six days before Passover, Jesus and his apostles went to the house of Mary and Martha in the town of Bethany near Jerusalem. Lazarus came to eat with Jesus and a large crowd gathered to see not only Jesus but Lazarus as well, since he had been raised from death. This caused the religious leaders who plotted against Jesus to make plans to kill Lazarus as well.

During the meal, Mary took a whole pint of very expensive perfume and poured it on Jesus feet and then cleaned off his feet with her hair. When Judas Iscariot, one of the apostles of Jesus, saw her anoint Jesus this way, he complained the perfume could have been sold and the money given to the poor. (Judas kept the money for the apostles and was stealing from them.) Jesus told Judas to leave Mary alone. Jesus informed him

Mary had intended to keep the perfume until he was buried, but had used it for him while he was alive.

The next morning, Jesus and his followers went to the Mount of Olives overlooking Jerusalem. Jesus sent two of his disciples to bring back a colt which would be tied up in the village of Bethphage. When they brought the colt back, the disciples put their cloaks on its back and Jesus mounted it and rode it into Jerusalem. The crowds of Jerusalem came out to witness Jesus riding into the city. Some threw their cloaks on the road in front of him while others cut palm branches from the trees and laid them in front of Jesus. The crowds shouted praises to the Lord and blessings on Jesus. The Pharisees were afraid when they saw this as they felt the crowds would always protect Jesus.

Once he had entered the city, Jesus went to the temple to prepare for Passover. When he arrived, however, he flew into a rage as he saw the moneychangers robbing the people who came to make sacrifices and offerings to the Lord. He overturned their tables and drove them out of the temple. The High Priest and the Pharisees grew angry at Jesus, but the crowds were amazed by him and they did not dare arrest him. Each day Jesus would teach in the temple and each night he would travel back to Bethany to sleep. The leaders of the Jews could not find any chance to arrest him.

Two days before the Passover celebrations were to begin, Jesus was eating at the home of a man known as Simon the Leper in Bethany. While he was there, a woman came into the home and poured expensive perfume over the head of Jesus. Judas again complained of the waste of money, but Jesus replied she was anointing his body for burial because he knew the time of his death was coming close.

Judas was overcome by Satan at this time and went in secret to the temple guards and chief priests. He asked them how much they would pay if he were to find a time and place for them to arrest Jesus without the crowds being around. The chief priests agreed to a price of thirty pieces of silver and Judas started watching for a time to betray Jesus.

The morning the Feast of Unleavened Bread began, Jesus and his followers went from Bethany to Jerusalem. Jesus sent two of his disciples ahead to find a particular man and tell him they would need the large room on the second floor of his house for the Passover feast that evening. Jesus and his apostles went to the house and waited as the meal was prepared.

As they were waiting, Jesus took off his robe and wrapped a towel around his waist. He washed the feet of his apostles where they would celebrate the Passover feast. Peter was ashamed to have Jesus wash his feet for him, but Jesus told him and the others he must serve them as an example that they should serve each other.

When the meal was brought out, Jesus and his apostles took their places reclining around the table and began to eat. While they were eating and talking, Jesus told them he was going to be betrayed and it would be by one of his own apostles. They could not believe it and argued it could not be true. John was leaning on Jesus while they ate and Peter told John to ask Jesus who it would be. When John asked Jesus, he replied it was the one he would give a piece of bread to once he had dipped it in oil. He took a piece of bread, dipped it and gave it to Judas Iscariot. When Judas took the bread, Jesus told him to go and do what needed to be done. Judas left the table, but the other apostles assumed he was going to handle a financial matter as he kept the money for the group.

(Mark 14:22-24) While they were eating, Jesus took bread, gave thanks and broke it, and gave it to his disciples, saying, "Take it; this is my body." Then he took the cup, gave thanks and offered it to them, and they all drank from it. "This is my blood of the covenant, which is poured out for many," he said to them. (NIV)

When the meal had ended Jesus and the apostles sang a hymn and left the house to go to the Mount of Olives just outside of Jerusalem. Along the way, Jesus told them how they would turn away from him when the time came, but he encouraged Peter to be strong and help the others when he regained his faith. Peter protested he would never turn from Jesus. Jesus told Peter that before the rooster crowed at dawn, there would be three times he would deny even knowing Jesus.

When they reached a place known as Gethsemane on the mountain, Jesus stopped and went to pray. He asked Peter, James and John to go with him to pray. Jesus prayed for himself, his disciples, and all believers. He knew what was going to happen and asked if there was any way the Lord could spare him from what he was about to endure. When Jesus had prayed a while, he found the three apostles with him had fallen asleep. He woke them up and returned to pray again. He was intently praying when an angel came to help strengthen him. When he had finished praying, he found his apostles asleep once again. He told them to wake up because his betrayer had returned.

As he was speaking to them, Judas came to where they were with a large group of soldiers and temple officials. He came to Jesus and kissed him on the cheek as a greeting. This was the way he agreed to identify Jesus in the night so the soldiers could arrest the correct man.

When the soldiers seized Jesus, Peter drew a sword and sliced off the ear of one of the servants of a temple official. Jesus told his disciples to stop resisting. He reached out and healed the ear of the servant. When the disciples realized Jesus did not intend to resist, they fled from the area.

The soldiers took Jesus into Jerusalem and Peter followed at a distance. Once Jesus was taken into the temple, Peter found his way to a fire nearby where he could keep warm. As he was sitting there, a servant girl asked if he was one of the disciples of Jesus. Peter said he wasn't. A short while later another man said he thought he had seen Peter with those who followed Jesus. Peter again lied and said he was not a disciple of Jesus. A third man then said Peter's accent was from Galilee, the same place Jesus came from. Peter angrily denied he knew Jesus. Just as he finished speaking, a rooster crowed to announce the dawn and Peter remembered Jesus had told him he would deny knowing Jesus three times before the rooster crowed. Peter wept and fled the warmth of the fire.

When Jesus was taken into the temple, he was brought before Caiaphas the High Priest. During the questioning, Caiaphas asked Jesus if he was the Son of God. When Jesus affirmed he was, the priests who were present ripped their robes and accused Jesus of blasphemy. The guards blindfolded Jesus and began hitting him. They mocked him and told him to use his gift of prophesy to name who had struck him each time.

Caiaphas then had Jesus taken to the Roman governor in Jerusalem, a man named Pontius Pilate. The leaders of the Jews had decided Jesus should be executed, but they did not have the authority to sentence him to death. When Judas heard the leaders of the Jews intended for Jesus to die, he went to them in shame at what he had done and told them he had betrayed an innocent man. The priests told him his guilt had nothing to do with them and turned away from Judas. Judas threw the money he had been paid to betray Jesus at the priests and left the temple. He then hanged himself. When the priests picked up the silver coins Judas had thrown, they knew it was blood money and could not go into the temple treasury. With the money, they bought a field from a potter to be used as burial ground for foreigners in Jerusalem.

When Jesus arrived at Pilate's house, he was questioned by the Roman official. Pilate could find no reason to sentence Jesus to death, but the religious leaders of Jerusalem were demanding the death sentence. Pilate sent Jesus to King Herod since he was from the region of Galilee and Herod had jurisdiction over him. When Jesus arrived, Herod was delighted. He hoped Jesus would perform a miracle for him, but Jesus remained silent and would not answer him. The men who accused Jesus of blasphemy stated the charges against Jesus, but Herod could find no evidence of a crime and sent him back to Pilate.

When Jesus returned to Pilate, the Roman official was concerned about what to do. While he had been sitting in judgment over Jesus, Pilate's wife had sent him a message telling him she had been disturbed by a dream about Jesus and told her husband he was judging an innocent man. She warned her husband not to be involved in his death. Pilate decided since it was the Passover and a tradition in Jerusalem was to free a prisoner during this time, he would suggest to the crowd that he free Jesus. But the leaders of the Jews had stirred the people up and when Pilate went to address the crowds and encourage them to ask for freedom for Jesus, the crowds responded they wanted a man named Barabbas to go free. Barabbas had led a rebellion against the Romans which had killed some men.

Pilate had finally had enough and he sent for Barabbas to be set free. He had a bowl of water brought to him, washed his hands, and told the crowd his hands were free from the blood of Jesus. He told them they could do to Jesus whatever they wanted. The crowd started chanting they wanted to crucify Jesus. Pilate tried to tell the crowd he could find no crime Jesus had committed, but the crowd became more agitated and demanded Jesus be crucified.

Pilate finally gave the order for Jesus to be crucified and the Roman soldiers took him from the palace. While the soldiers prepared Jesus to be crucified, they mocked him, slapped him, and spat on him. They dressed him in a fine robe and twisted some thorns together to sit on his head like a crown. They push the thorns into his head and beat him with a staff. They bowed before him in mockery and made fun of him as king of the Jews. They then took the robe off of him and put his own clothes back on.

The Roman soldiers gave Jesus his cross to carry and he was led with two other criminals out to a place called Golgatha. On the way, a man named Simon from Cyrene was told by the soldiers to carry the cross of Jesus for him. Once they arrived at the place of the crucifixions, the soldiers stripped Jesus of his clothing and started dividing it among themselves. They offered Jesus a drink of wine vinegar and when he refused, they placed Jesus on the cross and lifted him into place to await death. On each side of Jesus a criminal was raised as they were to be killed that day as well. The soldiers and some who came to witness the death of Jesus mocked him and told him to perform a miracle to save himself. One of the criminals hanging beside him joined in the mocking of the crowds, but the other criminal told him to stop the insults. He said Jesus was innocent while they were guilty. He then asked Jesus to remember him in death. Jesus responded the man would join him in Paradise on that day.

Pilate had a sign written in Aramaic, Latin and Greek that said: Jesus of Nazareth, King of the Jews. He posted it above Jesus so all who came by could see it. The leaders of the Jews protested what Pilate had posted, but he told them he would not remove it.

Among those gathered around the cross were Mary, the mother of Jesus, and some of the other women who had followed him throughout his ministry. The apostle John was also there. When Jesus saw John, he told John to take care of his mother. As the time approached for Jesus to die, he cried out to the Lord, calling him father, and asked why he had been abandoned in his misery. Jesus said he was thirsty and a sponge soaked in wine vinegar was lifted to him to drink. After he had taken a drink, he cried out in a loud voice and died.

At that moment the curtain in the temple split from top to bottom, a mighty earthquake shook Jerusalem, and the sun went dark. Tombs of righteous men broke open and many people in Jerusalem saw the dead walking around the city. The centurion and the other soldiers guarding the site of the crucifixions saw what had happened when Jesus died and confirmed in their own words Jesus was the Son of God.

The leaders of the Jews did not want criminals to be still hanging on crosses during the Sabbath, so they had the Romans break the legs of the condemned to speed their deaths. When they were ready to break the legs of the prisoners, they noticed Jesus was already dead. To make sure, one of the soldiers stabbed Jesus in the side.

Once it was confirmed Jesus was dead, a man named Joseph from Arimathea came to Pilate to ask for his body. Joseph was a member of the council of the Jews but was secretly a disciple of Jesus. Pilate was surprised to hear Jesus was already dead and told Joseph to take his body. Joseph and another member of the council named Nicodemus gathered Jesus' body and prepared it for burial with expensive herbs and perfumes. They wrapped him in fresh linen and placed him in a tomb near where he had died. It was a new tomb Joseph had carved out of the stone. Once they had placed Jesus in the tomb, they moved a heavy stone in front of the entrance. The women who had been near Jesus when he died saw where he was buried and went to a house to prepare spices and perfumes for his body.

When the leaders of the Jews saw where Jesus was buried, they asked Pilate to send soldiers to guard the tomb. They were afraid some of Jesus disciples would steal the body and claim he had been raised from the dead.

The next day was the Sabbath, the day of rest, so the women who had prepared the spices and perfumes for Jesus' body did not go to the tomb to tend to his body. The next morning they prepared to go the tomb. As they were going, there was a violent earthquake. An angel came from heaven in bright white clothing with a brilliant radiance around him. He rolled the stone of the tomb away and sat down to wait for the women. The soldiers who were guarding the tomb were frightened and amazed at what they saw. They rushed into Jerusalem and found the chief priests and told them what had happened. The chief priests quickly decided to pay the guards money to say Jesus' disciples had stolen his body in the night. They promised the guards they would be protected in their lie.

Mary Magdalene, who had followed Jesus since he had cast seven demons out of her, and a couple of other women arrived first at the tomb of Jesus. When they saw the stone was removed from the entrance they were afraid. The angel who was there told them they were searching for Jesus among the dead, but he was alive. He told them to tell Jesus' disciples he was raised. The women went back to where the eleven apostles and other disciples were staying. Mary Magdalene saw Peter and John and told them what she had seen. The three of them ran back to the tomb and Peter went in to see the burial clothes neatly folded where Jesus had been placed. Peter and John went back into the city not sure what to believe.

After they had left, Mary Magdalene stayed at the tomb and cried. When she looked in the tomb again, she saw two angels sitting where Jesus' body had been. They asked her why she was crying and she responded someone had taken the body of Jesus and she did not know where it was. She heard someone speak to her and turned to see a man there. She thought he was one of the men who tended the tombs and asked if he knew where the body was. Jesus answered he had come back to life. Mary Magdalene went to embrace Jesus, but he told her to go tell the apostles what she had seen.

Later that morning, two disciples of Jesus were walking from Jerusalem to Emmaus. They were talking about Jesus and what had happened to him when a man came up to them and began asking questions about what they had seen. They told him of Jesus and of his betrayal and crucifixion. They told him about how the women went to the tomb that morning and the body of Jesus was gone.

The disciples did not recognize the man walking with them was Jesus; their eyes were blind to the truth. Jesus started teaching them as he walked. He started with Moses and went through all of the teachings of the various prophets concerning the Messiah. When they reached Emmaus, the two disciples asked him to stay until they had their meal. Jesus agreed. When he prayed over the bread and broke it, their eyes were opened and they recognized Jesus. When they had recognized him, he disappeared from their presence. The two disciples hurried back to Jerusalem to tell what had happened to them.

When the eleven apostles heard the story of the two disciples just back from Emmaus, they did not know what to think. They did not believe Mary Magdalene when she said she saw Jesus at the tomb but now they had heard from two others who said they saw Jesus alive. The disciples had locked themselves in the house where they were staying because they were afraid. When they were eating their evening meal, Jesus appeared among them. He told them not to be afraid and showed his scars and wounds to prove it was not his ghost. They were amazed by all of this but their doubts still persisted, so Jesus asked for some food. They gave him some boiled fish and he ate it to prove he was alive.

A week later, they were still in Jerusalem when Jesus appeared to them again. Thomas the apostle had not been in the house when Jesus had appeared to the disciples and he refused to believe Jesus was alive until he had touched his scars with his own hands. Jesus told Thomas to take what proof he needed. Thomas then believed and cried for joy at seeing Jesus again. Jesus told the disciples they believed by seeing and said those who believed without seeing would be more blessed.

Jesus appeared and taught his disciples for forty days after his resurrection. One day he was teaching them on the Mount of Olives outside of Jerusalem. He gave them his blessing and told them to wait in Jerusalem until the Holy Spirit came to them. He was then taken up into the sky where a cloud hid him from view. As the apostles and disciples stood there looking up, two men in shining white clothes appeared next to them and asked why they were looking into the sky. They told the disciples Jesus was taken into heaven and one day he would return in the same way.

Early Church

Stories of the Apostles

The Upper Room

Story Found in Acts Chapter 2

fter Jesus had ascended into heaven, the apostles and the disciples who were with Jesus from the beginning were gathered in a house in Jerusalem. They met in the upper room of the house and prayed day and night waiting for the Holy Spirit who Jesus promised to send. On the day of Pentecost, there was a great wind which came into the house. Flames of fire rested on each of their heads as the Holy Spirit filled them. The disciples all began to speak in other languages and the noise from the house attracted a large crowd. Many scoffed at the believers for being drunk, but many of the foreign visitors in the town heard their own languages being spoken by the disciples. They heard of the wonders of God in their own languages and were amazed.

Peter stood up and addressed the crowd. He spoke of how this baptism of the Holy Spirit was a fulfillment of prophecies and told the story of Jesus. He told how Jesus died and came back to life. Peter explained how Jesus was the savior promised by the prophets of the past. When the crowds heard this, many asked the apostles what they should do. About three thousand were baptized and added to the numbers of disciples that day.

Ananias and Sapphira

Story found in Acts Chapters 4 to 5

The group of believers were living together and sharing all they had. From time to time a believer would sell something and give the money to the group. A man named Joseph, who everyone called Barnabas, sold a portion of land and gave the entire proceeds to the apostles to use as they saw fit for the believers.

A man named Ananias conspired with his wife to gain favor among the believers. He sold a plot of land and brought some of the money to the Apostles, but held back some for himself. When he brought the money to the apostles, he told them he was giving them all of the money he had received for the land. Peter asked him why he would allow Satan to persuade him to act with deceit. He told Ananias exactly what he had done and told him he had not lied to men, but to the Holy Spirit. When Ananias heard what Peter said, he fell dead at the feet of the apostles. The young men with the believers came and wrapped Ananias for burial and took his body away.

A short while later Sapphira, Ananias' wife, came to the house not knowing what had happened to her husband. When Peter saw her, he called her over and asked her how much money they had received for the property they sold. When she told him the same amount as her husband had stated, Peter asked her how she could have agreed to lie to the Holy Spirit. He told her the young men who had taken her husband to be buried were approaching the house at that moment. When she heard this, Sapphira dropped dead at Peter's feet. When the young men entered the house, they saw her body and took her to be buried with her husband. All in the church and those who heard of this event became fearful of lying to the Holy Spirit.

The Arrest of the Apostles

Story found in Acts Chapter 5

The believers would gather daily at Solomon's Colonnade at the temple. The apostles would heal many as they preached about the teachings of Jesus and his death and resurrection. People from miles around would bring their sick family and friends to the believers for hope of healing. Many believed if Peter's shadow would just touch a sick person, they would be healed.

The High Priest and his associates became jealous of the fame and good name the believers were developing and ordered the apostles arrested and put into prison. That night, an Angel of the Lord came and released the men from prison and told them to go and preach in the temple courtyard. The next morning the apostles went and started preaching in the temple courtyard just as the assembly of Jewish elders, called the Sanhedrin, was called to order by the High Priest. He ordered the apostles be brought from the prison, but when the captain of the temple guard came back he told how the prison was locked and the guards were still at their post, but there was no one in the prison. The men of the Sanhedrin were puzzled by this news.

As they were still wondering about what had happened, someone came into the assembly and said the men they were looking for were preaching in the temple courtyard. The captain and his men went to the courtyard and brought the apostles to the Sanhedrin. When the apostles arrived, they were addressed by the High Priest who reminded them they were told not to preach about Jesus. Peter replied they obeyed God and not men and they would continue to preach about Jesus and his resurrection.

When the Sanhedrin heard Peter's words, they were furious and wanted to stone the apostles. But a Pharisee named Gamaliel, who was respected by all men, asked the apostles be taken out of the meeting so he could speak to the Sanhedrin. He told the Sanhedrin in the past men had been raised up and had followers who proclaimed them as saviors. When those men had died, their followers had drifted away. He advised the Sanhedrin to let the apostles be left alone. He said if Jesus was just another man, his followers would drift away in time. But if Jesus were the Messiah, then the Sanhedrin would be fighting against God.

The Sanhedrin agreed to take Gamaliel's advice. They had the apostles brought back in and sentenced them to a public beating, told them to stop preaching about Jesus and then released. The apostles went from the assembly praising God for letting them be punished for his kingdom. They came back to the temple day after day preaching about Jesus.

Stephen

Story found in Acts Chapters 6 to 7

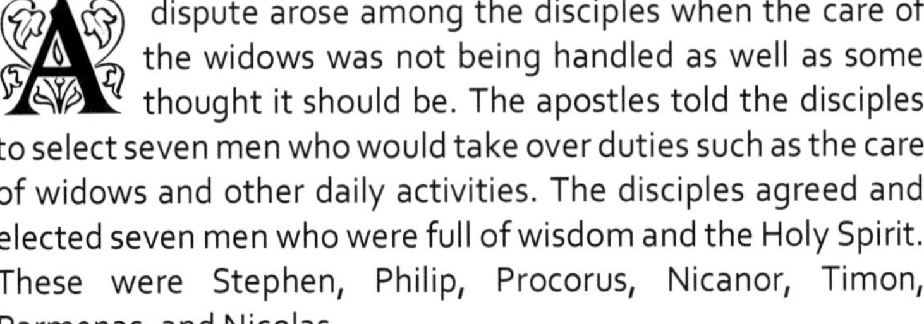

A dispute arose among the disciples when the care of the widows was not being handled as well as some thought it should be. The apostles told the disciples to select seven men who would take over duties such as the care of widows and other daily activities. The disciples agreed and elected seven men who were full of wisdom and the Holy Spirit. These were Stephen, Philip, Procorus, Nicanor, Timon, Parmenas, and Nicolas.

Miraculous signs and wonders occurred everywhere Stephen ministered, but a problem developed with a group of men from one of the synagogues. They argued with Stephen when he taught, but they could not win any points. They persuaded some men to accuse Stephen of speaking blasphemies against Moses and the Lord. The elders and the teachers of the law were stirred up by these accusations and seized Stephen and put him before the Sanhedrin.

The men who were his accusers said Stephen continually insulted the Holy places and the laws of Moses. They said he claimed Jesus would destroy the Temple and remove all the laws of Moses. As the Sanhedrin stared at Stephen during the accusations they could see his face took on the appearance of an angel's.

The Sanhedrin asked Stephen if the charges against him were true. Stephen stood and addressed the Sanhedrin. He told the history of the people of Israel from the time of Abraham. He pointed out the Patriarchs, the sons of Jacob, had sold their righteous brother into slavery. He told them Moses, who had spoken directly to the Lord, was rejected by the people of Israel while they were in Egypt. He railed against them for the history of Israel as it rejected and pushed aside every prophet who had come to them. He declared not only had they killed John the Baptist who prepared the way for the Lord's chosen one, but they also had killed the chosen one of God in their own jealousy and wickedness.

When he said this, those who were listening became enraged. They seized him and dragged him outside. They laid their cloaks at the feet of a young man named Saul and then proceeded to stone Stephen. Stephen kneeled in their midst and asked the Lord to forgive them of the sin they were committing, and then he died.

Peter

Story found in Acts Chapters 3 and 10 to 12

Peter and John went up to the temple one day to pray. As they passed through the gate known as Beautiful, they saw a man who was begging. He had been crippled and unable to walk since birth. He begged in the gate every day and on that day he asked Peter and John for some money. Peter and John looked directly at him and the beggar thought they were going to give what he asked. Instead, Peter told him they had no money, but they would give him something better. Peter told the man he would walk in the name of Jesus Christ of Nazareth. Peter then took the beggar by his hand and raised him to his feet. Instantly the man's feet and ankles became strong and the man started walking and jumping. He followed Peter and John into the temple loudly praising God.

Peter and John came to the place known as Solomon's Colonnade while the formerly crippled beggar was still holding onto them. He was shouting praises to God and jumping about in happiness. When many of the people saw him, they recognized him as the beggar from the gate Beautiful and gathered around him asking what happened. Peter addressed the crowd and told them it was the name of Jesus which healed him. He went on to tell the crowd about how Jesus had come to save them and the religious leaders had put him to death for his teachings. He told the amazed crowd how Jesus had been raised from the dead and was sitting in heaven next to God that very day.

The High Priest and the captain of the temple guard heard about this disturbance and went out to see what was happening. When they heard Peter address the crowd, they became angry at the words he spoke, but they could not do anything to him because they feared what the crowd would do. They had Peter and John brought before the Sanhedrin, the assembly of elders. They began to question Peter, but since the crippled man was standing with them, they could not think of any reason to stop Peter from speaking. They ordered Peter and John to stop speaking and preaching about Jesus, but Peter told the Sanhedrin they would not stop speaking about the events they had seen. The elders of the Jews were at a loss as to what they could do and sent Peter and John away.

After Stephen was martyred, the believers were severely persecuted in Jerusalem. The apostles and all of the disciples went away from Jerusalem for a time and traveled to various cities preaching the message of Jesus. In the town of Caesarea there was a man named Cornelius who was an officer in the Roman army. He and his family were devout, gave to the poor, and prayed regularly. One day when he was in prayer, an angel of the Lord came to him. He told Cornelius the Lord had heard his prayers and he was to be blessed for his care for the poor and his devotion to God. The angel told Cornelius to send men to the seaside town of Joppa and find a tanner named Simon. In his house he would find a man named Simon Peter. Cornelius sent two of his servants and a trusted soldier to find this Simon Peter and bring him to Caesarea.

At noon the next day, Peter went up on the roof of the house to pray. He became hungry and fell into a trance while praying. He saw a sheet come down from heaven full of unclean animals. A voice from heaven commanded him to kill and eat the animals, but Peter refused, saying he had never eaten anything unclean in his life. The voice admonished him not to call anything unclean the Lord had made clean. This vision was repeated three times and the sheet disappeared.

As Peter sat and wondered at what the vision could mean, the men from Cornelius had found the house of Simon the tanner and asked if Simon Peter was staying there. The Holy Spirit told Peter there were men looking for him at the front of the house and he should go with them. When Peter came down from the roof and went to the front of the house, he found the men. When he asked them why they had come to find him, they told him of the angelic message given to their master, Cornelius.

Peter and several other believers staying in Joppa went to the house of Cornelius in Caesarea. Cornelius had called all of his household together and invited Peter and the other believers to enter his house. Peter came into the house without hesitation and told all who were there, both Jews and Gentiles, how he had been shown the salvation of Jesus was for everybody and not just the Jews. As Peter was speaking, the Holy Spirit came on all those who were listening. The Jewish believers with Peter were amazed as they saw the Gentiles speaking in tongues when they were baptized in the Holy Spirit. Peter then declared no one could withhold the baptism of water from those to whom God had given his Spirit.

King Herod of Judea started persecuting the church about this time. He had the apostle James, the brother of John, put to death. When he saw the Jews in Jerusalem were pleased by this, he arrested Peter during the Feast of Unleavened Bread. Herod ordered sixteen soldiers to guard Peter to ensure he did not escape prison. Herod planned on bringing Peter to trial after Passover. The church in Jerusalem prayed for Peter to be released from prison, but soon Passover came and the next day Peter would be tried before Herod. That night, as Peter was sleeping in two sets of chains in between two guards in his cell, an angel of the Lord came to him. A bright light appeared in the cell and the angel woke Peter by hitting his side.

When Peter woke and saw the angel, he thought it was a vision. The chains fell off of his arms and the angel told him to get dressed. Once Peter was dressed, the angel led him out of the prison and into the streets of Jerusalem. After they were a full street away from the prison gate, the angel disappeared leaving Peter alone. When he realized he had not seen a vision, but was actual free from prison, Peter hurried to a nearby house where many believers had gathered to pray for Peter's release. When Peter knocked at the outer door to the house, a servant girl came and saw who it was. She recognized Peter's voice and was so excited she ran back into the house without letting him in. When she told those inside Peter was at the door they did not believe her. When she insisted he was there, they feared she had seen his ghost. Eventually she was able to persuade some to come and see for themselves. When they opened the door they were amazed Peter stood there. He told them to be quiet and explained to them how he had been let out of prison. He then told them to get word to the rest of the apostles about his release and left the house for another place to hide from Herod.

Philip

Story found in Acts Chapter 8

Philip left Jerusalem after the stoning of Stephen and went to a city in Samaria. He preached the message of Jesus and healed many people of illness and demon possession.

There was a man who lived in the city named Simon. This man was a magician and he amazed all in the city, both nobles and commoners. He bragged he was a great man and many in the city believed him because of the things he could do. After Philip came to the city and preached the message of Jesus, Simon soon became a believer and followed Philip.

When news reached the believers in Jerusalem that Samaria had accepted the message of Jesus, Peter and John were sent to help Philip in his ministry. When they arrived, they prayed for the recent converts. When Peter and John laid their hands on them, they were baptized in the Holy Spirit. When Simon saw what had happened he went to Peter and offered him money to buy the power he saw.

Peter rebuked him and told him the power of God was not for sale. Peter told Simon to repent of his sin so the Lord would forgive him. Simon asked Peter to pray he could be forgiven.

When Peter and John had finished preaching in the city, they traveled back to Jerusalem ministering in Samaritan villages along the way. After they had left, the Holy Spirit told Philip to travel south out of the city toward the road which led into Gaza from Jerusalem. When Philip arrived at the road, he saw an Ethiopian in a chariot reading a scroll. The Ethiopian was a eunuch in charge of the treasury for Queen Candace of Ethiopia. He had traveled to Jerusalem to worship at the temple of the Lord and was returning home along the road when he stopped to read.

Philip went over to the chariot and heard the man reading from the book of Isaiah. Philip asked the Ethiopian if he understood what he was reading. The Ethiopian said he could not understand if no one explained it to him. It was a section of prophecy but the Ethiopian did not know if Isaiah was referring to himself or someone else. Philip started with that piece of prophesy and explained how Jesus had come and fulfilled all Isaiah wrote about. He told him about Jesus' life, ministry, death and resurrection. As they traveled along, they came to a small body of water and Philip asked the Ethiopian if he wanted to be baptized as a believer in Jesus. Philip and the Ethiopian went into the water and Philip baptized him. When the Ethiopian came out of the water, Philip had been taken away by the Lord and the eunuch went back to Ethiopia rejoicing.

Philip had been taken by the Lord to Azotus and began preaching where he found himself. He eventually made it to Caesarea where he continued his ministry.

Paul

Story found in Acts Chapters 8 to 9 and 13 to 28

Saul was at the stoning of Stephen and approved of what the Jews did to the disciple of Jesus. He soon became one of the Jews in Jerusalem who started going door to door and arresting the disciples. Saul went to the high priest and obtained letters to give to the teachers at the synagogue in Damascus allowing him to arrest any of Jesus' disciples he found in the city and bring them back to prison in Jerusalem. While he was traveling to Damascus, a piercing bright light came from the sky and Saul fell to the ground.

A voice asked Saul why he was persecuting him. When Saul asked who was speaking, the voice answered he was Jesus. Jesus told Saul to continue traveling to Damascus and he would be told what to do. When Saul opened his eyes, he discovered he was blind. The men who were with him led him to Damascus, but Saul did not eat or drink for three days as he prayed to the Lord. While Saul was praying, he had a vision of a man named Ananias who came to the house Saul was staying in. In the vision when Ananias found Saul, he put his hands on Saul's head and his blindness was healed.

Ananias was a believer living in Damascus. The Lord spoke to him and told him to go to a particular house and ask to see a man named Saul of Tarsus. Ananias was afraid and told the Lord he had heard of the man and how Saul had cruelly treated the believers in Jerusalem. The Lord told Ananias Saul would be the messenger to the Gentiles and the Lord would show Saul the suffering he would endure for the name of Jesus. Ananias did as the Lord commanded and found the house Saul was staying in. When he saw Saul, he placed his hands on his head and told him Jesus had sent him to pray for Saul to be healed and filled with the Holy Spirit. When he said those words, Saul's vision was restored. Saul was baptized as a believer that day.

For a while, Saul stayed with the believers in Damascus and learned from them, but soon he was preaching the message of Jesus in the synagogues of the city. Everyone who heard Saul preach were astonished this was the man who had arrested and imprisoned the disciples of Jesus in Jerusalem. They thought he had come to arrest believers in Damascus and take them back to Jerusalem, and yet Saul preached the message of the believers to anyone who would listen.

Saul's preaching was effective and soon the Jews in Damascus started plotting to kill him. They watched the city gates every day to see when he would leave so they could find him without the crowds. Saul learned of the plot and the believers in the city helped him escape by lowering him over the wall one night. Saul returned to Jerusalem and tried to find a place to stay with the believers he had worked to imprison, but they did not trust him and thought he was laying a trap for them. Finally Barnabas took Saul to the apostles and testified for him. He told of Saul's experience on the road to Damascus, how he had met Ananias and the other believers in the city, and how Saul had spoken so bravely and effectively in the synagogues. When the apostles heard what Barnabas had to say, Saul was accepted by the believers in Jerusalem.

Saul spoke boldly in support of Jesus while in Jerusalem. He became involved in several debates with Jews from the Grecian cities. They tried to kill him after hearing him speak. When the believers learned how Saul's life was being endangered, they took him to Caesarea and put him on a ship headed to Tarsus.

Until the death of Stephen and the persecution of the church in Jerusalem, the message of Jesus was only spread to the Jews wherever the disciples went. When many of the disciples fled Jerusalem during the persecution, several of them went to Antioch and started telling the Greeks about Jesus. Many of those who heard the good news turned to the Lord and became believers. When the church in Jerusalem heard these reports, they sent Barnabas to Antioch. He found the reports were true and the church was growing quickly. Barnabas was a good man who was filled with the Holy Spirit and faith. He helped bring many people into the church there, and soon went to Tarsus to find Saul and bring him back. For a whole year Barnabas and Saul taught the believers in Antioch. Antioch was the first place the word "Christian" was used to describe the believers. After a prophecy was given that there would be a famine throughout the Roman Empire, the church in Antioch decided they would give what they could to help the churches in Judea. Barnabas and Saul brought the gifts from Antioch to the believers in Jerusalem. When they had finished in Jerusalem, Barnabas and Saul returned to Antioch accompanied by a young man named John, who also went by the name Mark.

In Antioch, the Holy Spirit told the church to send Barnabas and Saul to spread the good news of Jesus to other places. The believers prayed for Barnabas and Saul, laid their hands on them, and sent them on their way. They left Antioch with John as their helper and went to Cyprus where they preached in the synagogues in the city of Salamis. They traveled around the island of Cyprus preaching in each town until they came to the city of Paphos. The proconsul in this city was an intelligent man called Sergius Paulus. He asked for Barnabas and Saul to come to speak with him and tell him about Jesus. One of the proconsul's advisors was a Jew named Elymas Bar-Jesus who was a sorcerer and false prophet. When he heard what Barnabas and Saul were telling Sergius, he disputed what they said and tried to turn the proconsul away from their faith. Saul confronted Elymas and cursed him to be blind. Elymas immediately lost his vision and had to be led around by other people. When the proconsul saw what had happened and heard the teachings of Barnabas and Saul, he became a believer. It was on Cyprus that Saul started being called Paul.

Paul and Barnabas left Cyprus and headed into the region of Pamphylia. John left them when they arrived in Pamphylia and headed back to Jerusalem. Paul and Barnabas traveled to the city of Pisidian Antioch and sat in the synagogue on the next Sabbath. After the word of the law was read, they were invited by the Jews to speak if they wanted. Paul rose and gave a detailed and compelling sermon detailing how all of the prophets and poets pointed to the coming of Jesus. He told of Jesus' ministry and how he had been put to death by those who were jealous of him. He then told how Jesus had been raised from the dead and had promised eternal life to all who believed. The Jews were amazed and many of the people who attended the synagogue became believers. They asked Paul to return the next week to speak again.

When Paul and Barnabas returned the next week, almost the entire city had come to hear what Paul had to say. The Jews were jealous of Paul and Barnabas and began to speak against Paul as he told the good news of Jesus. Paul scolded the Jews for what they were doing and told the Gentiles the gift of salvation was extended by the Lord to them as well, if they believed in the name of Jesus. Many Gentiles became believers and the message of Jesus attracted much attention in the whole region. Eventually the Jews of the city stirred up enough trouble and conflict that Paul and Barnabas left the region for Iconium.

At Iconium, Paul and Barnabas again had much success among both the Jews and Gentiles. But disputes came up as some of the Jews in the synagogue spoke against what Paul and Barnabas were teaching. The two apostles stayed in the city explaining their teaching for a long time until they heard there was a plot to harm them. They left Iconium and went to the city of Lystra.

At Lystra, Paul was speaking when he saw a man who had been crippled since birth. When Paul looked at him, he saw the man was full of faith so he called to the crippled man to stand up and walk. The man jumped to his feet and began walking. When the crowds saw this, they believed Paul and Barnabas were gods. They thought Barnabas was Zeus and Paul was the messenger Hermes because Paul was usually the one speaking to the crowds. The people bowed to Paul and Barnabas and the priest of the temple of Zeus brought some animals to sacrifice to them. Paul and Barnabas tore their clothes and begged the people not to treat them as gods. They explained they were just men and the Lord was the true God. They finally succeeded in stopping the people from worshipping them. At that time, some Jews who opposed their teaching had arrived from Iconium and Antioch. They turned the crowd against Paul and Barnabas. The crowd stoned Paul and dragged his body outside of the city. They had thought Paul was dead, but when the believers gathered around Paul, he got up and walked back into Lystra. The next day Paul and Barnabas left for the nearby city of Derbe.

After they had preached and taught in Derbe and saw many people come to believe in Jesus, Paul and Barnabas retraced their steps back to Antioch. They stopped in each city they had visited and appointed elders to lead the believers. When they returned to Antioch, they told the church about everything which had happened, especially how the Gentiles were being converted.

Some believers came to Antioch from Judea and started teaching in order for a Gentile to be a believer, they had to be circumcised and follow the laws of Moses. A serious dispute broke out between those who came from Judea and those who lived in Antioch. It was decided Paul and Barnabas would go to Jerusalem and have a meeting with the apostles to determine what would be decided about the Gentiles. Paul and Barnabas were welcomed by the apostles and elders in the church in Jerusalem and the two men told of their trip. The council of believers heard arguments on all sides concerning the Gentile converts. The apostle Peter then spoke to the council arguing the Gentiles were purified by their faith and should not have a heavy burden placed on them.

After listening to everything, the council wrote a letter to the believers in Antioch. They said circumcision was not necessary, but the Gentile believers should abstain from eating food sacrificed to idols, should not engage in sexual immorality, eating animals which were strangled or eating any blood. Paul and Barnabas took the letter back to Antioch accompanied by two men sent from Jerusalem named Silas and Judas Barsabbas.

Paul and Barnabas decided they should go back to the cities they had preached in on their trip and encourage the church. Barnabas wanted to take John as their helper again, but Paul did not want him to go as he believed John had abandoned them on their trip. The disagreement over John was so severe, that Barnabas took John and sailed to Cyprus without Paul. Paul took Silas and went to Syria and Cilicia encouraging the believers in those regions.

When Paul and Silas arrived in Lystra, there was a believer named Timothy whose father was Greek and mother was a Jewess. Paul decided he wanted Timothy to accompany him and Silas on their journey, but Timothy was not circumcised. It was decided Timothy would be circumcised so the Jews they ministered to would not be offended. Paul and those with him traveled to many towns in the region encouraging the believers and seeing many people added to the church. When they came to the town of Bithynia, the Spirit of Jesus would not allow them to enter. They went to the town of Troas instead and that night Paul had a vision of a man standing in Macedonia asking him to come and preach.

The next day Paul and the others with him sailed to Macedonia and traveled to the chief city of that region, Philippi. When the Sabbath came, Paul , Silas and the others went out of the city gate to find where people went to pray. They went to the river and talked with the women who gathered there. One of the women was named Lydia. She was a seller of purple dyes and clothing and she worshipped the Lord. When she heard Paul speak, she became a believer and was baptized along with all of her household. She offered Paul. Silas and the others her house to stay in while they were in Philippi.

One day when the believers were going to pray, a slave girl who was possessed by a spirit who could tell the future crossed their path. The masters of the girl made money from her telling fortunes and she was a valuable source of income to them. When the girl saw the believers, she started following them and shouting. She was yelling that Paul and the others were servants of the Most High God and they were in the city to tell people how to be saved. For many days she would follow and shout until Paul had grown troubled by her activity. He turned to her and ordered the spirit leave her in the name of Jesus Christ. When the spirit left her, the owners of the girl were furious their source of income had been taken from them. The owners had Paul and Silas apprehended and taken to the magistrates in the town. They accused the men of stirring up trouble and advocating customs illegal for a Roman town.

The crowds turned against Paul and Silas and the magistrates had them stripped, beaten and thrown into prison. The head jailer put them in the most secure area of the prison and put their feet in stocks. That night Paul and Silas were singing hymns and the other prisoners were listening to them. A great earthquake shook the city and the stocks on the feet of Paul and Silas fell off. The doors to the prison were knocked open and the way was clear for any prisoner to escape. When the head jailer saw the doors to the prison were open, he decided to kill himself with his sword because he believed all the prisoners were gone. When Paul saw him, he shouted that none of the prisoners had escaped.

The head jailer called for lights to be brought and he went into the prison where he saw all the prisoners were still there. He fell before Paul and Silas and asked what he must do to be saved. Paul told him faith in Jesus was all that was needed. The head jailer had their wounds tended and Paul told him the good news about Jesus. The head jailer and his entire household were baptized that night.

The next morning the magistrates sent officers to the head jailer with instructions to release Paul and Silas. The head jailer told them they were free to leave, but Paul refused. He told the officers he and Silas were beaten without a trial and thrown into prison even though they were Roman citizens. He said they would not slip away from prison quietly, but the magistrates would have to come and escort them out of the prison. When the magistrates discovered Paul and Silas had citizenship with Rome, they were afraid. They came and led the men out of prison and tried to appease them with their words. After they left prison, Paul and Silas went back to the house of Lydia for a short while before leaving Philippi.

The next city on their journey was Thessalonica where they stayed at the house of a believer named Jason. Every Sabbath, Paul would go to the synagogue and speak about Jesus. He would use the scriptures to show Jesus was the Christ. Many Jews and God fearing Greeks believed, but other Jews stirred up trouble against the believers. They went to the house of Jason to arrest Paul, but could not find him or the others who traveled with him. They arrested Jason and some other believers they found there, and took them to the city officials. Jason and the others were fined and sent home. After nightfall, the believers sent Paul and Silas away.

In Berea, Paul found a synagogue full of Jews who were willing to examine the scriptures with him. Many people were added to the church, but when the Jews in Thessalonica heard Paul was teaching in Berea, they came to stir up trouble. The believers in Berea sent Paul away while Silas, Timothy and the others stayed. Paul was taken to Athens and his traveling companions planned to join him as soon as possible.

When Paul arrived in Athens, he was troubled by the amount of idols which were in the city. He went to the synagogues and marketplaces and told about Jesus. When some Greek philosophers heard him speaking, they were curious about what he was saying. They took him to a group called the Areopagus which discussed and debated ideas. They asked him what he was speaking about and he told them of Jesus and his resurrection. He used the language and ideas of Greek philosophy to teach them about the way to salvation. Some of the men and women of the group dismissed what he was saying as nonsense, but others asked him to return and speak again. Several men and women who heard Paul became believers while he was in Athens.

Paul left Athens and went to Corinth where he met a Jew named Aquila and his wife Priscilla. He worked with them as tentmakers while he preached in the synagogues. When Silas, Timothy, and the others caught up with him, Paul dedicated himself to teaching. Even though the leader of the synagogue and his household became believers, other Jews in the synagogues became abusive to Paul. He finally declared he would only preach to the Gentiles. Paul left the synagogue and went to the house of Titius Justus, a Greek who feared the Lord. One night Paul had a vision where the Lord came to him and told him to keep speaking boldly. He told Paul there were many believers in Corinth and he was safe in the city. Paul stayed in

Corinth for a long time and many people joined the church. Even when those who opposed Paul tried to stir up trouble, Paul and the believers were not persecuted by the authorities.

Eventually Paul decided to leave Corinth and travel with Aquila and Priscilla to Ephesus. He taught in the synagogue before heading on alone, leaving Aquila and Priscilla with the believers in Ephesus. He traveled to many towns encouraging the believers and speaking in the synagogues. Eventually he came back to Antioch for a time before traveling from town to town again. Word of Paul spread and he was well known among both believers and those who opposed the message of Jesus. Paul traveled in many regions and in many towns before he decided he needed to head back to Jerusalem and then go to Rome.

When Paul was in Ephesus a silversmith named Demetrius began stirring up the people of the city. Demetrius made most of his wealth from fashioning silver for the craftsmen of the city. Because a major temple to the goddess Artemis was located in Ephesus, many of the goods sold there were idols or shrines for the goddess. Paul and the church of Jesus were gaining so many converts and so large of a following that those who relied upon the worship of Artemis were starting to suffer financially. Demetrius gathered many of the craftsmen of Ephesus to try and do something against the believers in the city. They stirred up the crowds in the city by proclaiming how great Artemis was and searched for leaders among the believers. They found a couple of companions of Paul and took them to the large public theater in the city. Paul wanted to go speak to the crowd, but the believers and even some of the city officials urged him to stay in hiding until the danger passed. The crowd which gathered at the theater was not sure why they were all there. When one of the believers they had taken by force was put onto the stage, he tried to reason with them but when they saw he was a Jew, the crowds started chanting and shouting once again. Finally a city official came to the theater to address the crowds, Demetrius, and his conspirators. The official told them Ephesus had plenty of courts and judges available if there were any charges which could be brought against the believers. The crowds then dispersed and went home.

Paul soon left Ephesus and continued his travels to see the churches in the various towns. In Troas one night, a young man named Eutychus fell asleep while sitting on the edge of a window on the third floor of the building Paul was speaking in. He fell and died when he landed. Paul went out to him and threw himself on the young man. He stood back up and Eutychus was alive. The people went back into the building and finished listening to Paul until sunrise and they all went home, including the young man.

Paul soon felt he must go to Jerusalem with little delay. He decided against going back to Ephesus as it would take a long time, so he sent word for the leaders of the Ephesian church to meet him at a port on his way back to Judea. When he met them, he gave them instructions on how to handle various issues he knew would come against the church. He gave them his goodbyes and told them although he did not know what would happen when he arrived in Jerusalem, he knew he would never see any of them again. The leaders said their goodbyes to Paul and watched as he sailed to Jerusalem.

When Paul and his companions reached Caesarea, they met the prophet Agabus who prophesied Paul would be handed over to the Gentiles by the Jews in Jerusalem. When the believers in the city and those who traveled with Paul heard this prophecy, they begged him to stop his trip to Jerusalem. But Paul was determined to go to Jerusalem without delay.

Paul finally arrived in Jerusalem where the apostles and church elders greeted him warmly. He told of his journeys and how Gentiles were being added to the church in all of the regions he had been. The apostles were glad to hear the news, but they told Paul some of the Jewish believers had heard Paul was telling Jewish believers to stop following the laws of Moses and to stop practicing the customs of the Jews. Paul agreed to participate in the purification ritual at the temple to show the charges against him were false. The next day Paul purified himself and went to the temple to make arrangements for the offering he would make when the time of purification was over.

When the time of purification was almost over, some Jews who had confronted Paul in his travels saw him in the temple. They stirred up the crowds in the temple against Paul saying he had brought Greeks into the temple itself and he spoke out against the Jews everywhere he traveled. The crowds seized Paul and dragged him out of the temple. The commander of all of the Roman forces in Jerusalem was told of the trouble at the temple and hurried to the temple with his men to find out what had caused the disturbance. The crowd was beating Paul in order to kill him, but when the soldiers arrived, they left him alone.

The commander arrested Paul but he couldn't get a clear answer from the agitated crowd of what Paul had done. He had Paul bound and brought to the city barracks. When they reached the building, Paul asked if he could address the crowd. The commander allowed him to speak and Paul told the crowd what his background was and how he had as a young man stood and watched Stephen stoned to death for the sake of Jesus. He told how he had persecuted the church in Jerusalem and was on his way to Damascus to persecute the believers there when Jesus struck him blind and called him as a disciple. He told how he became a believer and came back to Jerusalem. He said while he was in Jerusalem, the Lord told him he was to go and speak to the Gentiles about Jesus.

When the crowd heard him say he was sent to the Gentiles by the Lord, they became enraged and demanded the commander kill him. The crowd became so violent the commander took Paul back into the barracks. He ordered one of his officers to flog Paul and question him about why the crowd was so upset. As Paul was being put into position to be flogged, he asked the officer if it was legal to beat a Roman citizen before a trial. The officer became afraid. He went to the commander and informed him of Paul's question. The commander went to Paul to confirm he was a citizen of Rome. When Paul confirmed it, the commander told him he had paid a lot for his citizenship and wanted to know what Paul had paid for his. Paul informed him he was born a Roman citizen. The commander became afraid of doing anything to Paul and decided he would order the Sanhedrin of the Jews to assemble in order to discover why Paul was being treated this way by the Jews.

Paul was put before the Sanhedrin the next day. When Paul said he had done nothing wrong and had a clear conscience, the high priest Ananias ordered him slapped across the face. Paul lashed out at the Sanhedrin when he had been slapped. When he regained his composure, he brought up the resurrection of Jesus. He did this because he knew some of the Sanhedrin were Pharisees who believed the dead would be raised one day, and others were Sadducees who did not believe in resurrection. The two sides started arguing among themselves so violently the commander of the Roman forces feared for Paul's safety. He had Paul taken away from the Sanhedrin and brought back to the barracks. The next night an angel of the Lord came to Paul and encouraged him. He said just as Paul had testified in Jerusalem, he would also testify in Rome.

The next day a large group of men presented themselves to the chief priests and elders of the Jews. They swore an oath to not eat until they had killed Paul. Paul's nephew discovered the details of the plot and went to Paul to let him know. After Paul heard the news, he had his nephew taken to the commander to tell him of the plot. When the commander questioned the young man, he discovered the plotters planned on having Paul brought before the Sanhedrin again where he would be ambushed and killed.

The commander called two of his officers and had them prepare a large group of soldiers. He told them to have two hundred foot soldiers, two hundred spearmen, and seventy horsemen ready to travel to Caesarea as an escort for Paul and those who traveled with him. The commander told his men to make sure Paul and his companions had horses as well and gave instructions they were to be brought to Governor Felix, the Roman official over the region. The commander had sent a letter with his men to give to Felix explaining why he had sent Paul. When Felix read the letter, he had Paul placed under guard until his accusers arrived from Jerusalem.

Five days later the High Priest Ananias came to Felix with men of the law. They made their case against Paul and Paul gave his defense to the governor. The governor was familiar with beliefs of those who followed Jesus and told both Paul and his accusers he would wait to give judgment until later. After Paul's accusers left Caesarea, Felix came with his wife, who was a Jewess, to hear Paul speak more of Jesus and what he taught. The governor was disturbed by what Paul said and sent him away. He was hoping Paul and his supporters would offer him a bribe for Paul's release, and so Felix kept Paul under guard for two years.

While Paul was being held in Caesarea, Porcius Festus was appointed governor. Festus traveled to Jerusalem soon after arriving in Judea and met with the Jewish leaders. They brought up their case against Paul and encouraged the governor to send Paul back to Jerusalem to stand trial. Festus told them he would be going back to Caesarea and if they wanted to send men to accuse Paul of a crime, he would listen to them there.

After Festus returned to Caesarea, the chief priests sent witnesses to accuse Paul. Paul spoke in his defense of the charges but Festus was not convinced one way or the other. He asked Paul if he would agree to go back to Jerusalem and be tried by the Jews, but Paul refused. He told the governor he was under Roman jurisdiction and he would not allow himself to be tried by the Jews. He appealed his case to Caesar which was his right as a Roman citizen. Festus spoke with his advisors and agreed Paul had the right to appeal his case to Caesar.

When King Agrippa came to Caesarea to greet the new Roman governor, Festus spoke to him about Paul's case. King Agrippa was curious about the case and asked to see and talk to Paul. When Paul was brought before the king, he told of his own conversion, his own ministry, and the good news of Jesus. When the king and governor dismissed him, they talked together about what Paul had said. King Agrippa told the governor if Paul had not appealed to Caesar, they could have released him.

Paul, his companions, and other prisoners being sent to Rome were put on a ship under the command of a centurion named Julius. The sea voyage was long and difficult at times. As the ship approached the island of Crete, a great storm came up and blew the ship into the middle of the sea. For fourteen days the storm battered the ship and the sailors started throwing cargo and gear overboard to keep it afloat. The storm blocked out the sun and it was dark all the time. When the sailors saw signs of land, they were afraid the ship would be smashed on rocks. But Paul told everyone on the ship an angel of the Lord had appeared to him the night before and promised not a single man would be harmed, although the ship would be destroyed. He encouraged everyone on the ship to eat so they would have strength when the ship went ashore. When they had eaten all they could, the sailors threw the rest of the provisions overboard to keep the ship from sinking. The next morning daylight showed a sandy beach ahead of them where they would ground the severely damaged ship. They ran for the beach but got stuck on a sandbar. The soldiers on the ship wanted to kill all of the prisoners so none would escape, but the centurion Julius would not allow it. He had those who could swim go from the ship first, and then made sure there was enough planks and boards to float those who could not swim to shore. When the crew and passengers reached shore, not a single man was missing or injured.

Islanders came to meet the men and told them they were on the island of Malta. The men of the island started building a fire for the shipwrecked men because it was cold and rainy. Paul went to gather wood for the fire when a viper bit him on the hand and latched on. Paul shook the venomous snake off his hand. The men of Malta believed Paul must have been a murderer, because after surviving the shipwreck, Justice was still going to take his life. They waited for Paul to fall over dead or show signs of being ill, but Paul was fine and in good health for as long as they watched him. The men of Malta changed their minds about Paul and thought he must be a god.

The chief official on Malta was a man named Publius who welcomed the shipwrecked men to his home and hosted them for three days. His father was bedridden with dysentery, but when Paul prayed for him, he was healed. The men of the island brought all of their sick people to Paul and they were cured of their illnesses. For three months the people of Malta took care of the men from the shipwreck and then supplied them for the last leg of their voyage when another ship was secured.

Paul finally arrived in Rome and the believers who lived there came to meet him and those who traveled with him from Caesarea. Paul was put in a private house with a guard by the authorities. After Paul had been in Rome for three days, he called the leaders of the Jews in the city to come to him. When they arrived, he told them what had happened in Jerusalem and how he had appealed to Caesar. They were open to what he said and were willing to listen to him speak about Jesus. Some believed, while others did not. Paul spoke constantly about the good news of Jesus for the entire time he was in Rome.

Thank you for reading *Bible Stories for New Christians*.

I wrote this book to fill a need I recognized. The stories of the Bible need to be easily accessible to new believers. Too often I see people come to the knowledge of Christ and the love of God, yet they're not given the basic background those who grew up in the Church take for granted. If there's a discipleship process in place, it often will start with an assumption of familiarity of the Bible. We ask new believers to understand the concept of Justification before they know who Jacob is.

While there are plenty of book which have simplified or streamlined Bible stories for children, it's difficult find these stories told in a straight-forward and non-sectarian way at an adult level.

I made it my purpose to only provide the straight narrative of the Bible without the use of commentary. I also attempted to not make presumptions on the part of the reader.

To those who grew up in the Church, these stories might refresh lessons you learned as children, or they might provide a different way of looking at a story you know well, or maybe you will read a story, or a portion of a story, and find you've never read it before.

To those who are new believers, this book will give you the basic understanding of many of the lessons and references you might find confusing as you read articles, listen to sermons, or go through a Bible Study class.

In no way would I suggest or recommend using this book as a substitute for the Bible. Read your Bible regularly. Read this book when you want to read a good story, or two, or thirty-nine from the Bible.

Wilson Harp